SHATTERING THE ILLUSION

SHATTERING THE ILLUSION

How African American
Churches of Christ
Moved from
Segregation to Independence

WES CRAWFORD

Abilene Christian University Press

SHATTERING THE ILLUSION

How African American Churches of Christ Moved from Segregation to Independence

ACU PRESS

ISBN 978-0-89112-228-9
LCCN 2012045733

Printed in the United States of America

Photos used by permission of the Center for Restoration Studies, Brown Library, Abilene Christian University, Abilene, Texas.

LIBRARY OF CONGRESS CATALOGING-IN-PUBLICATION DATA
Crawford, Wes, 1976-
Shattering the illusion : how African American Churches of Christ moved from segregation to independence / Wes Crawford.
pages cm
ISBN 978-0-89112-228-9
1. Churches of Christ--History. 2. African American churches--History. 3. United States--Church history. 4. Race relations--Religious aspects--Christianity. I. Title.
BX7075.C73 2003
286.6'3--dc23
2012045733

Cover design by Rick Gibson
Interior text design by Sandy Armstrong

For information contact:
Abilene Christian University Press
1626 Campus Court
Abilene, Texas 79601

1-877-816-4455 toll free
www.abilenechristianuniversitypress.com

To my mother, Brenda, who passed on her faith to me
and to my wife, Kim, who helps cultivate that faith still

Contents

INTRODUCTION

Race matters. Even within a religious body that at times has claimed virtual immunity from the pressures of its social and historical context, the ever present and powerful confrontation between white and black has greatly affected the formation of Churches of Christ identity. Without a convention to make official pronouncements on race relations or a conference to declare the formation of two denominations along the Mason-Dixon Line some may believe Churches of Christ have escaped the grasp of perhaps the most volatile issue in American history.[1] Nevertheless, one of the few denominations established on American soil did not avoid the effects of America's most intractable dilemma.[2]

A history of segregation within the Churches of Christ has obscured their evolution in the late twentieth century towards de facto denominational independence of their African American congregations. Predictably, much of that independence can be traced to the cultural and political effects of the Civil Rights Movement at mid century. This book seeks to recover that history. In addition, it seeks to prove that Churches of Christ journals, colleges, and lectureships shielded from view the full measure of the separation between African American and white members of the denomination.

This study contributes to the study of American church history in two ways. First, it challenges the illusion of racial unity among those congregations associated with Churches of Christ. African American and white members of this predominantly southern branch of the Stone-Campbell Movement mirrored the white-imposed segregation of their regional peers in the late nineteenth and early twentieth centuries; and, following the American Civil Rights Movement, the denomination remained divided as African Americans formally declared their independence from white paternalism and control. Second, this study reveals the power of unofficial denominational bodies to mask significant division existent within its ranks. Lacking centralized authority, Churches of Christ sought to mediate their theology through journals, colleges, and lectureships. As the only centralized voices of the denomination, these entities failed to address the division between African Americans and whites, thereby providing a false veneer of cohesion to insiders and outsiders alike. These three bodies not only failed to cohere African Americans and whites, they also helped maintain the illusion of racial unity within Churches of Christ.

Race and Racism

To set the stage for this study, one must become familiar with two key terms: race and racism. "Race" is a socially constructed phenomenon; therefore, one is incorrect to speak of the "white race" or the "African American race" as if lighter skinned individuals are necessarily and by nature classified separately from darker skinned individuals. In 1887, a Presbyterian leader made the statement, "The distinctions of race are drawn by God Himself."[3] He was wrong. Society has drawn the boundaries of race, not God. Such a statement may seem curious, for human beings are certainly born with different physical characteristics, such as skin color. To recognize the social construction of race, however, is to acknowledge that only certain physical features aid in race classification. As Michael O. Emerson and Christian Smith point out, though people have all sizes of feet and shapes of ears, those physical features are not used to classify one race from another.[4] Society has chosen only certain physical features among many as racial determinants. It not only uses a select group of physical features to determine race, it also attaches social meaning only to certain physical characteristics.[5] For example, a person with a large nose or red hair does not automatically have to fight the stereotypes of mental inferiority or financial hardship. A person born with black skin, however, often has to fight both.

Those members of society who have exercised their hegemonic power have attached significant meaning to white and black skin color. In his discussion of "scientific racism," Brad Braxton reminds his readers that countless white scientists, in their efforts to support the myth of white intellectual superiority, have attempted to prove that the skulls of white persons were larger than the skulls of black persons.[6] These quasi-scientific efforts, however, followed centuries wherein society attached positive connotations to white and negative connotations to black.

Some scholars have suggested that white racism toward African Americans began on another continent, arguing that even before American colonization began, the English had certain views of white and black. Of that time and place, wrote Winthrop Jordan, "white and black connoted purity and filthiness, virtue and baseness, beauty and ugliness, beneficence and evil, God and the devil."[7] During an era in which Shakespeare described beauty as "snow white" and ebony as "beautie still to lack," England discovered black Africans.[8]

Upon this discovery, English explorers, scientists, and clerics offered explanations for the black complexion. Although some borrowed more ancient and fanciful explanations like the Phaeton myth, which implied that Ethiopians inherited their black skin from Phaeton, a lad who drove his chariot too close to the sun, others proponents of naturalistic explanations postulated that darker skin somehow originated from the stronger heat of the African sun.[9] More common and tragic, however, were those explanations offered from scripture such as the Haminite myth. According to this view, black skin resulted from God's curse of Ham, following his sin against Noah in Genesis 9. In that text, God cursed Ham's descendents, the Canaanites, as slaves. Early Jewish scholars believed the descendents of Ham, those whom God had ordained slaves, were black. Jordan argued that this myth became prominent in Christian circles in the sixteenth century as Christian theologians became more interested in Jewish writings. Their discovery and utilization of the myth coincided with "the first great century of overseas exploration," which included explorations into Africa.[10]

As Europeans encountered Africans, they not only found biblical justification for dark skin and slavery, they also attached new meaning to blackness. Black Africans became the picture of savagery to white Europeans, and their treatment of African slaves bore witness to this fact.[11] African slaves were treated like other beasts of the field, packed on ships in tight quarters, and sent across the world. Unlike beasts, however, blacks also were viewed as sexual savages. In his description of Africa, Leo Africanus depicted Africans as savages with "great swarmes of Harlots among them; whereupon a man may easily conjecture their manner of living."[12] Writing in the mid-sixteenth century, Jean Bodin wrote that Ethiopia and lust went hand in hand.[13]

Other scholars such as Oscar and Mary Handlin have argued that whites attached negative connotations to blackness much later. During the eighteenth and nineteenth centuries, English colonists, argued the Handlins, sought to justify the emerging institution by referring to the Africans as barbarians and finding biblical justification for black inferiority.[14] In doing so, English colonists separated black slaves from other slaves, including whites.

Whether white racism preceded American slavery or vice versa, the end result remained constant: in America, black skin had meaning.

The picture of black Africans painted by sixteenth-century explorers and scholars as cursed, sexual savages ordained by God to servitude influenced generations of Euro-Americans. By the eighteenth century, as scientists set out to classify planets, diseases, and animals, men like Francois Bernier and Carolus Linnaeus took on the task of classifying humans as an integral part of the animal world; and the central physical feature they used to differentiate one human from the next was skin color. The next logical step was to rank humans from their lowest orders to their highest. Viewed as cursed, sexual savages, black-skinned humans were customarily viewed toward the bottom of the Great Chain of Being, while whites were consistently near the top.[15]

By the time of America's revolution, the idea of black inferiority was firmly embedded in the white, Western psyche. Even those whites who looked down upon slavery still held to the idea of black inferiority. Thomas Jefferson wrote, "in reason they [blacks] are much inferior, as I think one could scarcely be found capable of tracing and comprehending the investigations of Euclid; and that in imagination they are dull, tasteless, and anomalous."[16] Though Jefferson believed that the "moral sense" of blacks was as fully developed as in whites, he consistently argued that blacks were intellectually inferior to whites.[17]

From the pen of an American founder, one realizes, blackness had meaning. The portrait of blacks developed over centuries by scholars and politicians struck fear into the minds and hearts of Americans. In the antebellum period, white Americans feared slave revolts; after all, they had been taught that blacks were naturally savage. In the days following slavery, Harvard Professor Nathanial Southgate Shaler promoted his theory of retrogression, causing some white Americans to fear that in freedom African Americans would regress toward their natural barbaric state.[18] White Americans have used their fear to justify all manifestations of racism, including slavery, segregation, and paternalism.

Joel Williamson, in his book *The Crucible of Race,* reminds his readers that white racism has many faces, or mentalities. Specifically, Williamson traces three racial mentalities among whites in the southern post-bellum period: liberal, radical, and conservative. Racial liberals believed in the potential of African Americans; therefore, though few in numbers, they worked harder than any other group to ensure African American equality. Racial radicals existed at the other end of the continuum, believing African Americans incapable of moving beyond their natural state of barbarism. Radical groups such as the Ku Klux Klan (KKK) found inspiration from Shaler's theory and worked to purge America of African Americans. Racial conservatives existed in the middle of the long continuum. Conservatives did not actively work for African American equality nor did they believe African Americans would naturally gravitate toward a natural barbaric and savage state. Conservatives actively engaged in paternalistic efforts to help African Americans stay in their white-relegated place in society.[19]

Though each mentality viewed and interacted with African Americans differently, each shared the desire to protect their southern, organic society. Williamson's depiction of the southern, organic society proves helpful for any study of southern, American culture, especially one devoted to the topic of race. In describing that society, Williamson wrote, "In that order there would be various parts in the social body, and every part would have its place and function."[20] In order for the society to operate properly, slaves had to assume the role of the slave, and masters had to function as masters. Women took charge of the house, and men protected their families. Over time, these roles calcified in the southern United States and "dissent from within," as Williamson pointed out, "was inconceivable."[21] Dissent from without was largely ignored. As serious, public challenges to the southern, organic society emerged in the mid-twentieth century from within and without, social revolution was the result.

As one might expect, African Americans occupied one of the lowest places in the white-imposed hierarchical society. In the era of slavery, white masters lorded over their black slaves; in the post-bellum period, whites continued to keep blacks in their place through white-imposed Jim Crow segregation. Americans, both of the North and the South, modeled their society after the Victorian family: men protected women and provided for their families, and women served their husbands and took charge of the house. In the South, however, the roles were intensified in an effort to keep African American slaves in their place. For the southern, organic society to function properly, those at the top of the hierarchy had to maintain control over those below. As with the members of the Victorian family, every member of the social body of the South had its place and its function; however, African Americans posed a threat to the southern, organic society.

In the era of slavery, African Americans had their place. There were slaves, and there were masters. As long as slaves stayed in their places under the masters, most whites felt safe and content in their society. Emancipation threatened that society. Free African Americans, wrote Williamson, "were a contradiction in an organic world in which whites were free and Negroes were slaves."[22] In their efforts to maintain their social order, whites instituted racist laws to keep former slaves from challenging their hierarchy.

African Americans reacted to white racism on a long continuum between protest and accommodation. Albert Raboteau has shown that African Americans did not passively accept the racial status quo in the days preceding emancipation.[23] In the North, they established independent African American denominations; and in the South, through the "invisible institution," slaves worshipped independent from white society. Raboteau's scholarship indicates that African Americans never have fully allowed whites to dictate the course of their history. Even in the era of American slavery, slaves and freedmen resisted white domination.

In recent years, many church historians have challenged the long-held view that many African Americans of the post-bellum period willingly accommodated themselves to white authority, retreating instead inside the Black Church for leadership opportunities.[24] Sociologists long have suggested that most African Americans accommodated themselves to post-bellum society, accepting an inferior social status and looking forward to equality only in the next life, in heaven. W. E. B. Dubois, as one example, criticized his African American peers at the turn of the twentieth century for their other-worldly orientation.[25] In 1968, Benjamin Mays, longtime president of Morehouse College, argued that most African Americans held a compensatory view of God, a belief that God offered through the church or even heaven the freedom not afforded African Americans in mainstream American culture.[26] In his final published work, *The Negro Church in America*, E. Franklin Frazier, noted twentieth-century sociologist of African American religion, wrote: "The Negro church remained a refuge despite the fact that the Negro often accepted the disparagement of Negroes by whites and the domination of whites."[27] Carter G. Woodson, the "father of black history," referred to the Black Church of the early twentieth century as a "counter balance" to the more progressive and radical elements of African American society that sought to publicly challenge white racism.[28] Underlying these statements is the belief that most African Americans willingly accommodated to white authority in the public realm. Though each of these scholars acknowledged the militant efforts of particular black clergy against racist white regimes of church and state in the early twentieth century, they recognized efforts of accommodation far more than efforts of protest.

Recent scholarship has noted the balance of accommodation and protest existent within the African American community since the antebellum period. Hans A. Baer, Eugene Genovese, Vincent Harding, Manning Marable, Albert Raboteau, Merrill Singer, and Gayraud Wilmore are among numerous scholars to point out the activism, agency, and protest of African Americans from the days of slavery to the present. In the antebellum period, the Black Church engaged in extra-ecclesiastical activities that challenged the racial status quo, including the National Negro Convention and the Anti-Slavery Society. In the years following the Civil War, African American Christians continued their protest through their involvement with Reconstruction politics, the NAACP, and even some separatist efforts, such as Back to Africa movements.

Protest, however, was not the only path taken by African Americans. They understood well that whites held the power in the southern, organic society; therefore, most African Americans accommodated themselves to white authority, at least on occasion, for the sake of survival. Williamson argued that many African Americans played the role of the Sambo.[29] The name "Sambo" was the name customarily given to the second son in some African cultures, and it also became a popular name among American slaves. By the last generation of slavery, argued Williamson, many whites had developed a stereotypical image of all black people, a singular image that came to be known as Sambo. Williamson wrote:

> The Sambo of imagination was a child adopted into the white family, an adult black body with a white child's mind and heart, simultaneously appealing and appalling, naturally affectionate and unwittingly cruel, a social asset and a liability. Sambo had within him, then, two terrific and opposite capacities. Improperly cared for, he became bestial, an animal in human form and all the more dangerous because of his human capabilities. Properly managed, on the other hand, he was like a child—and dear.[30]

Williamson went on to write, "Sambo was a mask behind which black people might survive the holocaust."[31] When African Americans played the role of Sambo by refusing to look whites in the eyes or by proving through their pliant behavior that they posed no threat to white authority, they did so for survival's sake. Throughout American history, especially southern American history, as long as African Americans played their role well, many paternalistic whites provided for their well-being. As soon as African Americans stepped from behind the mask, however, paternalistic parents transformed, working diligently, sometimes violently, to put the Sambo back in his or her place.

African Americans never have solely adopted an accommodationist posture, and neither have they ever solely embraced the posture of protest. Indeed, this tension continually has existed within the African American community and within individual members of that community. In other words, African Americans were as varied as whites in their responses to the social constructions of black and white.

The previous paragraphs have illustrated that white racism against blacks did not originate in the American South, nor did it begin in the post-bellum period. Blackness and whiteness developed meaning over time and place. Society, not God or nature, constructed this meaning. For the purposes of this study, it remains important to examine more closely how one facet of that society, the church, addressed the questions of race and racism.

Racism and Christianity

American Christians have mirrored the racism of society since the days of colonization. Though a small minority, including John Woolman and the Quakers, challenged slavery long before most others, a vast majority of Christians and Christian denominations refused to challenge the racial status quo of American society.[32] Racist ideology was present even in Puritan New England. Samuel Willard, Congregational minister of South Church in Boston, spoke on the subject of chattel slavery during a 1703 sermon. Exposing his racist ideology, he said, "All servitude began in the curse."[33] For an influential Congregational minister to offer his support of the Haminite myth from a prominent pulpit suggests that the myth received wide acceptance in the eighteenth-century colonies. Cotton Mather, perhaps the best known church leader of his age, made a similar statement concerning slavery. Speaking to Christian slave-owners in 1706, Mather urged those masters to teach their slaves "that it is God who caused them to be servants."[34] Instead of challenging slavery or the societal definition of blackness, these leading Christian leaders agreed with and publicly endorsed the common racist ideology of colonial America.

Many white Christian leaders encouraged masters to evangelize their slaves, arguing that the gospel would make them more compliant. William Fleetwood, a bishop and member of the Anglican Society for the Propagation of the Gospel in Foreign Parts, told masters that Christianity posed no threat to slavery. In fact, he said that masters "are neither prohibited by the Laws [sic] of God, nor those of the Land [sic], from keeping Christian slaves; their slaves are no more at Liberty [sic] after they are Baptized[sic], than they were before."[35] Echoing the sentiments of Fleetwood, George Whitefield, the foremost revivalist of the early eighteenth century, wrote in his journal, "I believe masters and mistresses will shortly see that Christianity will not make their negroes worse slaves."[36] By the close of the colonial period, most Christian leaders associated slavery with blackness. Instead of joining abolitionists, most religious leaders found ways through scripture either to justify the meaning given to blackness by society or to create the racist ideology themselves.

Certainly, there were some white Christian leaders who disapproved of slavery in the colonial era, yet even those individuals and groups held to the notion of black inferiority. The Quakers, though they excluded slaveholders from membership of their denomination by the time of the American Revolution, never adopted the ideology of racial equality. African Americans such as William Bowen and Isaac Linegar sought membership into the Society of Friends for many years before finally being allowed to join.[37] Once Quaker meetings finally admitted African Americans, they were most often forced to sit in "special places" (against walls, under stairs, or in the gallery).[38] When a Quaker meeting house in Philadelphia was redesigned in 1756, the persons planning the building were instructed to allot suitable places for African Americans to sit.[39] Other abolitionists shared the ideology of black inferiority. Puritan Judge Samuel Sewall of Boston worked throughout his lifetime for the emancipation of slaves, yet he also said, "There is such a disparity in their conditions, colour [sic] and hair, that they can never embody with us, and grow up into orderly families, to the peopling of the land: but still remain in our body politick as a kind of extravasat blood."[40] The meaning of blackness had become so entrenched in the Western psyche that even those whites who worked most ardently for African American equality refused to view slaves and former slaves as their equals.

White Christian leaders continued to uphold the racial status quo into and beyond the Revolutionary Period. Abolitionism ultimately failed in its effort to eradicate slavery in the eighteenth century, and one cannot solely blame the South for its failure. Smith argued that the North shared many components of the South's racist ideology, and the two regions joined in their efforts to defeat abolitionists.[41] Most northerners and southerners agreed that slavery was not sinful in all circumstances. Northerners, like southerners, seriously questioned the abolitionist doctrine of immediate emancipation. Much like their southern counterparts, many northerners believed in the natural barbarism of blacks; therefore, the prospect of unleashing tens of thousands of savages in the country frightened as many northerners as southerners. Hence, even among those northerners who favored emancipation, many joined colonization societies, such as the American Colonization Society, which had the goal of sending freed slaves back to Africa.

By the time of the American Civil War, white southerners not only were in agreement with the ideology of black inferiority, but also were willing to go to war in order to keep African Americans in their place within southern society. In addition to offering Ham's curse as divine sanction and biblical justification for slavery, many southern religious leaders including George A. Baxter, Stephen Taylor, and George W. Freeman pointed to Paul's instructions to masters and slaves in Ephesians and Colossians.[42] The southern pro-slavery arguments centered on Paul's admonition that masters and slaves fulfill their respective duties toward one another and also that Paul's congregations had slaveholders, yet Paul never encouraged those members to free their slaves.[43] Robert Dabney, a Presbyterian theologian and ardent defender of slavery, wrote, "Here is our policy then, to push the Bible argument continually, drive abolitionism to the wall, to compel it to assume an anti-Christian position."[44]

The American Civil War and the debate over slavery divided North and South, but it also divided Christian from Christian; and both sides used the Bible as ammunition against the other. The biblical debate over slavery, however, did not begin in the nineteenth century. Two Boston lawyers, Samuel Sewall and John Saffin, engaged in this debate 150 years before the Civil War, and the debate continued to rage long after the treaty was signed between the North and the South. As E. Brooks Holifield wrote, long before biblical criticism made inroads into American Christianity, slavery forced Christian thinkers to ask critical questions about the history and development of scripture and doctrine.[45] Christian ministers and theologians had to choose between biblical literalism or an alternative reading of scripture that took into account the history and cultural context of biblical authors. During this era, many of those who chose to maintain a biblical hermeneutic based on literalism resided in the South. Southern white Christians used their hermeneutic to provide further support for their ideology of black inferiority.

In the century following the Civil War, southern white Christians used that same hermeneutic to justify white-imposed segregation and paternalism. Even after emancipation, white southerners worked to keep African Americans in their white-imposed place. Henry Tucker, prominent educator and minister of the Southern Baptist denomination, instituted a racial creed in 1883 after some members of his denomination accused him of being "unsafe" on the "Negro question."[46] In what Tucker called his "Confession of Faith," he asserted, "We do not believe that all men are created equal."[47] He went on to write: "We believe that our race is incomparably superior to any other. . . . As to the Negro, we do not know where to place him; perhaps not at the bottom of the list, but certainly not near the top."[48] Rufus B. Spain argued that Tucker's confession was that of virtually all of his fellow Southern Baptists.[49] Whether Spain's estimation is correct or not, certainly a large number of southern Christians, members and non-members of the Southern Baptist denomination, believed in black inferiority and worked throughout their lives to keep African Americans below whites in the southern hierarchy. To Tucker's name could be added countless others, including Charles Carroll, Richard Rivers, and William Brown.[50] Carroll asserted that blacks were not the descendents of Ham but instead a soulless beast. In his *Elements of Moral Philosophy,* Rivers wrote that whites no longer had the duty of master to slave to African Americans but instead of superior to inferior. This book was reprinted three times between 1887 and 1890, and it became a standard for the Methodist denomination. Brown, a bishop in the Protestant Episcopal Church, argued that blacks were digressing toward barbarism, and he advocated strict separation. Each of these Christians worked along with non-Christian members of society to reinforce the negative connotations of blackness.

The church continued to support racism and the ideology of black inferiority well into the twentieth century. In the early twentieth century, significant leaders in each of the three largest southern denominations offered public support for the KKK. Editors of the *Presbyterian of the South* wrote, "So far as we have been able to learn, the leaders of the Klan are honorable men."[51] The Southern Baptist Convention most often ignored the violence of the KKK but, on occasion, offered subtle support for the organization.[52] During the 1922 General Conference of the southern Methodist Church, a minister who discouraged the violence of the KKK, Will Alexander, was forbidden to read a paper in which he attacked the organization. Alexander later wrote that his experience in 1922 led him to cut ties with his longtime denomination.[53]

Though some southern white Christians made token efforts toward African Americans, such as the Race Relations Sundays instituted by the Federal Council of Churches, white members of southern denominations ordinarily modeled the racism of previous generations. Throughout the twentieth century, most white Christians in the South supported Jim Crow segregation, engaged in paternalistic gestures toward their African American regional counterparts, and embraced the societal construction of blackness.

African American Christians, on the other hand, have consistently challenged the ideology of black inferiority through a variety of accommodation and protest tactics since the era of American colonization. In the North, African American Christians instituted the independent church movement. Beginning in 1787 when Richard Allen and Absalom Jones protested white racism by walking out of St. George's Methodist Episcopal Church and Allen's subsequent establishment of the African Methodist Episcopal (AME) Church in 1794, African Americans in the North established numerous denominations independent of white control. Pressured during a worship service by white members of St. George's to end their prayers and to vacate their seats prematurely for white worshippers, Allen and Jones walked out of the church building with a sizeable African American contingent behind them. Their actions indicate that northern African American Christians did not passively accept white racism.

Southern African American Christians in the Colonial Period, likewise, refused to fully accept the racist status quo. Peter Randolph, one-time slave and Baptist preacher, wrote in his autobiography that many slaves, in protest against their masters, rejected Christianity altogether. Even if white masters forced their slaves to attend white worship services, some slaves, wrote Randolph, stood outside "selling refreshments, cake, candy and rum, and others would be horse-racing."[54] Many of those slaves who did become Christian grew tired of their white counterparts stressing the obligation of slaves to obey their masters; consequently, they would steal away from white society and their white masters in order to worship secretly in brush arbors. Their worship services were often much more emotive than white services. Mary Boykin Chesnut, a white visitor to a slave worship service, described the repeated shouting and clapping of the event, neither of which were customary for white services.[55] Slave preachers became influential figures in slave communities, offering messages of freedom to their peers through dramatic and image-filled sermons.[56]

In the post-bellum period, African Americans continued to reject white racism. As a bishop in the AME Church, Henry McNeal Turner urged African Americans to reject white racism and encouraged them to view God in their own image, black.[57] Turner perceived the plight of African Americans so dire in the United States that he encouraged African Americans to relocate to Africa. In 1883, Turner wrote, "I would make Africa the place of refuge, because I see no other shelter from the stormy blast, from the red tide of persecution, from the horrors of American prejudice."[58] In addition to Turner, many other African American ministers challenged white racism and encouraged others to follow in their footsteps. T. McCants Stewart, a New York AME minister, championed the cause of African American political independence from his post on the city's school board.[59] In 1865, J. W. Wood, a bishop in the AME Zion Church, supported a series of reforms for African Americans which included suffrage rights.[60]

During the twentieth century, long before the Civil Rights Movement, African American Christian leaders in the American South continued to push at varying degrees against white-imposed segregation and racism. African American religious intellectuals, such as Howard Thurman and Benjamin Elijah Mays, used their posts at historic black colleges to plant the seeds of the Civil Rights Movement in the minds of Martin Luther King Jr. and other mid-twentieth century protesters. Similar to Turner a generation earlier, Thurman encouraged African Americans to identify with a God like them. Comparing Jesus to "one with his back against the wall," Thurman wrote that Jesus fully understood the condition of a poor minority with little to few rights.[61] As president of Morehouse College, Mays spoke in chapel every Tuesday. Often following those chapel addresses, King would linger behind to have private conversations with his "spiritual mentor" about white racism, segregation, and potential African American responses to them.[62]

Though white society constructed meanings of white and black, African Americans refused to accept their definitions. The tension between white and black definitions often led to ideological and physical impasses. Especially in the American South, racism divided African Americans from their white counterparts. Racism also divided African American and white Christians in southern churches.

One such southern denomination, Churches of Christ, reflected their southern context. This study offers a closer look at this southern branch of the Stone-Campbell Movement. Within Churches of Christ, there have been racial liberals, radicals, and conservatives. Within Churches of Christ, African Americans have oscillated between accommodation and protest. Members of Churches of Christ have proven time and again that blackness and whiteness have meaning.

A Brief Outline

If one were to undertake the task of writing an exhaustive history of the American South, a substantial portion of that work, or perhaps the underlying theme of the entire book, would center on the confrontation of African Americans and whites. African Americans understood the society well; they had lived in the South as long as had whites. Left with few options, some African Americans chose to appease whites by staying in their place; others chose to publicly challenge the racial status quo. All African Americans moved back and forth on the long continuum between protest and accommodation. As white racial liberals, radicals, and conservatives consistently defended the hierarchic structure of society, African American protesters and accommodationists (in varying degrees and with varying methods) consistently worked against it. This book attempts to tell a microcosm of that larger story by examining one small slice of the southern, organic society, namely Churches of Christ.

This work consists of five chapters in addition to an epilogue. Chapter one presents a brief overview of denominational journals, colleges, and lectureships. Lacking official denominational bodies for their governance, Churches of Christ have relied on these three entities to mediate its theology. Denominational leaders have articulated their theological positions in journals, they have trained ministers in colleges, and they have spoken to large audiences at annual lectureships. In each of these venues, white leaders have given their audiences the impression of racial unity. Lacking other, more formal, venues for articulation or theological negotiation, those examining the denomination from within and without have seen an illusion of unity. Denominational journals, colleges, and lectureships have shielded from view the full extent of the division between African American and white members of Churches of Christ.

Chapter two examines Churches of Christ from the late nineteenth century to the dawn of the Civil Rights Movement. During this period, African Americans and whites remained separated through white-imposed segregation. The life and ministry of David Lipscomb and Marshall Keeble will receive special attention. Lipscomb, the most prominent white denominational leader of the early twentieth century oscillated between the poles of racial liberal and conservative in his days as editor of the *Gospel Advocate*. Even though he openly opposed segregated congregations, his rhetoric betrayed his allegiance to the racist ideology of his southern region. Keeble, the best known African American preacher in the history of Churches of Christ, has long been portrayed as a strict accommodationist, yet this study will show that, behind the scenes, even Keeble sought an end to white-imposed segregation. Keeble, like many of his African American peers, including Booker T. Washington, Whitney M. Young Sr., and Lucius Henry Holsey, oscillated between protest and accommodation throughout his career.

Chapter three focuses exclusively on the period of the American Civil Rights Movement. The revolutionary effects of that era affected Churches of Christ as much as any other southern denomination. During the 1950s and 1960s, African American members of the denomination declared their independence from white-imposed segregation and paternalism. Fred Gray and R. N. Hogan joined African Americans from other predominantly white denominations such as Gayraud Wilmore of the PCUSA in their public challenges of racism among white church leaders in journals, lectureships, and even the courtroom.

Chapter four turns to a pivotal event in the history of Churches of Christ race relations. In 1967, African American members sued white members over a series of events that transpired during the closing of Nashville Christian Institute, an African American denominational school. With this court case, African American members of Churches of Christ publicly asserted their independence from white control. In 1967, African Americans revealed a secret to their white counterparts: they had resented white-imposed segregation, paternalism, and racism for decades. Only in the aftermath of the Civil Rights Movement, however, did they collectively and publicly challenge the southern and denominational racist status quo.

Chapter five traces the development of African American Churches of Christ in the last quarter of the twentieth century. No longer even tokenly united to white Churches of Christ, African Americans turned their attention to their own school (Southwestern Christian College), their own journal (the *Christian Echo*), and their own lectureship (the Annual Southwestern Christian College Bible Lectureship). African Americans such as Jack Evans, Fred Gray, and J. S. Winston provided leadership for the denomination without the historic support of the *Gospel Advocate*, Abilene Christian University, or various white lectureships. In their physical separation from white members of Churches of Christ, however, theological separation has developed, especially in the arena of biblical hermeneutics.

The epilogue of this study looks to the future. In many respects the estrangement between African Americans and whites at the close of the twentieth century resembled another division in the history of the Stone-Campbell

Movement. In the waning years of the nineteenth century, those individuals and congregations that made up the eventual Churches of Christ looked increasingly dissimilar from eventual members of the Disciples of Christ. In both cases, physical estrangement, over time, led to theological estrangement. If history repeats itself, those living in the first decades of the twenty-first century could witness yet another significant division within Campbell's Movement, this time along racial lines.

CHAPTER 1

UNDERSTANDING CHURCHES OF CHRIST

Race matters. Race and racism have divided African American and white members of Churches of Christ as much as any other southern American denomination, yet key aspects of their identity have masked the extent of their separation. White denominational journals, colleges, and lectureships have created an illusion of racial unity; however, a closer examination of these sources as well as African American journals and speeches reveals its racially divided history. Chapters that follow will trace in detail how white denominational leaders used journals, colleges, and lectureships to conceal the racial divide in Churches of Christ. But first we begin with a closer look at these mediating influences and the roles they have played in Churches of Christ for more than a century.

Denominational Organization

Even though most southern white denominational leaders advocated and supported the racist regime of their region, they, at the very least, recognized and attempted to address the problem of race in their denominations. James S. Thomas and Joel L. Alvis Jr. provide windows into two such denominations.

In *Methodism's Racial Dilemma: The Story of the Central Jurisdiction,* Thomas recounts the manner in which the Methodist Church, a predominantly white denomination, debated about how to integrate its large African American constituency into the fabric of the denomination. When the Methodist Church united in 1939 (bringing together the Methodist Episcopal Church; the Methodist Episcopal Church, South; and the Methodist Protestant Church), the newly formed denomination maintained its single General Conference but structured six jurisdictional conferences to provide for its governance. Of the six jurisdictional conferences, geography defined five and race defined the other. These six jurisdictional conferences and one General Conference connected thousands of individual congregations by providing denominational programs, appointing ministers to serve at local congregations, and settling theological disagreements among members of the denomination. Alvis explores race relations in the Presbyterian Church in the United States (PCUS) in his book *Religion and Race: Southern Presbyterians, 1946-1983.* Not unlike Thomas, Alvis traces the path of the PCUS as it sought to move as a racially united denomination through the tumultuous years following the Civil War and into the era of the American Civil Rights Movement. In each of these predominantly white denominations, leaders recognized within their congregations problems centered on race and took steps to solve those problems.

The thinking and practices of these denominations were informed by the racist ideology of the southern, organic society. African Americans certainly did not have an equal voice with whites, and the centralized structures of these denominations did not bridge the chasm created by race. Indeed, many scholars agree that the centralized structures themselves resulted from the white leadership's desire to maintain control over African Americans in the post-bellum period.[1] African Americans of both denominations resented the white-imposed segregated structures, fearing they would discount or render silent their voices. The Plan of Union voted upon during the 1939 General Conference of the Methodist Church included the plan for the Central Jurisdiction. Of the forty-seven African American delegates to the General Conference, thirty-six voted against the plan; and eleven abstained.

In his 2008 study of the Methodist unification, Morris L. Davis explained how white Methodists in favor of union urged African Americans to set aside the "mere rights" for the greater good of unity.[2] In the early twentieth century, as American nationalism coincided with the rapid numerical growth of

Methodism, many denominational leaders viewed denominational unity not only in the best interest of Methodists, but also in the best interest of America. Methodist unification, argued its supporters, was in the best interest of the largest and most powerful Protestant denomination of the country. Despite passionate appeals against the establishment of the Central Jurisdiction by Robert Elijah Jones, an African American member of the Joint Commission, the Methodist Church went forward with their plans in 1939. Davis reported that as white delegates to the 1939 Uniting Conference cheered the decision and stood to sing "We're Marching to Zion," most of the eighty-seven black Methodist delegates remained seated in protest in one corner of the segregated auditorium.[3] The evidence suggests African Americans did not welcome "official segregation" within their denominations.[4]

Notwithstanding the racist ideology of southern denominational leaders, however, the central governing structures of the Methodist and Presbyterian denominations, much like other southern denominations, brought into the foreground the issue of race. Additionally, the white-imposed, segregated structures set in place by central denominational systems did, in fact, offer a certain level of cohesion, uniting African American and white denominational members. Even though racism and resentment dominated these denominations, their centralized bodies kept lines of communication open between African Americans and whites. Furthermore, their general conferences, synods, and assemblies disallowed whites of the denomination from ignoring African Americans altogether. The Methodist Church met to discuss African Americans in the denomination and made segregation official through the Central Jurisdiction. The PCUS met to discuss African Americans in the denomination and formed the Committee on Negro Work and the Black Presbyterian Leadership Council. These bodies did not end racism within their denominations, but they prevented white denominational leaders from ignoring their African American constituency.

Given the large number of African American members and ministers, one may wonder how predominantly white denominations could possibly ignore such a large constituency. In 2005, 3.2 percent of the entire membership of the Presbyterian Church (USA) or 74,000 individuals made up the African American membership of the denomination.[5] In 2007, the National African American Fellowship of the Southern Baptist Convention reported that one million of the denomination's 16 million members were African American.[6]

The 8.5 million members of the United Methodist Church include 319,000 African Americans.[7]

The question arises, however, as to what would happen in a denomination if it were left without the benefit of a general conference or synod to discuss the issue? How then would the denomination attempt to solve the race problem in its midst? Would the denomination meet to discuss the issue at all or would the issue of race remain ignored altogether? Churches of Christ, another predominantly white denomination, have a membership of just over one million people, 169,000 of whom are African American.[8] In spite of the denomination's large African American membership, white leaders (with the help of key African American leaders), virtually ignored the racism that dominated the denomination during the twentieth century.

Some of their ignorance may be traced to one of their most cherished ideals, namely congregational autonomy. Members of a denomination born in the age of Enlightenment, most Churches of Christ adherents prefer their autonomous congregational polity; and differences flourish accordingly. Woodmont Hills Church of Christ in Nashville, Tennessee, allows women to lead in the weekly Eucharistic service; Orient Street Church of Christ in Stamford, Texas, only allows women to teach children's Bible classes. Only a few Churches of Christ congregations have adopted the use of instrumental music during their worship services; others believe this act constitutes a blatant disregard for God's clear commands in scripture. Rubel Shelly, a well-known preacher in Churches of Christ, met for decades with other denominational leaders in Nashville while many of his Churches of Christ peers in the same city considered this type of interaction anathema.[9] Congregational leaders within the denomination are Trinitarians, modalists, and Arians; they are premillennialists, postmillennialists, and amillennialists; they are exclusivists, inclusivists, and universalists. Despite these examples of variation, thousands of congregations bearing the name "Church of Christ" on their marquees cover the American landscape, each one somehow united to the next. This phenomenon, coupled with the apparent lack of any structural system of cohesion, begs the question, "What provides cohesion and direction for this seemingly disconnected denomination?"

Lacking an official governing body, Churches of Christ have sought direction through denominational journals, colleges, and lectureships. For more than a century, these three entities have helped Churches of Christ leaders mediate differences in theology, worship, and even race relations. Lacking a general conference or assembly, denominational leaders addressed key theological issues from the pages of the *Gospel Advocate,* the lecture halls of Abilene Christian College, and the annual Tulsa Soul Winning Workshop. The editors, administrators, and lectureship directors of the various platforms provided a service to the denomination by permitting certain leaders the opportunity to articulate their theological positions to members of Churches of Christ; however, those same editors, administrators, and lectureship directors also served as a filter for the denomination, allowing some information to flow freely while blocking other voices and positions.

Throughout the late nineteenth and early twentieth centuries, Churches of Christ journals, colleges, and lectureships virtually ignored the white racism that pervaded the American South. On the rare occasion that a white editor, administrator, or lectureship director did mention African Americans, he always presented an illusion of racial unity. When African American leaders allowed their resentment to spill to the surface, especially in the 1960s, white leaders continued to ignore denominational racism; consequently, the chasm that always separated African American and white members continued to increase. In order to better understand these mediating forces in Churches of Christ, the following paragraphs explore them in greater depth.

Churches of Christ Journals

In 1909, W. T. Moore stated, "The Disciples of Christ do not have bishops, but they have editors."[10] Lacking hierarchical structures or personalities and devoid of denominational conferences, synods, or assemblies, men such as Alexander Campbell and David Lipscomb used their posts in the *Millennial Harbinger* and the *Gospel Advocate,* respectively, to mediate the theology of the Stone-Campbell Movement. Denominational journals have served as forums where laypersons and leaders have been able to articulate their theological positions, attempting to inform and influence members' positions on matters of doctrine, polity, and, on occasion, race.

Without examining every issue or era through which periodicals influenced Churches of Christ, this study examines two key events in the early years of the Stone-Campbell Movement. The events serve as windows into two important concepts of this project, namely race relationships and denominational coherence. The first event centers on the denomination's response to American slavery.[11] The second reflects the role played by denominational periodicals in the division between Churches of Christ and Disciples of Christ in the late nineteenth and early twentieth centuries. Both events exemplify the inability of the journals to maintain denominational cohesion.

Not unlike most other American religious bodies in the nineteenth century, the Stone-Campbell Movement was plagued by the issue of slavery. The moral dilemma created by this issue rendered it, like the rest of the nation, divided. Pro-slavery proponents, James Shannon among them, articulated the biblical precedent for slavery.[12] John Boggs and other abolitionists used venues such as the *North-Western Christian Magazine* to espouse their view that slavery constituted blatant sin.[13]

The most influential opinions concerning slavery, however, found expression in the writings of Alexander Campbell's *Millennial Harbinger*. Though the Stone-Campbell Movement lacked an official president, head bishop, or pope, Campbell wielded much influence on the denomination by virtue of his debating ability, his inclusion as an author in numerous publications, his editorship of the *Millennial Harbinger*, and his establishment of Bethany College. By the 1830s, Campbell already had published *The Living Oracles* (his translation of the New Testament), edited the *Christian Baptist* for nearly a decade, and served as a delegate to the 1829 Virginia Constitutional Convention. As the debates over slavery were raging in America, Campbell's voice was one often heard within his denomination.

Campbell sporadically addressed the slavery issue over a thirty-year period (from 1830-1860).[14] Like most other early leaders of the denomination, the union of all Christians existed as one of Campbell's primary concerns. This quest for unity persuaded him from siding with either abolitionists or proponents of slavery; therefore, he often received sharp criticism from both. Unmasking his chief concern, Campbell wrote: "To preserve unity of spirit among Christians of the South and of the North is my grand object, and for that purpose I am endeavoring to show how the New Testament does not authorize an interference or legislation upon the relation of master and slave, nor does it in letter or spirit authorize Christians to make it a term of communion."[15] Campbell attempted to ward off division within his movement by articulating a middle position on the slavery issue.

Campbell built his position on two essential ideals of the Christian Church, restoration and unity. The first of these ideals, restoration, arises from Campbell's biblical hermeneutic. Seeking the pattern of first-century Christianity as identified from the pages of the New Testament, he found no scriptural warrant for abolitionism. In his epic 1845 series, he stated: "As Christians, we can lawfully, under Christ, go no further than to exact from Christian masters and Christian servants all that is comprehended in those [biblical] precepts."[16] Again, in the same year, Campbell wrote, "There is not one verse in the Bible inhibiting it, but many regulating it. It is not, then, we conclude, immoral."[17]

These statements would seem to support Campbell's identity as a southern Virginian aristocrat.[18] In reality, however, Campbell did not approve of slavery. During the 1829 Constitutional Convention of Virginia, he lobbied for anti-slavery legislation, but the eastern aristocracy of the state defeated the bill.[19] On the first page of the first issue of the *Millennial Harbinger,* Campbell listed one subject of interest for the new periodical: "Disquisitions upon the treatment of African slaves, as preparation to their emancipation and exaltation from their present degraded condition."[20] On another occasion, he described slavery as "that largest and blackest blot upon our national eschutcheon, that many-headed monster, that Pandora's box, that bitter root, that blighting and blasting curse."[21]

Though Campbell disagreed with slavery, he should not be compared to nineteenth-century abolitionists such as Theodore Dwight Weld. An educator who came under fire at Cincinnati's Lane Seminary in 1834 for his radical abolitionist views, Weld found biblical justification for emancipation, which he outlined in his pamphlet, *The Bible Against Slavery*. Weld publicly condemned slavery as an institution against the will of God; Campbell never made any such proclamation.

Given Campbell's rejection of slavery, coupled with his unwillingness to work actively toward its abolition, he fit the description of Joel Williamson's "racial conservative."[22] Campbell's racial ideology rested on African American inferiority. As evidence of Campbell's ideology, one should look no further than the first paragraph of his epic treatise on slavery from the *Millennial Harbinger.* As he discussed the prospect of granting freedom to the nation's slave population, he wrote: "One thing is most evident, that without intelligence or virtue on the part of the people, such chartered rights are dangerous investments."[23] Campbell shared the conviction of many racial conservatives that African Americans lacked the mental capacity of whites. Racial conservatives of the nineteenth-century South, though they rejected slavery, still felt uneasy about the prospect of releasing so many thousands of slaves into the general population. Instead, many of them, like Campbell, worked diligently for the American Colonization Society (ACS), hoping to colonize Liberia with former American slaves. In his work with the ACS, Campbell joined other evangelical proponents of colonization such as Congregationalist Jehudi Ashmun who traveled to Liberia in 1822 to help lead one such colony.

Foreseeing the national debt quickly satisfied, Campbell urged the government to use the money ordinarily appropriated to that end for colonization of American slaves in Africa.[24] Although some African Americans, such as Edward W. Blyden, saw the ACS as a "humane, philanthropic, and far-seeing work," many others, such as Martin R. Delaney, Richard Allen, and James Forten, viewed the ACS with contempt, believing the society was a ploy of whites to rid America of African Americans.[25] Jess O. Hale argues that Campbell's involvement with the ACS stemmed from his desire to ease the economic burden of the South as it moved to a free labor economy.[26] Though economics certainly may have played some role in Campbell's association with the ACS, Hale fails to recognize any other possibilities, including racism. Campbell's conviction that a Union full of freed slaves constituted a "dangerous investment," most likely influenced his ACS involvement. In his study of the formation of the ACS, Henry Noble Sherwood argued that racism played a central role in the society's formation. Charles Fenton Mercer, an early supporter of the ACS, justified his position before the President of the United States by suggesting that the rapidly increasing free black population "endangered the peace of the State."[27] Many white racial conservatives, including Campbell, viewed the ACS as a better alternative than abolitionism.

More important for this study than Campbell's personal views on slavery, however, was his position as leader of a unity movement. He and Barton W. Stone were the most prominent figures in the early days of the Christian Church. Stone, like Campbell, was an author, debater, and editor; and he also received notoriety from his leadership at the Cane Ridge Revival, which took place at his home congregation in August of 1801. A further indication of his place within the movement comes from his role in the union meetings of 1831. When the Christians of Middle Tennessee and Kentucky joined the Disciples of the Ohio Valley, Stone was chosen to represent his peers in the meeting with the Campbellites.[28]

The Campbellites and Stoneites were not the only American religious groups of the early nineteenth century to seek unity. Abner Jones and Elias Smith, also recognizing the divided state of religion in America, joined in order to create the Christian Connection in 1802. E. Brooks Holifield argues that, following the American Revolution, these leaders created a "cultural commotion" spreading across the American landscape with "renewed force."[29] Campbell and Stone joined many other like-minded American religious leaders of the early nineteenth century in their quest to unite Christians of all denominations; yet, in the days leading up to the Civil War, both leaders were having difficulty maintaining unity within their own denomination. Having just witnessed the fissure within the Methodist and Baptist denominations, Campbell wrote his 1845 *Millennial Harbinger* series, hoping to avoid such a division in his own denomination.[30] In the years prior to the Civil War, Campbell did not find his primary motivation from abolitionists, proponents of slavery, state's rights supporters, or morality. Unity was his chief aim. From 1830-1860, Campbell sought to become a mediator within the denomination, urging abolitionists, proponents of slavery, and every individual in between to remember the most important ideals of the church. In his mind, those ideals were restoration and unity.

Richard Hughes rightly points out that Campbell seemed unable to grasp that these twin ideals, restoration and unity, were "mutually exclusive terms."[31] The kind of restoration advocated by Campbell, especially from the *Christian Baptist*, necessarily lent itself to sectarianism. As Campbell alienated everyone or every group that did not share his vision of the primitive church, he made unity nearly impossible. A denomination built upon these two ideals was destined for conflict and division, and would find itself in desperate need of a mediating influence. Campbell attempted to play that role in the mid-nineteenth century.

Commenting upon Campbell's role as mediator within the Christian Church, T. Brian Pendleton writes: "This mediating position offers a window into the mind of a leader who sought to strengthen the Disciples' ability to weather the storm of slavery in a manner many other religious groups did not."[32] In an attempt to measure the influence of denominational journals within Churches of Christ, one must ask the pivotal question: What were the effects of Campbell's words in the *Millennial Harbinger*? Was Campbell successful in maintaining denominational unity or not?

Alexander Campbell was the foremost first-generation leader of the Stone-Campbell Movement, which includes Churches of Christ. From his editorial post at the *Millennial Harbinger* he sought to offer direction on the subject of slavery and prevent his movement from splintering during the Civil War.

Barton Stone, the other namesake of the Stone-Campbell Movement, offered leadership and cohesion to his movement through his roles as author, debater, and editor.

Numerous scholars of the Stone-Campbell Movement have followed the lead of Moses E. Lard, a mid-nineteenth-century editor bishop, who argued that the Stone-Campbell Movement was the only fellowship of Christians not to divide in that period.[33] Winifred Ernest Garrison and Alfred T. DeGroot estimated that during the period in question there were 1,241 Stone-Campbell congregations in the North and 829 in the South with just over 100,000 total members.[34] Though the majority of members lived above the Mason-Dixon Line, the denomination certainly had large representation in both slave and free states. Despite this large representation, Campbell's denomination, in their estimation, did not divide over the slavery issue. Unlike the Methodists, Baptists, and many other American denominations, the Stone-Campbell Movement remained intact for another quarter century; and the issues that eventually divided Disciples of Christ and Churches of Christ, though certainly influenced by sectionalism, did not include slavery.[35] Another supporter of this view, Jess Hale, believes that Campbell's denomination eventually divided over the use of instrumental music in worship, not slavery. He cites Campbell's ability to moderate the slavery discussion within the denomination through the *Millennial Harbinger* as the chief factor preventing formal division. While others may have "aggravated passions," Hale writes, "Campbell did try to moderate the matter."[36]

According to Garrison, DeGroot, and Hale, Campbell succeeded. Certainly, two denominations with their own independent structures did not arise from the formerly united Stone-Campbell Movement in the mid-nineteenth century, one situated in the North supporting the abolitionist cause and the other situated in the South supporting slavery. Nevertheless, one should not dismiss the possibility of division along these lines.

In some respects, the plight of the Stone-Campbell Movement mirrors the Episcopal Church of the same period. The Episcopal Church avoided a formal division during the period of the Civil War, and it also avoided separate, racially defined conferences. These factors alone would lead some to believe the Episcopal Church experienced far less turmoil over the race issue than did its denominational counterparts; however, Gardiner H. Shattuck's recent work reveals that official division is not the only kind of division.[37] From the days of the Civil War to the Civil Rights Movement, the Episcopal Church, though a unified denomination, addressed racial tension through separation and paternalism. African Americans within the denomination even had their own school, Bishop Payne Divinity School in Petersburg, Virginia, and various subsidiary organizations, such as the Conference of Church Workers among Colored People. The governing body of the Episcopal Church never allowed an official division to occur, but the denomination maintained separation in other ways. The Stone-Campbell Movement maintained its separation for different reasons.

Campbell's words in the *Millennial Harbinger* concerning slavery and even the reactions of subsequent denominational leaders to them may have created a picture of denominational unity; but, upon closer inspection, one realizes that this picture is only an illusion. Campbell succeeded in warding off an official division only because the denomination lacked an official governing body to declare the reality of such a division. A separation did begin to manifest itself between what eventually became the Disciples of Christ and the Churches of Christ shortly after the end of the war ; and, just as slavery was the root cause of the Civil War, it also can be called the root cause of the division between Churches of Christ and Disciples of Christ.

Slavery divided North from South. Slavery caused southern Americans to distance themselves from their northern counterparts and to form their own unique and separate identity. Following the Civil War, Stone-Campbell Movement congregations in the South distanced themselves from their northern counterparts and even began to solidify themselves around new clusters of influence: the *Gospel Advocate* and Nashville Bible School. Henry E. Webb, in his discussion of a northern journal, the *Christian Standard*, which became the most important early publication of the Disciples of Christ, writes that many northern congregations began to identify with the *Christian Standard* while most southern congregations identified with the *Gospel Advocate*.[38]

A perusal of the *Gospel Advocate* from the years following the Civil War reveals a distinctly southern character. Stemming from his desire to highlight Lipscomb's counter-cultural, premillennial worldview, Hughes discounts the sectional bias of the *Gospel Advocate* in the post-bellum period, stating that Lipscomb's anti-northern rhetoric simply reflected the editor's disdain for all human governments.[39] Hughes is correct to a certain degree; but, in his attempt to prove Lipscomb's premillennialist tendencies, he downplays the strong pro-southern and equally strong anti-northern language of Lipscomb during this period. Though Lipscomb denied any sectional bias in an 1866 article, he wrote in the same paragraph, "that we had not a single paper known to us that the Southern people could read without having their feelings wounded by political insinuations and slurs, had more to do with calling the ADVOCATE into existence, than all other circumstances combined."[40] He went on to write in the same article that the editors of the *Gospel Advocate* had the habits and feelings of the southern people in mind.[41] Several years later, in one telling statement concerning his views of both northerners and southerners, Lipscomb said southerners respect the Bible and religion more than their northern counterparts, who are more prone to "infidel theories."[42] Lipscomb also wrote an article defending the character of southerners against the attacks of Isaac Errett, then editor of the *Christian Standard*.[43] Accusing his northern counterparts of ignoring the efforts of southerners to improve the condition of freed persons, Lipscomb argued that southerners were in fact more benevolent than northerners to former slaves.[44] The animosity present in Lipscomb's tone suggests a strong sectional division between the editors of the *Gospel Advocate* and the editors of the *Christian Standard*.[45]

Though the denomination lacked an official governing body to declare division, articles from the two leading journals of the Stone-Campbell Movement following the Civil War suggest the presence of two factions, one situated primarily in the North and the other situated primarily in the South. Regardless of Campbell's attempt through the *Millennial Harbinger* to steer his denomination away from schism, the Stone-Campbell Movement did, in fact, experience an ideological divide much like the rest of the country in the central decades of the nineteenth century.

One should compare this situation in the Stone-Campbell Movement with other religious groups of the period. When disagreements arose between northern and southern Baptists over the right of slaveholders to become missionaries, many southern Baptists withdrew their support from the Triennial Convention, founding instead the Southern Baptist Convention in 1845.[46] A similar division occurred within the Methodist Episcopal Church in 1844. When the General Conference of 1844 mandated that Bishop J. O. Andrew, a Georgian, free his slaves or vacate his ecclesiastical office, the southern delegates to the General Conference rebelled, forming their own denomination, the Methodist Episcopal Church, South.[47] Members of Campbell's denomination in the South had no such central organization from which they could rebel. Instead, leaders perpetuated an illusion of unity through their denominational journals by calling attention to their ability to avoid the plague of division that spread to other mid-nineteenth-century denominations. A perusal of denominational journals from the latter half of the nineteenth century, however, shatters that illusion. Northern and southern members of Campbell's denomination articulated separate views on slavery, race relations, congregational worship, and church governance from their various periodicals. The denomination's inability to formalize division gave the impression of continued union, but the words of the "editor bishops" clearly reflected the failure of Campbell's unity movement to avoid division.

Campbell's mid-nineteenth-century series on slavery offers only one example of the mediating practice of denominational journals. In the days preceding the American Civil War, Campbell sought unsuccessfully to maintain the unity of northern and southern members of his unity movement. His message, coupled with the lack of formal division, however, convinced many subsequent leaders that they had succeeded where many other American denominations had failed. Campbell's actions helped perpetuate an illusion of unity in the nineteenth century.

Before examining the second mediator of Churches of Christ theology, one should also note one other denominational publication, namely the *Christian Echo*. Founded in 1902 by George Philip Bowser, the *Christian Echo* became the sole journal published by African American members of Churches of Christ. Throughout the twentieth century, editors and authors from this journal helped to mediate the theology of African American Churches of Christ. As subsequent chapters will show, however, Bowser and the editors that followed him used the *Christian Echo* to articulate a distinct identity from their white denominational counterparts. Whereas some African American leaders such as Marshall Keeble maintained close ties to the white leadership, Bowser, through the *Christian Echo*, planted the seeds for African American independence early in the twentieth century.

White Churches of Christ journals continued to perpetuate an illusion of unity throughout the twentieth century, though not between northern and southern members of the denomination. Instead, white editors and authors perpetuated the illusion of unity between African American and white members of Churches of Christ. In their construction of this illusion, however, editors and authors did not work alone.

Churches of Christ Schools

Christian educational institutions are the second mediating influence in Churches of Christ. For nearly two centuries, faculty and administrators within the Stone-Campbell Movement colleges have prepared ministers and articulated their theological positions to their members. The first of these educational institutions to influence the Churches of Christ branch of the Stone-Campbell Movement opened its doors in 1891 as the Nashville Bible School (NBS). For most of its existence, this institution has been recognized as David Lipscomb College, though in 2006 its name was legally changed to its present Lipscomb University.[48] Lipscomb met with James A. Harding almost a century earlier, in 1888, to discuss the possibility of creating a college where the Bible would provide the heart of the curriculum.

In addition to representing the first educational institution within Churches of Christ, NBS also provided seeds for other institutions within the denomination, including Harding University, Abilene Christian University, and Nashville Christian Institute, a school founded and operated by African American members of the denomination. J. N. Armstrong graduated from NBS in 1893, became a faculty member shortly thereafter, and eventually left to co-found a school in Bowling Green, Kentucky, with James A. Harding, Potter Bible College. Following the closing of Potter Bible College in 1913, Armstrong became president of Harper College in Kansas. Harper College merged in 1924 with another junior college, Arkansas Christian College, creating a new institution, Harding College. Additionally, A. B. Barrett, the first president of the institution that eventually became Abilene Christian University (then named Childer's Classical Institute), studied under Lipscomb and Harding at NBS. Andrew Mizell Burton, an insurance magnate and substantial benefactor to David Lipscomb College, along with Athens Clay Pullias, longtime president of David Lipscomb College, provided financial support and leadership to Nashville Christian Institute. The influence of Lipscomb's school reached far beyond the walls of its classrooms: in addition to its formidable role in training countless denominational leaders who passed through its own halls, it also influenced Churches of Christ through at least three other educational institutions.[49]

A second institution worthy of note began in the early twentieth century. Founded the same year the United States Religious Census revealed the division between Churches of Christ and Disciples of Christ, Abilene Christian College (ACC) reflected the conflict between the two groups. According to the charter, trustees "must be members of a church of Christ which takes the New Testament as its only sufficient rule of faith, worship and practice, and rejects from its faith, worship and practice everything not required by either precept or example."[50] During the 1919-20 school year, ACC became the first fully accredited four-year liberal arts college among Churches of Christ. With its academic credentials and its place of influence within the denomination, ACC produced world-renowned biblical scholars, such as Everett Ferguson, Abraham Malherbe, William Martin, and J. J. M. Roberts, and also helped steer a predominantly pacifistic denomination in the legacy of Lipscomb to one that strongly supported the American military efforts in both WWI and WWII.[51] Perhaps the most lasting influence of ACC, however, began in 1918 when then President Jesse P. Sewell inaugurated the first ACC Bible Lectureship. William S. Banowsky, influential twentieth -century preacher within the denomination, has referred to the ACC Lectureship as the "mirror of the movement," arguing that by viewing the lectureship themes and sermons over the twentieth century, one can understand Churches of Christ during the same period.[52]

Harding University, a third influential Churches of Christ educational institution, began in 1924 in Morrilton, Arkansas.[53] J. N. Armstrong, former president of Harper College, became Harding's first president. From its present location in Searcy, Arkansas, Harding College provided leadership in the denomination's premillennial controversies of the early twentieth century[54] and also led the nationalistic charge against Communism under the presidency of George S. Benson, former missionary to China. During his tenure, Benson launched an anti-Communism campaign under the National Education Program, whose slogan became "Where Christian and American ideas go hand in hand"—a far cry from Lipscomb's premillennial and counter-cultural ideals articulated in his 1913 work, *Civil Government*, in which he encouraged Christians to abstain even from voting.

A fourth influential college in Churches of Christ, Southwestern Christian College (SWCC), opened its doors in 1950 in Terrell, Texas, and continues to stand as the only African American college in the denomination. As subsequent chapters will reveal, SWCC came to embody the independent character of its founder, G. P. Bowser. In the second half of the twentieth century, African

American members of Churches of Christ have clustered around SWCC and remained largely disconnected from white members of the denomination. The school trains ministers for African American congregations, hosts an annual lectureship for its African American constituency, and guides its African American constituency through the publications and meetings of its faculty and administration.

Each of these Churches of Christ colleges has mediated the denomination's theology as students have passed through its classrooms. As preachers have gained certain perspectives on scripture and ministry by studying and applying what they have learned at ACC and David Lipscomb College, they have, in turn, passed on their knowledge to thousands of Churches of Christ congregations around the world. Before they shaped students on their campuses, however, college faculty and administration made decisions about which theological issues to address. Although Harding attacked communism and ACC worked to change the longtime pacifistic posture of the denomination, both institutions largely ignored the presence of white racism in Churches of Christ and the Civil Rights Movement in the American South.

Brown vs. The Board of Education mandated schools to desegregate in 1954, yet most colleges associated with Churches of Christ reluctantly adhered to this law; for most of them it took nearly a decade following the court's decision to comply. ACC desegregated its undergraduate school in 1962, David Lipscomb followed in 1963, and Harding made the same decision in 1964. Even after these schools finally opened their doors to African Americans, many accused them of making the change solely for the purpose of receiving federal aid. William Floyd, an African American, summed up the feelings of many members when he wrote: "The Church of Christ has placed itself on the sideline of the greatest moral struggle of our times. Without exception, every one of our southern Christian colleges have waited until it was safe before they integrated. And when they finally integrated (mildly), they blew trumpets and waved flags and sent articles to newspapers announcing their courage and humanitarianism."[55]

In contrast to Churches of Christ colleges, two other private Christian colleges in Abilene, the same location as ACC, desegregated much earlier. Morris Baker, an African American, entered McMurry University as an undergraduate student in 1959; and Sammye Marie Stafford received a master's degree from McMurry University in 1956.[56] Hardin Simmons University, a Baptist college, began admitting African Americans into their undergraduate program in 1961.[57] Billy Curl was the first African American to enroll at ACC as an undergraduate student, but he did not begin attending classes until 1962.[58] In 1960, an African American member of Churches of Christ, Floyd Rose, applied for admission to ACC but was rejected because of his skin color. Instead, he was forced to go across town to McMurry, a Methodist school.[59] Rose became an outspoken leader for African American rights; and, as late as 2008, he continued to encourage African Americans to engage in civil disobedience to challenge unjust laws.[60]

African American members of Churches of Christ, led by R. N. Hogan, editor of the *Christian Echo,* consistently criticized white denominational colleges for their unwillingness to comply with the Supreme Court's 1954 decision. Hogan regularly referred to ACC, David Lipscomb, and Harding as "so-called Christian colleges" during this period, indicating his belief that their actions not only broke the law, but also went against the principles of Christianity.[61]

If one's orientation to American southern culture during the 1950s and 1960s rested solely on white Churches of Christ colleges, one would hardly notice that the South was undergoing a social and moral revolution. White Churches of Christ colleges ignored both the Civil Rights Movement and the calls for change from their African American constituents. In doing so, white leaders perpetuated the white racism that had dominated Churches of Christ since its beginning and also shielded from view the full measure of the separation between African Americans and whites.

In addition to the influence of Churches of Christ colleges, one other school, Nashville Christian Institute (NCI), deserves special mention. The history of NCI began in 1922, two decades before the first students arrived. When the Southern Practical Institute, another African American school, closed shortly after it opened in 1920, many African Americans sought to open a school without the patronage of whites. A fundraising effort began within the African American community to build a school owned by, operated by, and established for the benefit of African Americans. Key leaders such as P. H. Black, G. P. Bowser, T. H. Busby, J. D. Fowler, and Annie C. Tuggle provided financial support toward this effort.[62] On June 15, 1920, this African American contingent purchased a seven-acre tract of land in north Nashville on Hefener Avenue, near Fisk University.[63] An old twelve-room, brick building existed on the property, which the group planned to convert into a schoolhouse to be opened in 1923. The school did not open in 1923, nor did it open for another seventeen years. During this period, the old building functioned as a periodic site for Bible classes to keep the property tax-free. Economic hardship for many years and, finally, the Great Depression kept their dream from becoming a reality until 1940. Despite these early hardships, the aforementioned African Americans and others continued to fund this effort without the financial assistance of whites.

One should not overlook the pride felt by the African American community toward this independent effort. P. H. Black wrote of these times: "We are but few in number, and we are having a hard pull, but by the help of God, we have shouldered the responsibility to erect and maintain an institution which means to us that men can be better educated along this line; we must admit that the colored people need it."[64]

In 1939, the city of Nashville entered into negotiations with the all-African American Board of Trustees of NCI to purchase the property on Hefener Avenue. These negotiations resulted in a trade of property: the city took the Hefener Avenue property, upon which they built Ford Green Elementary, and the NCI board took control of the Ashcraft City School Building on 24th Avenue North plus a sum of money in excess of $10,000.[65] Classes began in this building in 1940.

Though African American leaders of the denomination made it an early goal to establish a school for African Americans akin to the NBS, which included a college, NCI never offered courses above the twelfth-grade level. Their curricula included grades one through twelve. Its first students were adult African American men and women, and classes were offered only at night. During its first few years, NCI remained unaccredited; but, by 1942, the school opened as a fully accredited elementary and high school. The Board of Trustees, though pleased with the school's opening and accreditation, soon realized NCI would not remain a service to African Americans long if it did not seek help. The African American independence of NCI lasted only a few years. Within three years of its opening, whites took control.

In 1943, A. M. Burton turned his attention to NCI; that same year marked the end of racial autonomy for the school. Burton previously had opened a school for African Americans in 1920, the Southern Practical Institute. Even after that effort, he hinted that his inclination to move in this direction had not been squelched. He wrote in 1924 to Marshall Keeble: "It may be that some time this winter we can start a night school, or Bible class, to meet once or twice a week and develop more of the younger colored people into preachers."[66] In 1943, he found his opportunity. He even had plans to expand NCI on a thousand acre tract of land in Sumner County; but, when the residents close to that property expressed their reservations about the new project, he used $50,000 of the money he had set aside for the new land to build a new building on the school's north Nashville site.

Burton's involvement with NCI reinforced the racist status quo of the American South. When he helped the school financially, he also joined the Board of Trustees as president and suggested the composition of the board be changed to include six white members and four African Americans.[67] From this point forward, though Burton and others might have rescued the school from bankruptcy, resentment began to build in the African American ranks. Evidencing this sentiment, Hogan wrote: "These men who claim to be Christians are guilty of robbing poor Negroes who struggled and gave of their meager income in order to build a Christian School for their children who were denied the privilege of attending the white so-called Christian school."[68]

One's perception of Burton's involvement with the school depended on one's racial vantage point. Speaking of the same event, J. E. Choate, a white man, said Burton "took a lively interest in the school and decided to support it."[69] The ideology of white superiority provided the backbone for the paternalistic system that dominated America in the early twentieth century. African American members of Churches of Christ, like their peers in the larger American context, publicly resisted that ideology in the years leading up to the Civil Rights Movement. Their resistance eventually turned into outright rejection.

NCI stood in a long line of southern African American schools operated by whites. Fisk University, a Nashville school associated with the United Church of Christ, was established in 1866; but the school did not have its first African American president until 1947. Meharry Medical College, a school established by the Methodist Episcopal Church in 1876, also in Nashville, did not have its first African American president until 1952. Paine College, an African American school established in 1882 by the Methodist Episcopal Church, South, did not have an African American president until

Andrew Mizell Burton spent his life engaging in philanthropic efforts, many of them related to African American education. He is pictured here at a groundbreaking ceremony with Marshall Keeble, who was often a recipient of those funds during his preaching career.

1971. Though these schools eventually challenged the racist status quo of the South, they, much like NCI, spent much of their existence under the thumb of white control.

Unlike other schools of its region, NCI always had African American leadership, at least in name. Very early in its history, Keeble replaced A. C. Holt, another African American, as the school's president.[70] For the next two decades Burton and Keeble provided the financial resources to keep the school open, Burton through his own money and Keeble through his fund-raising ability in both the white and African American corners of Churches of Christ.[71] This partnership between Burton and Keeble, white and African American, became the norm for NCI until the school's closing in 1967.

NCI became the center of a biracial effort to educate African American young men and women, but the ultimate goal of many supporters of the school was to train preachers. NCI became known as a "preacher factory" among many members of the denomination for its prolific ability to send out preachers to the African American community.[72] In the first eight years of its operation alone, the school trained over four hundred individuals for ministry.[73] Such prominent African American leaders within the denomination as Jack Evans, Fred Gray, and Robert Wood received an NCI education.

In these respects, NCI may be compared to another, better-known southern school for African Americans, Tuskegee Institute. Established in 1881 as a cooperative effort between white city officials and African Americans, that school educated generations of African American leaders but also modeled the white paternalism so common in the South. Robert J. Norell reports that Lewis Adams, an African American city leader, promised Alabama democrats that he would find African American supporters for their party if those same politicians worked to seek funds through the state legislature for an African American normal school in Tuskegee.[74] Through this arrangement African Americans received a school and whites received two gifts in return. First, they received the votes promised by Adams. Second, through their efforts, they were able to see themselves as "morally responsible beings who were doing their duty."[75]

In addition to providing a school for African Americans, however, white Tuskegee leaders also laid the foundation for social revolution. During the Civil Rights Movement, students from Tuskegee led African Americans in civil disobedience and protest against white segregation. Likewise, though white leaders in Churches of Christ failed to realize the end result of their paternalistic gestures in the early 1940s, alumni of NCI would eventually lead the charge against white denominational racism in the late 1960s.

In the 1880s, Tuskegee gave the impression that whites and African Americans in the South had learned cooperation. NCI painted the same picture in the 1940s. In addition to providing an education for African Americans, NCI served a secondary function: the school masked the division between African American and white members of the denomination. The *Gospel Advocate* regularly included articles about the great work being done at NCI, and Keeble provided regular columns to the journal on the school's behalf.[76] Large white lectureships invited Keeble to speak about and raise money for the school.[77] White speakers were regularly invited to speak and teach on the campus of NCI.[78] Through these key mediating forces, many white members were allowed to believe that African Americans and whites partnered to provide a valuable service to the denomination.

Unrevealed by journals, colleges, and lectureships, however, was the fact that many African Americans resented the white paternalism and racism that dominated the school. Jack Evans said white speakers at NCI's annual lectureship customarily arrived late to their sessions, just in time to speak, and left before the end of services, a practice that angered many African American members of the denomination.[79] Those African Americans who initially raised the money to start NCI felt betrayed by whites who came in and "stole their school" in the early 1940s.[80] Though they resented the activities of whites for nearly three decades, African Americans refrained from publicly challenging white leaders of the school until 1967, when the white-controlled board made the decision to close the school and place its remaining assets in the only recently desegregated David Lipscomb College.[81] Until that time, NCI functioned as a mask, shielding from view the full measure of the division between African Americans and whites.

White and African American schools helped mediate the denomination's theology throughout the twentieth century, but they also worked together to perpetuate white racism and paternalism until the 1960s. These schools, along with denominational journals, succeeded in masking the wide chasm separating African American and white members of Churches of Christ. Their efforts were strengthened by a third mediating influence, lectureships.

Churches of Christ Lectureships

A relative latecomer to the Stone-Campbell Movement, lectureships served as a substitute for the Disciples of Christ's American Christian Missionary Society, an institution which many members of Churches of Christ increasingly viewed with suspicion. One editor who helped shaped the mindset of those who would become first generation members of Churches of Christ, Benjamin Franklin, wrote: "It is not the missionary work to which we are opposed, but empty plans, schemes, and organization, after sectarian models."[82] Quite reactionary against their increasingly estranged peers, leaders within Churches of Christ shied away from any hint of centralized control.

Far from a meeting of leaders designed to order the future path of Churches of Christ, lectureships provided numerous forums for members and leaders to fellowship and network with one another while attending classes and keynote addresses by some of the most well-known preachers.

Churches of Christ scholars have recognized the lectureship's place within the denomination. Douglas A. Foster dubbed these meetings "our national conventions."[83] This label provides a helpful metaphor for understanding lectureships, but one must be careful not to attach too much authority to these meetings. Lectureships are like national conventions in that they bring together thousands of people for fellowship and discussion of denominational issues. They are unlike conventions, however, in that they stop short of handing down position papers (as the PCUS General Assembly did in 1954), constructing a common statement of faith (as the Southern Baptist Convention does periodically with their Baptist Faith and Message), or organizing their congregations into easily governed districts (as the Methodist General Conference did in creating the Central Jurisdiction in its 1939 meeting). Churches of Christ lectureships help mediate the theology of the denomination by providing a forum for theological discussion and debate.

One also should note the plurality of lectureships within Churches of Christ; Scores of lectureships take place each year. Most of these occur on the campuses of Christian colleges and schools of preaching; but some of the best attended lectureships occur at other locations, such as the Tulsa International Soul-Winning Workshop, held annually at the Oklahoma state fairgrounds. The large number of lectureships, in addition to their varied theological platforms, helps one understand their inability to provide a single, centralized voice for Churches of Christ. In reaction to the perceived liberality of many school-sponsored lectureships, many preaching schools instituted their own lectureships—most notably the Denton Lectures (held each year in Denton, Texas), the Florida School of Preaching Lectures (held each year in Temple Terrace, Florida), and the Memphis School of Preaching Lectures (held each year in Memphis, Tennessee). Nonetheless, lectureships provide a forum for connection and also a venue for leading preachers to articulate their theological positions to thousands of people who meet in Churches of Christ buildings across the globe. The "national conventions" of Churches of Christ provide a loose connection, a connection that allows factions within the denomination to either accept or reject the positions of its leaders or even to inaugurate new conventions altogether.

One example of the mediating power of lectureships occurred in 2006, the one-hundred-year anniversary of the official division between Churches of Christ and Disciples of Christ. Significant leaders of both Churches of Christ and Independent Christian Churches, the third major branch of the Stone-Campbell Movement, planned events to commemorate the anniversary of the division with gestures of unity. Lacking general conferences or assemblies, leaders of both denominations chose their largest lectureships to publicly declare their desire for unity. During the 2006 Tulsa International Soul-Winning Workshop, lectureship directors invited Christian Church ministers to share the stage with Churches of Christ ministers. Christian Church leaders reciprocated a few months later at their 2006 North American Christian Convention held in Louisville, Kentucky. Lectureship sermons centered on church unity and cooperation. In one pivotal moment at the North American Christian Convention, Jeff Walling (minister of the Providence Road Church of Christ) traded Bibles with Dave Stone (minister of the Southeast Christian Church) during a keynote address the two preachers shared. Walling and Stone, two well-known ministers of their respective denominations, received a standing ovation from the crowded auditorium of the Louisville Convention Center.

The responses of many members of Churches of Christ to these unity efforts allow witnesses to observe the influence of denominational lectureships. In October of 2006, the administration of Freed-Hardeman University responded to these unity efforts by hosting a lectureship on their own campus. During their meeting, church leaders publicly criticized those who believed exchanging Bibles could erase the differences between the two groups.[84] These three 2006 lectureships display the mediating power of Churches of Christ lectureships. During each gathering, denominational leaders articulated their views on church unity, but the leaders came to no consensus or official position. In fact, one lectureship sparked another one. For over a century, Churches of Christ lectureships have provided platforms for preachers and other leaders to mediate theology by articulating their position on a wide array of ecclesiastical issues.

With their efforts in 2006, lectureship directors introduced the subject of church unity into Churches of Christ colleges, publications, and pulpits. The preacher of the largest Church of Christ in the world, Rick Atchley, and the former preacher of the largest Independent Christian Church in the world, Bob Russell, co-authored a book in 2006 entitled *Together Again: Restoring Unity in Christ after a Century of Separation*, which was co-published by two of the largest publishing companies of each denomination.[85] The sermons and publications centered on this issue in 2006 display the influence of Churches of Christ lectureships.

With few exceptions, Churches of Christ lectureships failed to address the issue of race relations in the twentieth century, and only one white lectureship speech ever directly confronted the issue of white-imposed segregation.[86] Consequently, these issues never moved into public discourse among members of the denomination. Among African Americans, only Marshall Keeble received regular invitations to speak at white lectureships; and African Americans in attendance at these lectureships were seated in the balcony, away from the white members.[87] Though the lectureships provided venues for fellowship and networking, the lack of an African American presence at the best-attended lectureships forced them to the margins, thereby separating them from key aspects of denominational life. Churches of Christ lectureships, in other words, aided in the separation of African Americans and whites.

Conclusion

From the birth of Churches of Christ in the late nineteenth century until the end of the twentieth century, journals, colleges, and lectureships helped mediate theological discussions. White leaders most often ignored the topics of paternalism, segregation, and racism by failing to write, teach, or speak about them. At other times, they lauded the efforts of African American and white cooperation. Through their efforts, white leaders created an illusion of racial unity; however, as the twentieth century progressed, African American challenges to the racial status quo became more regular. By the late 1960s, through their own journals, colleges, and lectureships, African American members of Churches of Christ, once and for all publicly displayed their resentment and shattered the illusion created by their white counterparts.

Chapter 2

SEGREGATION

Race matters. If race did not matter, Churches of Christ would not exist as a racially divided denomination; however, African American and white members of Churches of Christ have maintained separation from one another ever since the inception of the denomination. Hap C. S. Lyda indicates that a small number of independent African American congregations existed within the Stone-Campbell Movement even before the American Civil War.[1] As Churches of Christ emerged as an independent denomination in the post-bellum period, mostly in the southern United States, African Americans and whites continued in their separate status through white-imposed segregation. Though denominational journals, colleges, and lectureships shielded from view the full measure of their separation, African Americans and whites remained segregated until the dawn of the Civil Rights Movement.

Though from emancipation to the mid-twentieth century Churches of Christ existed and moved back and forth upon the long continuum between racial radicalism and racial liberalism, white members continued to mandate their separation from African American members. During the same period, African Americans attempted to engage their denomination amid white-imposed segregation. Their strategies of accommodation and protest produced mixed results.

White-Imposed Segregation

In *The Crucible of Race* Joel Williamson described racism as a "mental condition, a disorder of the mind in which internal problems are projected upon external persons."[2] Racists seek to address their own inadequacies by asserting their power over others, enforcing upon them an identity that is not real. In doing so, racists rob others of the right to establish their own sense of self. Throughout American history, whites have enforced a false identity upon African Americans, robbing them of the right to establish a satisfying identity of their own.

White racism had an ironic effect upon African Americans. During the era of slavery, African Americans sought freedom from whites, but as many gained their independence, they built families, farms, and churches that looked surprisingly similar to those of whites. Williamson wrote, "Even as they moved away in the physical sense, they gained the freedom they needed to be more like whites."[3] Throughout the antebellum period, whites not only enforced a false identity upon African Americans, they also created the false impression that their own identity, a white identity, was superior to all others. As some African Americans left slavery, they sought not only their freedom but also a new and superior identity. This African American "exodus to whiteness" persisted until the period of Reconstruction. As African Americans moved in mass away from the white world following the Civil War, there grew "a pride in blackness, a pride that sprang in part from having survived great tribulations together."[4] The disengagement of African Americans from the white world in the post-bellum period gave rise to racial solidarity and afforded African Americans the space needed to create their own identity apart from the scrutiny or racist influence of whites.

Despite the efforts of African Americans to create their own identity, however, whites continued their attempts to enforce the racist status quo into the twentieth century. Williamson's work looked closely at the period between 1880 and 1915. During this period, he argued, three racial mentalities (liberal, radical, and conservative) provided the template for white responses to African Americans. Following the Civil War, racial conservatives worked diligently to return African Americans to their appointed "place" in the southern, organic society. In the 1880s, racial liberals wanted to push the former slaves toward racial equality. By the 1890s, however, racial radicals had silenced the liberals by their militant tactics, which included mob violence and lynching. After the 1920s, racial conservatives supplanted the liberals and radicals and set the agenda on race relations until the Civil Rights Movement of the 1960s.

A perusal of Churches of Christ journals from the late nineteenth and early twentieth centuries reveals the presence of these three mentalities' making their appearance, and they appeared in the same order as described by Williamson; however, each appeared at least a generation later than his timetable suggests for the nation as a whole. The following paragraphs tell the story of how racial liberals, radicals, and conservatives helped maintain white-imposed segregation in Churches of Christ from the late nineteenth century until the 1960s.

Without question, the most influential white leader in Churches of Christ in the post-bellum period was David Lipscomb. He lived most of his life within the united Stone-Campbell Movement, but he is best remembered as the first true leader of the separated Churches of Christ. As editor of the *Gospel Advocate* from 1866 until his death in 1917 and as co-founder of NBS (an institution that eventually took his name as its own following Lipscomb's death), he provided a significant voice within the denomination for more than one generation.

Lipscomb was born in 1831 to parents who abandoned their Baptist faith to follow Alexander Campbell. When he was only three years old, Lipscomb's parents became convinced that the Bible condemned slavery; so they moved their family from Franklin County, Tennessee, to Illinois and freed their slaves. The following year, after Lipscomb's mother and three of his siblings died, his father moved the family back to Tennessee. After the death of his young mother, Lipscomb received much of his motherly tutelage as a child and an adolescent from an African American woman, and African Americans were among many of his early playmates.[5] His early, positive interactions with African Americans led Lipscomb to challenge many common racial perspectives held by white southerners in the early twentieth century. A resident of Tennessee the rest of his life, Lipscomb attended Franklin College under the tutelage of Tolbert Fanning, whom he joined following the Civil War in making the *Gospel Advocate* a fixture in Churches of Christ households.

On certain occasions, Lipscomb resembled a racial liberal more than any other Churches of Christ leader in the late nineteenth century; but, at other times in his career, his rhetoric more closely aligned him with conservatives. In other words, Lipscomb had complicated, and perhaps paradoxical, views on race. Just as individual African Americans moved back and forth along the vast continuum between accommodation and protest, individual whites also vacillated from time to time between racial mentalities.

If one reads only Lipscomb's words from a May 1868 article in the *Gospel Advocate,* one may be tempted to place him squarely in the racial conservative category. In that article, Lipscomb provides his support for the Haminite myth. Though his primary purpose was to encourage more involvement among whites in the evangelization of African Americans, Lipscomb wrote plainly, "There is but one way to deliver our fellowmen from the curse of

From his position as editor of the *Gospel Advocate,* David Lipscomb shaped the identity of Churches of Christ more than any other individual in the late nineteenth and early twentieth centuries. His position on racism and segregation in the church created a pattern that would last until the Civil Rights Movement era.

God—deliver them from the sin that calls down the curse, and then God will see that the curse is removed."[6] He also wrote, "What a crown of joy at the last day, to have been God's instrument in delivering a race from a curse, hanging over them since the days of Noah."[7] According to Lipscomb, only when African Americans encountered the Christian gospel would they be freed from the curse that had haunted them since the days of Noah's son.

Many Christian slaveholders justified slavery on the basis of God's curse on Ham, which they perceived as advocating the perpetual servitude of blacks.[8] Even if Lipscomb believed African Americans to be the progeny of Ham, he did not believe they were restricted by God to perpetual servitude. Lipscomb believed the gospel could deliver African Americans from their curse.[9]

The Haminite myth was not the only piece of racist ideology adopted by Lipscomb. Several years later, his rhetoric concerning an African American child disclosed his allegiance to a myth concerning African American women. In his attempt to defend a young African American girl's right to attend worship at a white congregation, Lipscomb wrote, "She is not forward but deports herself modestly."[10] Such a statement seems out of place when referring to a young child. Why would anyone even suspect a young girl to deport herself immodestly? Winthrop Jordan traces the origins of a myth accepted by whites, which suggested black women were especially passionate and more prone to sexual sin than white women.[11] Apparently, Lipscomb adhered to this myth, and the casual way in which he inserted it into his article without qualification or further comment suggests the degree to which he and his readers were comfortable with such racist convictions.

Also aligning him with other racial conservatives, Lipscomb consistently encouraged whites to educate and evangelize African Americans in order to lift them from "degrading barbarism."[12] To his predominantly white audience he wrote, "a weighty responsibility rests upon us."[13] On another occasion, he called it the "duty of Christians to teach and instruct the negroes [sic] and in every way encourage them to lives of godliness and righteousness and purity."[14] Racial radicals discouraged African American education, believing the former slaves incapable of learning. Instead, they advocated the strict separation of African Americans and whites. Lipscomb, however, routinely encouraged white members of Churches of Christ to help African Americans, obviously believing them capable of "godliness, righteousness, and purity."

Like many racial conservatives (and unlike many liberals), Lipscomb did not support the immediate change of social and political relations. He believed that the gospel would heal the relations between African Americans and whites, and that the "social conditions will adjust themselves."[15] Those abolitionists who worked for emancipation and courageous whites who advocated African American equality in the post-bellum period challenged the societal racial status quo, but Lipscomb never pushed for African American civil rights. He was content, instead, to work for African American uplift within his denomination. With these efforts, Lipscomb became the individual most closely resembling a racial liberal in Churches of Christ.

The episode that most closely aligned Lipscomb with racial liberals centered on a series of articles he wrote in the *Gospel Advocate* in 1907. In that year, a correspondence concerning the equality of African Americans and whites in ecclesiastical life occurred between S. E. Harris, E. A. Elam, and Lipscomb. The discussion began when Harris wrote a letter to Elam, then front page editor of the *Gospel Advocate* and close friend of Lipscomb, requesting that Elam desist his practice of bringing "the colored girl that lives in your house" to the white congregation that Elam regularly attended. Harris' letter sparked a heated correspondence that eventually enticed Lipscomb to involve himself. The *Gospel Advocate* printed the entire series of exchanges under the title "The Negro in Worship—A Correspondence."[16]

Harris argued that Elam's African American guest should attend a nearby African American congregation in order to maintain congregational peace and order. More than anything else (correct doctrine, evangelism, community outreach), Harris viewed congregational peace as the ultimate pursuit of the church. He began his first response to Elam by revealing his primary motivation: "I was shocked to get such a letter from you, as I thought you would rather have peace at Bellwood than division, but it seems you had not."[17] This same topic served as his final admonition to Elam: "We would like everything to be run nicely and in order."[18] Later, in his discussion with Lipscomb, Harris seemed to advocate peace at all costs, writing, "Can any one [sic] be a Christian and cause division, whether he thinks that thing is wrong or not?"[19] This desire for peace and order stemmed from the southerner's desire to protect their organic society, and it dominated the rhetoric of Churches of Christ leaders and laypersons until the 1960s.

Lipscomb, the third party in this conversation, provided the strongest voice against ecclesiastical segregation up to this point in the denomination's history. He revealed his disdain for racially segregated congregations. Unlike both Harris and Elam, Lipscomb characterized such segregation as a moral issue, not simply a social one. He referred to forced segregated worship as "a sin against God."[20] Whereas racial conservatives worked diligently to force African Americans into their "place," Lipscomb spoke openly against segregating African Americans from whites in ecclesiastical settings; nevertheless, not even Lipscomb advocated the desegregation of society.

More than any other white public figure in Churches of Christ at the turn of the twentieth century, Lipscomb advanced the cause of African American rights; yet, even Lipscomb helped maintain the white-imposed segregation that held sway over the denomination for much of the century. In a final analysis, Lipscomb must be labeled a racist, albeit a benign racist; yet, decades following this exchange in the *Gospel Advocate*, both African American and white leaders within Churches of Christ called attention to Lipscomb's bravery and revolutionary ideas.[21]

In spite of Lipscomb's acceptance of the Haminite myth and the myth about the heightened sexual desires of African American women; and, in spite of his conviction that African American uplift depended on white educational and financial support, history has labeled Lipscomb a champion of African American rights! If Lipscomb was the foremost champion of African American rights in Churches of Christ during the early part of the twentieth century, it is no wonder that the denomination remained committed to white-imposed segregation. Lipscomb's favorable characterization by denominational hagiographers may be attributed to the dearth of white racial liberals in the denomination. As civil rights activists in Churches of Christ battled against racial conservatives in the 1960s, Lipscomb remained the only white leader from the past to which they could point who challenged the racial status quo, even in the slightest.

Lipscomb, however, was not alone. Other white Christian leaders in the early twentieth century oscillated between the poles of conservatism and liberalism and, as a result, aided in their denomination's maintenance of the racial status quo. For example, Atticus Haygood was a racial liberal who spent his life advocating African American education. In 1881, Haygood, while President of Emory College, published *Our Brother in Black* wherein he praised northern churches for their efforts to educate African Americans and criticized southerners for not doing the same. In the same book, Haygood discussed the single race of humanity.[22] In recognition of his service to the enterprise of African American education, John F. Slater appointed Haygood as general agent of the Slater Fund, a million dollar trust for the purpose of offering a Christian education to African Americans.[23] Yet in spite of his dedication to uplifting African Americans through education, Haygood never stopped believing in the inferiority of blacks. In 1881, he wrote that "only lunatics and visionaries" would seek to educate African Americans in white schools.[24] Though Williamson labels Haygood a "racial liberal," the latter fits perfectly the former's definition of "racial conservative," because Haygood never wavered in his belief of black inferiority.[25] Haygood, like Lipscomb, resisted simple classification.

Haygood and Lipscomb certainly helped the cause of African Americans in the early twentieth century more than many of their southern, white peers; but the inconsistency of these denominational leaders helps one understand the enormity of the boulder blocking the path of African Americans. If racial liberals helped maintain white-imposed segregation, how much more did conservatives and radicals block their path toward equality?

The presence of racial radicals in Churches of Christ is evidenced in the series of *Gospel Advocate* exchanges between Lipscomb, Elam, and Harris. Not only did Lipscomb himself use rhetoric characteristic of radicals, Harris initiated the correspondence based on radical racist ideology. Harris sought to maintain peace in his congregation by having Elam bring the African American child to a neighboring African American congregation, but he also obviously feared the child's influence on white children in his congregation. He stated plainly, "She is black, and therefore subject to the temptation of her race."[26] At the heart of the racial radical ideology is the idea of black retrogression first advocated by Nathanial Shaler and Phillip Alexander Bruce, which asserted that, following emancipation, blacks would revert back to their native savage state.[27] Racial radicals feared African Americans would regress further and further away from the civilization they had learned during slavery, attack defenseless white women, and finally destroy the southern, organic society. Though Harris attempted to veil his racism by consistently appealing to the peace of the church, his rhetoric betrayed his racist ideology.

Another racial radical in Churches of Christ, Foy E. Wallace Jr., did not mask his racism in the slightest. Unlike Harris, Wallace became a prominent leader in the denomination as a preacher, editor, author, and debater in the early twentieth century. During his career, he edited four denominational journals: the *Gospel Advocate* (1930-1934), *The Gospel Guardian* (1935-1936), the *Bible Banner* (1938-1949), and *Torch* (1950-1951). Using these forums, he provided a leading voice on a wide array of issues, ranging from premillennialism to race relations.

In the *Bible Banner* in 1941, Wallace ridiculed white women for shaking hands with African American preachers, African American preachers for holding meetings with whites in attendance, and some "upstart preachers" who talked about social equality.[28] Through reading his vitriolic rhetoric, one witnesses firsthand the mind of a racial radical.

Underlying Wallace's rhetoric seems to be his jealousy of popular African American preachers within Churches of Christ, including Marshall Keeble and R. N. Hogan. He wrote at length about a meeting he conducted in the weeks following one by Keeble at the same location. Apparently a certain white man became excited over Keeble's style and teachings; but, when Wallace preached the same message a short time later, the man grew offended. In spite of the obvious, Wallace concludes his article with the words: "And if any of the white brethren get worked up over what I have said, and want to accuse me of being jealous of the negro [sic] preachers, I will just tell them now that I don't even want to hold a meeting for any bunch of brethren who think that any negro [sic] is a better preacher than I am!"[29] Wallace's racial ideology would not allow him to fathom the possibility of African American equality, much less African American superiority.

In an article written just weeks later, Wallace unearthed another layer of his racist ideology when he wrote, "These men [Keeble and Luke Miller] know their work and do it. They know their *place* and they stay in it" (italics added).[30] Wallace could tolerate African Americans as long as they stayed in their white-designated place.

In addition to challenging African Americans who moved out of their places and the whites who helped them, Wallace also praised N. B. Hardeman, an influential white leader in Churches of Christ, for helping to maintain the racial status quo. Following a sermon delivered by Hardeman in Harlingen, Texas, a group of African Americans came to the front of the auditorium to shake his hand. Wallace held up Hardeman's response as a model to follow. According to the editor of the *Bible Banner,* Hardeman told the group that "he could see all of the colored brethren he cared to see on the outside after services, and that he could say everything to them that he wanted to say without the formality of shaking their hands."[31]

Wallace, the racial radical, advocated the white-imposed segregation common in Churches of Christ in the first half of the twentieth century. His rhetoric as an editor and his influence as a preacher and debater helped spread his ideology throughout the denomination for more than fifty years. Though most other writers and preachers did not mirror Wallace's blatant racism, his views nonetheless influenced race relations in Churches of Christ. As evidence of his ability to influence the denomination, one only needs to notice that Keeble sent a reply to Wallace immediately after the latter published his scathing article.[32] Keeble's response will be examined in subsequent paragraphs; but, regardless of his rhetoric, the fact that he replied at all indicates something important. When white leaders of Churches of Christ spoke or wrote on the subject of race relations, members, even African American members, noticed and reacted. In other words, whites imposed their ideology on the

Foy Wallace provided a "racial radical" voice within Churches of Christ in the middle decades of the twentieth century through his position as editor of the *Bible Banner.*

denomination in the early years of the twentieth century, thereby aiding the separation between African Americans and whites.

Far more than either liberals or radicals, racial conservatives set the racial agenda in Churches of Christ in the years before the Civil Rights Movement. In this respect, Churches of Christ fit well into their southern American context, because racial conservatives set the agenda for all other southern denominations, including Southern Baptists, Methodists, and Presbyterians in the first half of the twentieth century. In each of these denominations, white leaders engaged in paternalistic activities, seeking to do for African Americans what, in their minds, African Americans could not do for themselves. In each of these denominations, white leaders maintained their belief in the inferiority of blacks, and worked diligently to keep African Americans in their place, a place well beneath whites in the white-constructed social hierarchy.

Williamson provided a helpful metaphor for those seeking to understand the mindset of the racial conservative. Whereas the radical viewed blacks as beasts, rapidly retrogressing toward their natural state of savagery, conservatives, wrote Williamson, viewed blacks as children in need of protection and assistance.[33] Ironically, southern racial conservatives did not view themselves as keepers of the racial status quo; instead, they viewed themselves as saviors and protectors of African Americans. Northern reconstructionist outsiders intruded into the South, disrupting the southern way of life and forcing former slaves to move out of their place in society. Southern racial radicals had sought to eradicate African Americans from the South through lynching. Conservatives, in their own minds, arrived to protect their former slaves from harm and to return them safely to their rightful place in society.

Andrew Sledd, an Emory professor, was one of the first conservatives to challenge racial radicalism in the twentieth century. Writing in 1902, Sledd called lynchers "murderers"; and supporters of lynching, he labeled "blatant demagogues" and "political shysters."[34] Not long after Sledd's publication, he received such pressure from southerners who viewed lynching as an act of God, punishing guilty and deterring would-be rapists, that he resigned his post from Emory and fled to the North. Consistent with other racial conservatives, Sledd did not stay and fight. Williamson asserts that the great majority of conservatives made one attack against radicalism and then retired to other tasks.[35] Another southern racial conservative, John Spencer Bassett, wrote a similar article in 1903 in which he characterized Booker T. Washington as the second greatest man (after Robert E. Lee) to appear in the South since the Revolutionary Period.[36] Bassett, like Sledd, received immediate criticism from southerners; but he was able to retain his position at Trinity College, in large part because he folded under the administrative pressure put on him by Trinity's president. He indicated in a private meeting with the chief school administrator that he never had meant to insinuate that Washington was "great," only that he was "remarkable" for his ability to accomplish all that he had in spite of the inferiority of blacks.[37]

Racial conservatives continued to attack and retreat from racial radicals in the early years of the twentieth century; but, by the 1920s, they had gained their place of influence in southern society, a place they would occupy for decades to come. Their ideology, which centered on white paternalism and African American inferiority, dominated southern society and southern Christianity, including Churches of Christ.

The southern white racial conservatives in the early twentieth century Churches of Christ were too many to count, but they included such figures as Benton Cordell Goodpasture, Reuel Lemmons, and James Fowler. Perhaps the greatest example of racial conservativism, however, arose in the person of Andrew Mizell Burton, a white millionaire and philanthropist in Churches of Christ who helped establish or fund three separate African American educational institutions (Silver Point School, Southern Practical Institute, and Nashville Christian Institute) over a fifty-year period and who also funded the ministry of Marshall Keeble and other African American ministers. Burton accumulated great wealth through his Life and Casualty Insurance Company,[38] but he did not keep his wealth to himself. Some estimate that, for many years, Burton gave away approximately 90% of his income to philanthropic causes,[39] including David Lipscomb College and various efforts toward African American education.

Paternalism dominated his interactions with African American members of Churches of Christ. Not only did he give his own money to build African American schools, he also urged other white members to participate in these efforts as well. An excellent example of Burton's paternalism centers on his efforts with the Silver Point School. The newly established African American school quickly fell into financial trouble, and Burton was asked to help. After conducting a thorough study of the school, he petitioned whites through the *Gospel Advocate* to send money to help.[40]

A. M. Burton typified racial conservatism in Churches of Christ in the twentieth century. He used his tremendous wealth to fund African American education and the ministry of Marshall Keeble, yet he never challenged the racial status quo within Churches of Christ.

This plea for help, as well as many others like it, gave the impression that African Americans and whites worked in harmony with one another. In fact, the money gained from others, coupled with Burton's own donations, resulted in the purchase of new lots, the construction of a new brick chapel, and the erection of a dormitory for female students. If one's only orientation to Churches of Christ was the *Gospel Advocate,* one would assume African Americans and whites worked well with one another. The journal, however, not only provided contact between these two racial factions; it also shielded from view the full measure of their separation.

The *Gospel Advocate* reported the plea for help and the results of the campaign, but it neglected to mention another important fact. During this period, the board of directors also added a few new faces, including six whites.[41] Even though the Silver Point School began as an African American venture, it quickly turned into an institution under the leadership of whites. Several years later, Burton again would be asked to help with another African American school, NCI; and, once again, he simultaneously gave money and added a dominant number of white members to that institution's Board of Directors.[42]

Burton's actions demonstrate his belief in black inferiority. He viewed African Americans as children in need of a helping hand; and, throughout the early twentieth century, he offered his hand numerous times. Nevertheless, not once in his efforts did he relinquish control or authority of those institutions to African Americans. Instead, he consistently insisted on white leadership. A more blatant example of his insistence on maintaining the racial status quo took place in 1920.

In that year, Burton offered G. P. Bowser, a prominent African American preacher and teacher in Churches of Christ, the post of principal at a new school for African Americans in Nashville, Southern Practical Institute. Burton asked Bowser to serve the school as principal and another of his friends, C. E. W. Dorris, a white man, to serve as the school's superintendent. On the first day of the school's operation, Dorris mandated that African Americans enter the building through the back door. Offended by the proposition of asking African Americans to enter their own school in such a way, Bowser objected to the superintendent and asked him to reconsider his position. Dorris refused. By the end of the week, Bowser resigned his post at the Southern Practical Institute and rejoined his family in Louisville. Regardless of his concern for African American education and regardless of his friendship with Bowser, Keeble, or other African American leaders, Burton failed to intervene in this situation. Instead, he allowed Dorris to enforce the racial status quo, white-imposed segregation.

The white-imposed segregation exemplified in the Southern Practical Institute episode of 1920 reinforced the separation between African Americans and whites within Churches of Christ. As Bowser left Nashville and resigned his post from the school, he also urged African Americans to withdraw their support from the school.[43] Just six weeks after Bowser's resignation, the school closed for lack of students. This episode in Churches of Christ history makes plain the distance between African Americans and whites, but it also shows that many African Americans were unwilling to accept white-imposed segregation, even in 1920. Their protest in that year would be duplicated many times in the Civil Rights Movement period, thereby allowing the estrangement between these two racial factions to widen. White journals, however, routinely failed to report these episodes of African American protest. Instead, they allowed their predominantly white constituency to see only the created illusion of racial unity.

Much like other southern denominations of the late nineteenth and early twentieth centuries, Churches of Christ had in their midst racial liberals, radicals, and conservatives; and each in his or her own way worked to reinforce the racial status quo of the southern, Victorian, organic society. Never once in this period did a convention, synod, or assembly address the distance between African Americans and whites, because Churches of Christ lacked such venues. Instead, the journals, schools, and lectureships remained silent on the issue altogether. As a result, the estrangement between these two racial factions went largely unnoticed or, at least, unaddressed.

During this same period, however, African Americans did recognize the product of white-imposed segregation. This type of interaction between these two racial factions forced African Americans to the margins of the denomination. Between the Civil War and the Civil Rights Movement, African American members of Churches of Christ interacted with white racial liberals, radicals, and conservatives; and, over time, the former learned to survive in a world dominated by the latter. In order to survive in a world dominated by white-imposed segregation, African American members of Churches of Christ moved back and forth on the long continuum between accommodation and protest.

African Americans never have adopted a solely accommodationist posture, and neither have they ever solely embraced the posture of protest. Indeed, this tension has existed within the African American community and within individual members of that community since the colonial era. This study provides proof of this hypothesis by exploring the lives of African American leaders within Churches of Christ like G. P. Bowser, Fred Gray, R. N. Hogan, and Marshall Keeble, men who did not fit easily in either category.

Though accommodationists and protesters had different tactics, they shared a common goal, namely African American advancement. This phenomenon is illustrated in the careers of Booker T. Washington and W. E. B. DuBois. Washington has come to be known as the quintessential African American accommodationist of the twentieth century, yet he shared many of the same goals as DuBois, the one largely responsible for the founding of the NAACP. Williamson characterized their differences and commonality well when he wrote: "The principal and professor both wanted full political and civil rights for black people, though they might differ as to how to achieve those goals."[44] These two influential African American leaders exemplified the complexity of the continuum between accommodation and protest. African American protesters in the twentieth century challenged laws and worked for civil rights for the purpose of voting. African American accommodationists in the same period worked for economic development for the purpose of racial solidarity. Both accommodationists and protesters strategically used the system to achieve their goals.

As August Meier rightly points out, however, no group of African Americans or individual African American fell simply into one category or the other. In reality, "the attempts to hold to both clusters of ideologies—or to parts of both—or to shift from one to the other" was the plight of most African Americans in the early twentieth century.[45]DuBois wrote in 1903: "One ever feels his two-ness,—an American, a Negro; two souls, two thoughts, two unreconciled strivings; two warring ideals in one dark body, whose dogged strength alone keeps it from being torn asunder."[46] In addition to the inner struggle described by DuBois, the unreconciled strivings of accommodation and protest and of conciliation and agitation also waged war within the African American community and within individual African Americans.

Within Churches of Christ, accommodationists and protesters employed different methods in their struggles against and within white-imposed segregation. The two principle leaders of African American Churches of Christ in the first half of the twentieth century, Keeble and Bowser, illustrate how two divergent methods were employed toward the same end. Whereas Keeble more often accommodated himself to white-imposed segregation, Bowser consistently pushed against it; nevertheless, both men sought African American equality within their denomination.

The remainder of this chapter explores the life and ministry of Marshall Keeble, an African American who worked within white-imposed segregation to establish schools for African Americans and to preach the gospel to countless people, both African American and white. In the early twentieth century, Keeble represented a large portion of the African American constituency in Churches of Christ that publicly accommodated themselves to the segregated system of their denomination. Keeble and his peers, like other African Americans of their period, employed their methods to achieve equality; but, by the 1960s, the failure of their strategy had become apparent.

The Life and Ministry of Marshall Keeble

Marshall Keeble was born on December 7, 1878, in Rutherford County, Tennessee, to parents who lived most of their lives in slavery. The Keeble surname, first bestowed on Marshall Keeble's[47] grandfather by his southern slave owner, was a name of some prominence in the antebellum South. John Bell Keeble served as a longtime dean of the Vanderbilt Law School, and Major Horace Pickney Keeble, who purchased Marshall's grandfather, was a prominent lawyer in Murfreesboro, Tennessee. During the Civil War, Marshall's grandfather traveled with the Major as his personal valet. The Major had few slaves; but those he did own worked closely with the family, performing chores around the house and the small farm. Marshall's father and grandfather learned to read and write through the private instruction of their "master" or "mistress" in the family parlor.[48] From his earliest days in Rutherford County, Marshall worked closely with whites. His ability to work within a system controlled by whites led to his effectiveness as a preacher in Churches of Christ.

Keeble's effectiveness as a preacher has become legend. He reportedly baptized more than 40,000 people (many of whom were white) and established over three hundred congregations in his sixty years of preaching. His success as an evangelist, as well as his ability to befriend individuals across racial lines, earned Keeble unprecedented fame within the denomination. During his lifetime, he was appointed an honorary tribal chief in Nigeria and given an honorary Doctor of Laws degree from Harding College.[49] Frank G. Clement, governor of Tennessee, recognized him for his contributions to the community in which he lived; and Athens Clay Pullias, president of David Lipscomb College, counted Keeble among his friends.[50] Following his death on April 20, 1968, Keeble's admirers continued to bestow honors upon him. Goodpasture, longtime editor of the *Gospel Advocate,* conducted Keeble's funeral before over three thousand guests (white and African American) at the Madison Church of Christ in Madison, Tennessee, then the largest Churches of Christ congregation in the world. Weeks after his funeral editors from leading denominational journals devoted special editorials and entire issues to Keeble's memory.[51] More than three decades after his death, Nashville city officials unveiled a historical marker detailing Keeble's extraordinary achievements on April 12, 2000.

Students of history generally and Churches of Christ specifically must wonder how an African American achieved such stature in the first half of the twentieth century in the American South. In the shadow of Jim Crow and on the eve of the Civil Rights Movement, Keeble enjoyed ministerial success among all classes of people. Perhaps an explanation of this quandary arises from an examination of a memorial written of Keeble by Karl Pettus. Three months following the deaths of two important African American religious leaders, Keeble and Martin Luther King Jr., Pettus carefully highlighted the reasons that Keeble gained the approval of white church members. Through his editorial, Pettus attempted to distance Keeble from the more well-known civil rights icon by calling attention to the former's "more peaceful demeanor" and his refusal to participate in marches or riots.[52] White members surely admired Keeble for his success as an evangelist, but the qualities that made his name commonplace among his white counterparts were his humility and public acceptance of the white-imposed segregated system that governed the American South. Whereas they viewed King as a loud troublemaker, they viewed Keeble as a quiet, unassuming gospel preacher.

This self-effacing gospel preacher assumed an accommodative posture toward his white peers. Refusing to join the crusade for racial equality led by King, the Southern Christian Leadership Conference, or the NAACP, Keeble worked within white denominational power structures of the mid- twentieth century to raise money for African American education. His non-threatening demeanor afforded him unusual "compliments" among the power brokers of his southern Christian denomination. J. P. Sanders, former dean of George Pepperdine College, commented that many white people forgot Keeble was a "Negro."[53] Sanders told of an occasion when he sat on a stage seated next to Keeble before an African American audience. Sanders found himself thinking, "Brother Keeble and I are the only two white people here."[54] No evidence suggests that Keeble invited such opinions of himself or that he would have welcomed such racist comments; nevertheless, his refusal to publicly challenge the status quo of his era and his willingness to work within the white power structures granted Keeble favor in the minds of many white leaders.

In 1931, J. W. Brents, who served many years in the Bible Department at NCI, wrote that Keeble "knows his place and at all times scrupulously keeps it."[55] Keeble never publicly challenged the social norms of the South by encouraging African Americans to strive for better jobs, more prestigious titles, or advanced degrees. Having never gone beyond the seventh grade himself and having worked as a coal and vegetable huckster in central Nashville for many years, he modeled the lifestyle he encouraged. He made his aspirations (or lack thereof) clear to white members of the denomination. Referring to African Americans as "your cooks, house girls, farm hands, chauffeurs, and nurses," Keeble cautioned whites not to neglect domestic missions among African Americans in favor of foreign missions. Doing so, Keeble argued, would be a mistake, "because if we can get the gospel to those who serve your homes and care for your little ones, you can put more trust in them and save them from ignorance of the blessed gospel of Jesus Christ."[56]

Keeble accommodated himself to whites in order to gain a hearing among white leaders and to ensure financial support for NCI. Evidence suggests he was successful in his endeavor. A decade following the above words by Keeble, A. B. Lipscomb, who followed in his uncle's journalistic footsteps as editor of the *Christian Leader,* wrote of Keeble: "We have never made a better investment

Marshall Keeble provided a bridge between African American and white Churches of Christ throughout his life. He often acquiesced to white racism out of necessity in order to further the cause of African American education.

for the Lord nor any which brought such quick and happy results." Speaking of Keeble's preaching, Lipscomb said, it "not only created a new religious and moral status for the negro element but it has brought to this community a new citizenry capable of thinking in terms of the Bible." But for Lipscomb, the benefit of this new citizenry meant that "now we have better farm hands, better porters, better cooks, better housemaids than ever before."[57] White leaders in Churches of Christ were open to accepting African Americans who "knew their place," especially gifted preachers like Keeble.

J. E. Choate, one of Keeble's biographers, frequently referred to Keeble as "*our man* Keeble" (italics added).[58] This phrase allows historians to recognize an important aspect of Keeble's relationship with whites. Though they may have appreciated his humility or accommodating style, Keeble's relationship with many whites rested on racism, not friendship. Choate's description of Keeble's relationship with white leaders of Churches of Christ resembles the relationship of a slave to a master. In Choate's mind, Keeble was "our man." Keeble's interaction with white leaders through lectureships, journals, and colleges may have granted him certain denominational privileges; but those same privileges did not result in an end to racism within Churches of Christ.

The most vivid illustration of Keeble's accommodating style appeared in the pages of a denominational journal in 1941 during his correspondence with Foy Wallace Jr. This study already has recounted Wallace's attack on African American preachers from his *Bible Banner*, calling attention to their practice of shaking the hands of white women after their meetings. He became indignant that some white women "lowered themselves" to that level "just because a Negro has learned enough about the gospel to preach it to his race."[59] He also criticized another African American preacher for sharing a bed with a white preacher on a mission trip, referring to such behavior as "a violation of Christianity itself."[60] After expressing openly his disgust with African Americans who favored social equality, he reminded his readers of Keeble, an individual who "could not be spoiled" by such activities. But even Keeble did not escape the venom of Wallace, who concluded his article by stating, "But if I ever hear of them [Keeble and Luke Miller] doing anything akin to such as this I will take back every good thing I have ever said of them."[61] Though Wallace's racist comments cause even the most passive personality to turn red, Keeble's response boggles the mind. Even though Wallace did not ask for a response, Keeble sent the following letter to the editor of the *Bible Banner*:

Dear Sir and Brother in Christ:

For over thirty years I have tried to conduct my work just as your article in the *Bible Banner* of March suggested. Taking advice from such friends as you have been for years has been a blessing to my work.

So I take the privilege to thank you for that instructive and encouraging article. I hope I can conduct myself in my last days so that you and none of my friends will have to take back nothing they have said complimentary about my work or regret it.

Please continue to encourage me in my work and pray for me.

Fraternally yours,
M. Keeble[62]

Wallace published Keeble's letter in the *Bible Banner* and attached his own thoughts about Keeble beneath his signature. Wallace wrote: "This letter is characteristic of the humility of M. Keeble. It is the reason why he is the greatest colored preacher that has ever lived."[63] Wallace, like many other white leaders in Churches of Christ, applauded Keeble's unassuming and accommodating style.

The above exchange provides a window into Keeble's public personality. Publicly, Keeble seemed the quintessential accommodationist; but to naively accept the radical accommodationist portrait of Keeble ignores some events from his life that took place out of the public eye and beyond the view of his white counterparts in Churches of Christ. The following evidence proves that there is a stark distinction between the illusion of Keeble created by white denominational leaders (and perpetuated by Keeble himself) and the reality of Keeble's ministry and persona.

In an interview with this author, John Mark Tucker, author and former Dean of Library and Information Resources at ACU's Brown Library, spoke of a side of Keeble not revealed in the *Bible Banner* or the *Gospel Advocate*. [64] Tucker, a young white man, was invited in 1964 to speak at NCI's daily chapel. Following Tucker's comments, Keeble stepped to the microphone and lauded the upbringing Tucker had received from his father, a personal friend of Keeble. Here, beyond the view of Burton, Goodpasture, or Wallace, Keeble expressed in tears his anxiety over the 1964 presidential election. In that year, Republican nominee Barry Goldwater challenged Democratic candidate

Lyndon B. Johnson. One should recall that Goldwater led the effort against the Civil Rights Act of 1964, arguing the state could not legislate morality. The former president of NCI spoke to the students of freedom, slavery, the right to vote, the right to educational and economic equality, and his dream for an integrated society. He even expressed his longing for a prophet like Moses to lead his people to freedom, a prophet, he said, like Lyndon Johnson. Finally, Keeble prayed to God, asking for a president who would "place blacks squarely on the road to freedom."[65]

A year later, Tucker was with Keeble and another man, Denny Crews, driving in Brookline, Massachusetts, the birthplace of John F. Kennedy. As the men drove to dinner, Crews pointed out Kennedy's first home. Keeble shouted, "Stop the car!" The aged Keeble exited the car, stood in front of the home, and stated, "All this we have now, he [Kennedy] was the starting of it."[66] The same man who publicly thanked Wallace for his encouraging racism also privately welcomed the Civil Rights Movement.

Some African Americans members of Churches of Christ apparently also understood the difference between the public and private Keeble. In a 1987 article from the *Christian Echo,* Harry Kellam compared Keeble to King, writing that the former disliked segregation as much as the latter.[67] Of particular interest is Kellam's retelling of an event that occurred during his time as a student at NCI in 1963. During the height of the Civil Rights Movement, students from NCI were invited to participate in a civil rights march in downtown Nashville; and they immediately received a stern warning from the white president of the school, Willie Cato, and other staff and teachers not to participate. White leaders also urged Keeble to demand that NCI students not participate. Instead of honoring their demands, however, Keeble told the students to "do what you feel best."[68] The students of NCI marched along with other African American students from Tennessee State University and Fisk University, resulting in the desegregation of all downtown restaurants.

In light of this new information, Keeble seems to resemble Booker T. Washington. Washington has been characterized by historians as the quintessential African American accommodationist of the late nineteenth and early twentieth centuries. Not a public advocate for equal social rights, Washington uttered the now famous statement, "In all things that are purely social we can be as separate as the fingers, yet one as the hand in all things essential to mutual progress."[69] Washington's accommodationist style invited the attention of Americans, both African American and white. His popularity earned him invitations to the White House by Presidents Grover Cleveland and Theodore Roosevelt, the praise of Clark Howell (then editor of the Atlanta *Constitution*), and, perhaps most importantly, an untold amount of financial support for Tuskegee Institute by white philanthropists.[70]

In addition to his public persona, however, one must also take into account his covert efforts for African American equality. Meier suggests that in spite of his "accommodating tone and verbal emphasis upon economy as the solution to the race problem, Washington was surreptitiously engaged in undermining the American race system by a direct attack upon disfranchisement and segregation."[71] Meier supports this assertion by calling attention to Washington's involvement with numerous covert efforts for African American rights, including his financial support of court cases involving discrimination in the matter of representation on juries and railroad segregation.[72] In 1899 Washington lobbied against the Hardwick disfranchisement bill in Georgia, and in 1900 he sought money to fight the electoral provisions of the Louisiana constitution.[73] In a work published after his death, Washington discussed his views of segregation, saying an African American's choice not to constantly express his or her embitterment was not proof that he or she did not feel it.[74] Like Keeble, Washington spent much of his adult life raising money for African American education from white philanthropists. Although neither man made it a practice to jeopardize his fundraising efforts in the white community, both men privately challenged the racist status quo of America.

Present-day African American leaders in Churches of Christ recognize Keeble's motives. Jack Evans, current president of SWCC, recently commented that Keeble "should be judged in light of his own times." He went on to say that "without Keeble's work we wouldn't have many of the African American congregations we have today."[75] African Americans in the early twentieth century, including Washington and Keeble, accommodated themselves to white authority out of strategy. Keeble's strategy helped him raise thousands of dollars for NCI, establish hundreds of African American congregations across America, and earn a place of notoriety in Churches of Christ.

Another figure who had much in common with Keeble was Whitney M. Young Sr., father of the better known civil rights activist, Whitney M. Young Jr. The elder Young spent most of his life as an administrator and teacher at Lincoln Institute, a school for African Americans that adopted the accommodationist posture advocated so strongly by Washington. Relying heavily upon white support for Lincoln, Young rarely publicly challenged the racist status quo of Kentucky. Throughout his life, Young wrote and spoke on the virtues of vocational education, hard work, and piety. As Dennis C. Dickerson has suggested, however, Young also "searched for any cracks or openings in Kentucky's Jim Crow system to advance his students and other blacks beyond the restraints of racial segregation and second-class citizenship."[76] Though Young rarely spoke openly about racial prejudice or discrimination, he joined the Kentucky Division of the Southern Regional Council in the 1950s and celebrated the 1954 decision of the Supreme Court. Dickerson wrote that Young was indebted to the leadership style of Washington. Both emphasized diplomacy in their dealings with whites, and both promoted racial integration whenever they could. Both men were "pragmatic leaders,"[77] who allowed their ultimate goals to be governed by the racial realities of America. Keeble also could be called a pragmatic leader.

Keeble played the role of the Sambo as a necessary price to pay for a larger hearing among both African Americans and whites. His accommodating style made white members of Churches of Christ, like Wallace, more comfortable with their African American counterparts. Keeble modeled himself as an unthreatening individual, though in the safety of NCI and in the company of other African Americans, he was covertly insurgent. He was safe enough to write articles for the *Gospel Advocate, Bible Banner,* and *Firm Foundation*. He was safe enough to speak on the campuses of Abilene Christian College, David Lipscomb College, Harding College, and Freed-Hardeman College. He could provide keynote addresses at their lectureships. Given the limited meaningful contact between African Americans and whites in the early twentieth century South, Keeble provided to white members of Churches of Christ the face for their African American constituency, and the white leaders found that accommodating face pleasing to the eye.

Most denominational studies of Keeble's life,[78] as well as larger volumes with sections on Keeble,[79] highlight the accommodationist viewpoint of Keeble. More recent scholars, however, have questioned the "Uncle Tom" stereotype so commonly given to him. Darrell Broking, in his 2003 master's thesis, for example, suggests Keeble understood his audience well and used the system to his advantage. As one piece of evidence for his theory, Broking recounts Keeble's comments during a meeting for white people: "God doesn't want you to call a man unclean because he is black. God created him. Don't call him common or unclean."[80] Broking suggests this episode reveals an often unseen aspect of Keeble's character, an aspect that understood well the political benefits of playing the part of "Uncle Tom." He goes to great lengths to disprove the theories articulated by J. E. Choate, Goodpasture, and others, arguing instead that through a "grand strategy" Keeble sought to eradicate the color line in Churches of Christ.

In attempting to challenge Choate's obvious hagiographic portrayal of Keeble as the perfect, accommodating, "Negro" evangelist of the twentieth century, Broking may assume too much of Keeble. The above statement of Keeble, for example, does not necessarily cast him among civil rights activists. Not many of Keeble's audiences in Churches of Christ viewed African Americans as "unclean," so Keeble's statement to the contrary would not ellicit controversy or signal his "grand strategy" to end racial strife. Whether Keeble had a grand strategy or not remains a matter of speculation. Nevertheless, the evidence offered by Tucker and Kellam certainly challenges the long held opinion of Keeble as a strict accommodationist.

Given Keeble's openness to civil rights marches, one wonders what decisions he would have made had he lived past 1968, especially as one considers the career of other African American leaders whose ministries resembled Keeble's, such as Bishop Lucius Henry Holsey. A generation older than Keeble, Holsey spent much of his ministerial career advocating African American assimilation from his post as bishop in the Colored Methodist Episcopal (CME) Church in America. During Holsey's lifetime, the CME Church endured a strained relationship, based upon white paternalism, with the Methodist Episcopal Church, South (MEC, S). The MEC, S formed the CME Church to accommodate its African American members who remained in the denomination following the Civil War (an era in which many African Americans chose to join independent African American denominations).[81]

Like Keeble, Holsey publicly acquiesced to the white paternalism offered African Americans by the MEC, S. As an educator of African Americans, Holsey routinely spoke before white audiences raising money for his educational endeavors. Also like Keeble, Holsey made shocking statements regarding race relationships. On the subject of slavery, for example, Holsey wrote: "the Negro race has lost nothing by it, but has gained a thousand pounds sterling silver where it has lost a penny."[82] On another occasion, he wrote: "I have no complaint against American slavery. It was a blessing in disguise to me and to many."[83] During the 1882 MEC, S General Conference, Holsey said before the assembled crowd of white denominational leaders: "We have looked, and still look, to you for guidance an [sic] counsel. We ask your sympathy, aid, and cooperation in redeeming your friends and former slaves from the long night of darkness and degradation."[84] Statements such as these earned Holsey a hearing among white denominational leaders for many years.

Holsey championed the cause of assimilation until the 1897 decision of the Richmond County School Board to close the all-black Ware High School. After the school board voted to close the school, African Americans filed a lawsuit to secure implementation of the "separate but equal" treatment under the law. Many of Holsey's friends were among the financiers of this lawsuit. This episode in Augusta's history, changed race relationships in that city, and also changed Holsey from an assimilationist to an advocator of black nationalism.[85] Afterward, Holsey advanced the idea of a separate black state, believing African Americans and whites could not live peacefully in the same vicinity. One must assume that Holsey did not develop his disgust with racial prejudice overnight and that the 1897 decision of the Richmond County School Board simply pushed his private concerns into the public eye. Neither Holsey nor Keeble accepted the idea of African American inferiority, yet both of them worked within a system dominated by white-imposed segregation for many years. If Keeble had lived beyond 1968 and into the period where many of his African Americans friends publicly expressed their animosity toward white denominational leaders, one wonders if he also would have tempered his apparent acceptance of segregation.

Keeble was no "Uncle Tom," but he did rely upon white aid most of his life. Much like other ecclesiastical and social organizations, Churches of Christ in the early twentieth century were dominated by white paternalism in matters of racial interaction. White racial conservatives routinely built church buildings in which African Americans could congregate for worship and also paid the salaries of their ministers. White members often viewed the African American community as a target missionary field; and not a small number of African Americans encouraged them in their efforts, Keeble chief among them.[86]

A. B. Lipscomb wrote an article in his *Christian Leader* in 1931 that typifies Keeble's acceptance of the white paternalism so common to his age. The article describes a meeting Keeble held in Valdosta, Georgia. Lipscomb seems primarily concerned with raising awareness within the white community of African American mission efforts and also to encourage fundraising for them. Lipscomb wrote: "We have never made a better investment for the Lord, nor one that brought such quick and happy results. Brother Keeble unhesitatingly says that, without this moral and financial support, he could have done little or nothing."[87] White leaders such as Lipscomb (both David and A. B.), Burton, and Goodpasture sponsored African American individuals and congregations in their ministry efforts, but that does not mean these ministries lacked any African American aid. African Americans helped their own congregations through their own financial contributions.[88] Nevertheless, many African American ministries stayed alive through the support of the white community, and Keeble's was no exception to the rule.

During his tenure as president of NCI, Keeble regularly solicited his white counterparts for money.[89] The white community responded and helped the school to remain open for over two decades. W. E. Brightwell, the "New and Notes" editor of the *Gospel Advocate,* wrote in 1948: "It [NCI] is an orphan upon our doorstep . . . crudely pieced together out of second hand and salvaged materials." He concluded his comments by reminding his readers, "Where the next ton of coal will come from was a real concern."[90] The unofficial and unspoken arrangement between Keeble and white leaders, however, did not solely benefit the African American community. The letters exchanged between white preachers, supporters of the school, and Keeble seem to describe a normal mode of operation. White individuals and congregations sent money to help NCI; Keeble then visited those congregations and held meetings for African Americans (bringing along students from the school); and a new African American congregation began in that community, supplied often with a preacher from the Institute.[91] African Americans received a school and an education. Whites received more members into their churches and gratification for their work among African Americans.

The contact Keeble maintained with his white counterparts through journals, schools, and lectureships gave the impression of a racially united denomination. That illusion was nowhere more visible than through NCI. In addition to inviting white leaders to the school, Keeble made a habit of taking trips with "his boys" to white congregations across the nation to preach, sing, or recite scripture from memory. White audiences were reportedly amazed at the speaking ability of the young boys as well as their capacity to memorize long portions of scripture.[92] In addition to providing a ministry service to local white congregations, these excursions also provided a window into the fine education offered at NCI. Upon witnessing the "show," white members felt more comfortable sending money to support this African American mission effort; and they became more convinced of the good race relations in Churches of Christ.

White paternalism took place not only through institutions such as NCI, but individuals also gained much from the financial contributions of wealthy white patrons. Keeble received support from various individuals, but no person contributed more to his ministry efforts than A. M. Burton. Keeble's success as an evangelist came to Burton's attention early in the former's career. In a letter dated September 19, 1924, Burton said to Keeble, "It is indeed interesting to calculate just what we could do if we had seventy-five or one hundred colored preachers like you."[93] Throughout the remainder of his life, Burton attempted to help Keeble clone himself in the African American community by spending vast financial resources on his mission trips, educational efforts, and family needs.[94] Late in Keeble's life, Burton even funded a mission trip for Keeble to Nigeria.[95]

As Keeble became more bonded to the white constituency in Churches of Christ, he attempted to connect large numbers of African Americans to whites in the denomination. Keeble said on various occasions, "After establishing a new congregation, the first thing I do is to get them to order the quarterlies published by the *Gospel Advocate*."[96] In the 1940s, the Gospel Advocate Company attempted to use the influence of Keeble to publish a new journal similar in form and content as the *Gospel Advocate* but aimed specifically at the African American community. This new journal, the *Christian Counselor*, boasted Keeble as its editor but lasted only a short time, due to a small list of subscribers. For those who did favor such a journal, the *Christian Echo* already had a foothold. Following the failure of the *Christian Counselor*, the *Gospel Advocate* editors invited Keeble to write a regular column in their journal in a new section entitled "the colored page."[97] These regular articles reinforced the false perception of the connection between African Americans and whites.

The failure of the *Gospel Advocate* to make significant inroads into the African American community provides further evidence of the inability of Churches of Christ to bridge the gap between African Americans and whites. Their foremost journal (and strongest articulator of denominational identity) failed to connect with African Americans. Lacking this connection, African Americans continued along their trajectory away from their white denominational peers. Most whites, however, never noticed their absence.

Keeble also attempted to connect African Americans to whites through denominational colleges. In the early twentieth century, the segregated system forbade African Americans from attending white colleges, but Keeble's place in Churches of Christ permitted him the opportunity to speak regularly on college campuses. His place also granted him special honors by the white administrators of those colleges. In 1965, newly named president of Harding College, Clifton L. Ganus Jr. flew to Dallas to meet George S. Benson (former president of Harding College) and Keeble on a fundraising trip for NCI. During this meeting, President Ganus conferred upon Keeble the honorary Doctor of Laws degree from Harding College.[98]

Regardless of Keeble's connection to white denominational colleges, most African Americans never bonded in similar fashion. Few other African Americans ever received invitations to speak on their campuses; in fact, all Churches of Christ colleges remained segregated institutions until the last years of Keeble's life. Keeble enjoyed the favor of white leaders because he refrained from publicly challenging their racism. In Keeble, they saw a powerful and successful preacher who stayed in his white-relegated place.

White lectureships also welcomed Keeble with open arms. Keeble spoke at every major Churches of Christ lectureship during his lifetime, including the lectureships on the campuses of Abilene Christian College, David Lipscomb College, Freed-Hardeman College, Michigan Christian College, and Lubbock Christian College.[99] Always drawing one of the largest crowds at the lectureships, Keeble often used these occasions as fundraising opportunities for the NCI.[100] Keeble also used these occasions to express his perceived connection between African American and white members of the denomination. During the 1952 Harding College Lectures, Keeble said:

> The first thing I discovered in my early ministry was that my schooling was very limited, but I was able to read books of sermons written by our educated brethren, who write to these papers and they will never know what they have meant to me in preparing me to meet these intellectual giants who defy the church of Christ, and overthrow the faith of many of us.

> I am still reading articles in these papers written by brethren who graduate at our great colleges, and these articles have prepared me and enabled me to meet educated men, whom I have debated with and the people thought I defeated them. I was debating, but I want you brethren who are educated to know that it was you that won the debate, and I am proud of the colleges that prepared you, so I could read your articles in our papers, and read your books of sermons.[101]

Notice Keeble's use of the phrase "our papers," denoting his membership in the denomination. Nevertheless, other African Americans did not enjoy the same membership privileges. Though Keeble's regular addresses gave the impression of unity, none existed. Keeble became a regular preacher on the lectureship circuit; his African American peers did not. If African Americans and whites had enjoyed the unity Keeble and white leaders modeled in journals, colleges, and lectureships, African American members of Churches of Christ would not have been forced to sit in the balconies of those colleges during annual lectureships, and they certainly would not have been forced to attend non-Churches of Christ colleges in Abilene and Nashville.

Conclusion

Though Keeble spoke at white lectureships, preached at white congregations, and wrote in white denominational journals, his life and ministry failed to bind the racially separated Churches of Christ. By the mid- twentieth century, the denomination remained as separated as ever, and perhaps even more so. By the 1960s, the end of Keeble's life, fewer and fewer African Americans were publicly accommodating themselves to white-imposed segregation. White racial conservatives continued to engage in paternalistic gestures as the Civil Rights Movement came of age; but by that era, African American members of Churches of Christ had begun the next phase of their journey toward independence.

CHAPTER III

INDEPENDENCE

Race matters. During the 1950s and 1960s, white members of Churches of Christ finally were forced to recognize the problems created by race. For nearly a century, journals, colleges, and lectureships had helped maintain separation between African American and white members of the denomination, but with the advent of the American Civil Rights Movement, African American members, much like their regional peers, became more public in their protest, thereby bringing into the open their deep-seated resentment against white-imposed segregation, paternalism, and racism. As the Supreme Court and civil rights activists gained the upper hand in their battle against Jim Crow, African American members of Churches of Christ helped perpetuate denominational division by declaring their independence from white leaders.

Early twentieth century African American leaders such as G. P. Bowser helped lay the foundation for the more public protests of R. N. Hogan and Fred Gray in the 1950s and 1960s. Together these men labored to challenge and finally reject white-imposed segregation in Churches of Christ. If segregation set the agenda for race relations in Churches of Christ in the early decades of the twentieth century, African American independence changed the racial climate beginning in the period of the American Civil Rights Movement.

The Foundation of Independence

In the decades preceding the American rights movement, many African American leaders, as we have seen, chose a more accommodative posture toward white authority and control. Some scholars have concluded that African Americans endured a period of deradicalization in the first decades of the twentieth century, a period that finally ended with the arrival of the Civil Rights Movement in the 1950s. The chief proponent of this view, Gayraud Wilmore, believes the period of "deradicalization" of the Black Church began following the death of Henry M. Turner in 1915.[1] Without a radical leader in the Black Church to challenge racial prejudice, segregation, or white paternalism, he argues, African Americans retreated into their own institutions, refusing to offer a prophetic voice against racial segregation and prejudice.

Wilmore's deradicalization thesis demands closer scrutiny. Numerous scholars, such as Dennis C. Dickerson, Mark Chapman, Randall M. Jelks, and Thomas I. S. Mikelson have pointed out the shortcomings of Wilmore's position in recent years, each highlighting the many influences upon civil rights activists by African Americans living in the period Wilmore has labeled "deradicalized." [2] Though Howard Thurman, Benjamin Mays, Mordecai Johnson, and George D. Kelsey did not lead mass boycotts or lunch counter sit-ins, these religious intellectuals disseminated ideas that encouraged the activism of the Civil Rights Movement among such leaders as Medgar Evers, Martin Luther King Jr., James Farmer, and James M. Lawson Jr.

From these early twentieth-century religious intellectuals, civil rights activists inherited the view of segregation as sin, the picture of Jesus as an ally of the oppressed, and the desire to pursue racial reconciliation. Through Johnson's presidency of Howard University from 1926-1960, Mays' tenure as dean of Howard's divinity school and later term as president of Morehouse College, Thurman's time as dean of Rankin Chapel at Howard, and Kelsey's many years as a professor at Morehouse, African American students, many of them seminarians, were encouraged to resist the ideals of racial inferiority and seek equality. Some African American activists moved beyond ideas in the pre-Civil Rights Movement era. Adam Clayton Powell Jr. led marches in the 1930s and 1940s, and Archibald J. Carey was a benefactor to the Congress of

Racial Equality (CORE).[3] In no way can these ideas and actions be considered "deradicalized."

The fermenting of ideas that led to the Civil Rights Movement began much earlier than the 1950s. In 1930, a group of African American students at Yale Divinity School organized the Upsilon Theta Chi Society, which hosted a seminar including the likes of Mays and A. Philip Randolph. In the midst of Wilmore's "period of deradicalization," African American intellectuals at this conference discussed educational, economic, and various social issues that discriminated against African Americans.[4] Randolph, though not a religious person, was the son of an AME Church minister and still connected to many leaders within the Black Church.[5] In 1940, twenty-three years before the historic event that took place in front of the Lincoln Memorial, Randolph threatened President Franklin Roosevelt, saying he would lead a March on Washington if the federal government would not outlaw racial discrimination in wartime defense plants. With Executive Order 8802, Roosevelt gave into Randolph's demands and established the Fair Employment Practices Committee to enforce the new law.[6] The activism and fermenting of ideas among African American leaders in the early twentieth century was so great that, by 1948, William Stuart Nelson compiled a book, *The Christian Way in Race Relations*, that included numerous essays written by African American religious intellectuals in which they outlined their then mature thoughts concerning racial prejudice, segregation, and black freedom.[7]

Though no African American members of Churches of Christ held positions of president or dean of colleges in the early twentieth century, seeds of protest were certainly planted by men like G. P. Bowser, who mentored the future activist editor of the *Christian Echo*, R. N. Hogan. If not for the influence of Bowser, Hogan may never have publicly led a charge against the white-imposed segregation of Churches of Christ colleges. Ideas matter, and the ideas of Bowser set in motion a movement toward independence among African Americans in Churches of Christ.

G. P. Bowser was born on February 17, 1874 in Maury County, Tennessee. Though his grandfather, Frank Sowell, was a pioneer preacher in the Stone-Campbell Movement, Bowser did not gain his first Christian instruction from either Churches of Christ or Disciples of Christ. Following the death of his father, Bowser's mother moved to Nashville and placed her five children in Walden Institute, a school founded by northern whites for African American students. As a result of Walden Institute's affiliation with the Methodist denomination, the Bowser family began attending the Bethel AME Church in Nashville in 1889. Though Bowser's mother, Charity Elizabeth Bowser, retained her membership in a Stone-Campbell Movement congregation in her hometown, she raised her children in the AME Church.

Bowser's early affiliation with the AME Church may help present scholars understand his more militant approach to race relations. As African Americans in early twentieth-century Churches of Christ publicly acquiesced to southern racism, Bowser provided a voice for racial equality and independence. Bowser likely learned more than arithmetic and reading from the Walden Institute. Unlike Churches of Christ, African Americans within the AME Church had a long history of independence from white control. Beginning with the 1787 exodus from St. George's Methodist Episcopal Church by Richard Allen, the AME Church led the parade of African Americans out of white controlled denominations. Though Bowser spent most of his adult life in Churches of Christ, his early years within the AME Church provided for him a foundation unlike many of his African American peers within Churches of Christ. Like other African American denominations, the AME Church provided opportunities for African American leadership at the highest level and independence from white authority and control. Bowser modeled this independence for many decades in Churches of Christ.

By 1896, Bowser had married Fannie Billips and had entered the ministry through the AME denomination. Unable to support his family on his meager salary, however, he became disenchanted with ministry, left the AME Church, and even questioned his belief in God for a time. Nevertheless, by 1897, he had regained his faith in God; and, through his friendship with an evangelist named Sam Davis, became acquainted with the denomination in which his grandfather had preached for so long. He joined the Stone-Campbell Movement at about the time of the division between Churches of Christ and Disciples of Christ. Feeling more comfortable with the conservative-minded (and less affluent) leaders of the Gay Street and Lea Avenue Christian Churches, Bowser joined Sam W. Womack and Alexander Cleveland Campbell in the formation of a new congregation, the Jackson Street Church of Christ.

During this period, these African American leaders, including Bowser, maintained a connection to white denominational leaders. Some of these African American leaders even sent regular articles to the *Gospel Advocate*.[8]

George Philip Bowser, often wearing the label "The Father of African American Education" in Churches of Christ, is pictured here with his wife. He initiated a stream of African American protest within the denomination.

The connection between African American and white members of Churches of Christ, largely built upon white paternalism, continued until the late 1960s; but during his lifetime Bowser planted seeds that would grow into African American independence.

Students of African American religious history may find helpful insight into the life and work of Bowser by examining another African American leader within a predominantly white denomination, William Henderson Franklin. An African American leader within the Presbyterian Church, USA in the late nineteenth and early twentieth centuries, and a Bowser contemporary,

Franklin spent much of his career building African American agencies within a historically white denomination. A 1901 law prohibiting integrated education in Tennessee, Franklin's desire for African Americans to help themselves, and the necessity for sources of income beyond those of the Presbyterian Freedmen's Board moved Franklin, an integrationist, to dedicate most of his life to establishing African American structures within the Presbyterian Church, USA.[9] Like Bowser, Franklin provided a voice for education within his denomination. Also like Bowser, Franklin encouraged African American autonomy within a predominantly white religious body.[10] The life and work of these leaders underscores the existence of African American agency and leadership within seemingly white dominated denominations. Regardless of their independence, however, both men learned the art of working both cooperatively and independently within the white power structures of their denominations.

Much like Franklin, Bowser, early in his career, joined his peers in soliciting and receiving the aid of his white denominational counterparts. Nowhere was this more evident than in the arena of education. The same 1901 law that prohibited Franklin from seeking integrated education within the Presbyterian Church also prevented African Americans from attending such institutions as Lipscomb's NBS; but, during this period, they lacked financial resources to begin such an effort independently of whites. In 1905, S. W. Womack, Alexander Cleveland Campbell, and Bowser met with Lipscomb to seek his advice and financial assistance before starting a school for African American members similar to NBS.[11] Lipscomb encouraged them to begin the process solely through the African American community, but he also promised to offer any help they needed in the future.[12] Instead of challenging the laws that restricted African Americans from attending NBS, Lipscomb and other white racial conservatives honored their promise to these men by pouring thousands of dollars and hours into the project of educating African Americans.

The first school established within Churches of Christ for African Americans began on January 6, 1907 at the Jackson Street Church of Christ. The founders made it their goal to offer African Americans an elementary and secondary education, using the Bible as the primary textbook. Among members of Churches of Christ, Bowser has sometimes worn the label "father of black education" or the "black David Lipscomb."[13] As with most other efforts toward African American education, Bowser took the lead in this educational effort; and, when he moved to Silver Point, Tennessee, three years later, the school followed. Although the school came to be known by various names throughout its existence ("Putnam County Normal, Industrial, and Orphan School," "Silver Point Christian College," and "Silver Point Christian Institute"), the most recognized name for the institution has become the "Silver Point School."[14] Like Franklin's Swift Memorial Institute in Rogersville, Tennessee, the Silver Point School, also in Tennessee, while drawing on white support, was viewed as belonging to African American Churches of Christ members.

Although its first board of directors consisted solely of African Americans (Henry Clay, Womack, and Campbell), the Silver Point School drew upon the financial resources of whites throughout its existence.[15] In 1913, Bowser hired Annie Tuggle as a teacher in the school, but her most lasting service came from her fundraising ability. When classes were not in session, she traveled across the country, soliciting funds from prominent church members, including Lipscomb. Shortly before his death, she traveled to Nashville, requesting his help. At the time of the meeting, Lipscomb did not have any personal funds to contribute; but he promised to help her in the cause by sending other resources to Silver Point.[16] To this end, Lipscomb called upon A. M. Burton to conduct a study of the Silver Point School in 1916.

Upon the completion of his study of the Silver Point School, Burton contributed money to the school and, through the *Gospel Advocate*, encouraged others to do the same. He also changed the racial make-up of the school's board, giving whites majority control, although during this period Bowser became publicly frustrated with white members of the denomination. One notices the beginnings of a transformation of Bowser during his days at Silver Point. In a 1913 *Gospel Advocate* article, Bowser wrote that he would no longer appeal to the white community for assistance, since his continual requests in the journal had brought only meager results. Their "unwillingness to help" proved increasingly frustrating to Bowser and caused him to publicly criticize whites for their lack of support.[17] Here one begins to see the fundamental difference between Bowser and Keeble. The latter lived his days in the shadows of Burton, Goodpasture, and other white leaders; the former eventually turned his back on the white community, opting instead to seek educational uplift through the work and resources of the African American community alone. His frustration with raising money reached such a level that, in 1918, he suddenly resigned from his post at Silver Point and moved to Louisville, Kentucky, to establish a work among African Americans under the guidance of the Highland Church of Christ, a predominantly white congregation. Without his leadership and sufficient funding, Silver Point School closed in 1920.

Shortly after Bowser arrived in Kentucky, Burton offered him the post of principal at a new school for African Americans in Nashville's Southern Practical Institute. Southern Practical Institute joined a long list of African American schools in Nashville operated by white denominations. For example, within the same city were Fisk University, Meharry College, Tennessee A & I, and American Baptist Seminary. Each of these institutions, like Southern Practical Institute, relied upon white philanthropy during its earliest years. White Nashvillians in Churches of Christ undoubtedly knew of these other denominational institutions, and in 1920, they established their own school.

After much deliberation, Bowser returned to Nashville, accepting the position on a tentative basis; but he left his family in Louisville, anticipating a return in the near future. His reluctance to move his family proved wise, for he returned one week after Southern Practical Institute opened its doors. His brief tenure as principal of this school became a turning point in Bowser's understanding of race relationships in Churches of Christ. When Dorris refused to allow African American students to enter their own school through the front door, Bowser said, "human dignity" would not allow him to support the superintendent's decision. By the end of the week, Bowser had resigned his post at the Southern Practical Institute. In his departure, he also urged other African Americans to withdraw their support from the school.[18] The school closed six weeks later. Following his experience with the Southern Practical Institute, Bowser rejected once and for all the paternalism which had become so common in Churches of Christ by that time and began to rely instead on independent, African American leadership.

The events of 1920 resulted in the closing of the Southern Practical Institute; but, more importantly, they signaled the birth of a new independent African American movement in Churches of Christ. As an influential African American within the denomination, Bowser set a new course for race relationships. Turning his back on white racism, Bowser set out on a path toward independence. Physically, Bowser moved from the center of white influence, Nashville (the home of the *Gospel Advocate* and NBS), to the West (first Louisville, then Ft. Smith, Arkansas, and finally Detroit). Symbolically, Bowser moved away from white leadership by cutting his ties with the *Gospel Advocate,* Burton, and the other sources of white power and control. Certainly, Bowser's actions did not change race relationships in the denomination in a single moment: many African Americans remained connected to the *Gospel Advocate,* Burton, and NBS for fifty more years. Nevertheless, Bowser's actions did create a new stream within the African American community, a stream that began with Bowser and would run through future leaders such as R. N. Hogan, Jack Evans, Levi Kennedy, and J. S. Winston. These men, who would rise to prominence by the 1950s and 1960s, learned from Bowser and articulated his positions during the tumultuous decades in the mid-twentieth century.

One first witnesses the presence of this new, independent stream during Bowser's efforts with yet another African American school in Ft. Smith, Arkansas. Continuing his dream of educating African Americans late in his life, Bowser did not appeal to white members of Churches of Christ through the *Gospel Advocate* for money. Instead, he solicited the African American community through the *Christian Echo,* a journal he started in 1902. Until this time, Bowser had used both the *Christian Echo* and the *Gospel Advocate* to advance the cause of African American education; but after 1920 he abandoned white sources of influence.

Bowser's words from the *Christian Echo* reflect not only his need for financial resources, but also his view of two separate racially defined factions within Churches of Christ:

> It is grievous as well as shameful to think of 30,000 Negro disciples and not a school among *us*. When will *our people* throw off the "yoke of indifference" and decide to do something to educate *our boys and girls* under Christian influence? Our white brethren from the beginning of the Restoration, saw the need for schools and at once went to work with telling results. Will you preachers please line up with me in a determined way for a Christian school? Let me hear from you.[19] (italics added)

In the above statement, one should not overlook Bowser's distinction between African Americans and whites ("us," "our people," "our boys and girls"). A year later, in an appeal to African Americans, he wrote: "The white disciples saw the need of prepared men and, hence, have established many institutions. This is needed among the colored, and we will never be able to impress the intelligent until leaders are better prepared."[20] In the same issue, he blamed the "Board System" of the Silver Point School for its closing and then appealed to his African American peers to help support their own school, writing, "Five cents per month from half of the colored people will suffice to meet all needs."[21] Even in the 1920s and 1930s, Bowser recognized the vast separation between African Americans and whites in Churches of Christ. In the same period in which Keeble and the white editors of the *Gospel Advocate* worked hand-in-hand to create an illusion of racial unity, Bowser and a handful of African Americans were beginning to acknowledge their separation from whites and, at the same time, lay the foundation for African American independence.

Another of Bowser's *Christian Echo* appeals seems worthy of note due to the comparison he sets up between his institution and Nashville Christian Institute. After calling attention to the effort among whites and African Americans to raise money for NCI, Bowser wrote: "If however that money was placed in Fort Smith, Ark it would accomplish much more good."[22] With these

Pictured here late in his life, G. P. Bowser offered an alternative voice to the more accommodative one heard by Marshall Keeble. Bowser's proteges helped move African American Churches of Christ decidedly toward independence.

words, Bowser not only asserted his independence from white paternalism, he encouraged others to join him in an independent African American educational venture. By 1939, he encouraged African Americans to send their money to a new kind of effort, one that would be led exclusively by African Americans.

Bowser Christian Institute in Ft. Smith began, not from the hands of white philanthropists, but instead through the efforts of J. S. Winston (a student of Bowser). Winston called a meeting in 1938 for African American leaders in Dallas, which was followed by a similar meeting in Ft. Smith. These gatherings, along with Bowser's appeals through the *Christian Echo,* encouraged the African American community to support its own school. The Bowser Christian Institute existed for eight years (1938-1946). It housed a printing press for the *Christian Echo,* hosted an annual lectureship for African American members, and served as a training ground for future African American leaders.

Bowser's final educational project originated not through his own leadership but through the leadership of his students. In 1950, just months before Bowser's death, Winston drove his mentor to Dallas, Texas, and the site of a new school that opened later that same year, Southwestern Christian College. In the first years of the twenty-first century SWCC existed as the only African American college affiliated with Churches of Christ. Jack Evans, the current president of SWCC, credits Bowser with founding the school.[23] In the years following the Civil Rights Movement, as more African American members of Churches of Christ declared their independence from white-imposed segregation, paternalism, and racism, SWCC became an important mediator of theology among African American Churches of Christ.

Bowser died in 1950, the same year classes began at SWCC. His ideas and his activism laid the foundation for African American independence in Churches of Christ. Bowser's students built upon that foundation by publicly protesting white racism in the 1950s and 1960s.

African American Independence

Bowser's most devout protégée, R. N. Hogan, led that charge toward independence. During a preaching trip in Arkansas, Bowser came in contact with a nine-year-old boy whose father just recently had died. The boy's mother requested that Bowser take her son, Hogan, to raise.[24] Hogan grew up under the tutelage of Bowser, learning from him the same independent spirit that disallowed the latter from serving as principal of the Southern Practical

Institute. Hogan helped move Bowser's independent spirit into the African American mainstream during his tenure as editor of the *Christian Echo*. Even while Keeble spoke at the many white lectureships, fully engaging the dominant white racist ethos of his day and helping to perpetuate the illusion of racial unity, Hogan began his decade-long attack on white denominational colleges for their unwillingness to follow the Supreme Court's mandate to desegregate. When Hogan began his time as editor of the *Christian Echo*, white racism reigned in Churches of Christ; by 1967, however, African Americans had sought independence and had found it.

Hogan left no room for doubt concerning his position on white-imposed segregation and racism when he proclaimed boldly in 1959: "That being a respecter of persons is a sin is without question, for the Bible plainly says that it is a sin."[25] Racial prejudice, according to Hogan, had "caused multiplied thousands to lose their souls."[26] Contrary to the many white journal contributors who equated racial injustice with other social problems, Hogan adamantly declared segregation a moral issue, and one deserving the full attention of the church.

From the stream of his mentor, G. P. Bowser, Richard Nathaniel Hogan used his post as editor of the *Christian Echo* to challenge racism in white Churches of Christ colleges.

Though Hogan challenged many denominational bodies, he reserved his most vehement attacks for white Churches of Christ colleges. Between 1954 and 1966, Hogan used the *Christian Echo* to call into question the integrity of college presidents and boards of trustees for their refusal to desegregate.[27] "Christian college" had become a common designation of these institutions among members of Churches of Christ, perhaps reflecting the historic sectarian tendency of viewing themselves as the only Christians. Hogan, understanding well this history, attacked his white peers at the heart of their self understanding. One of his most common tactics involved comparing unfavorably David Lipscomb College, Harding College, Abilene Christian College, and other "so-called Christian schools" to denominational institutions. He wrote in 1959: "One of the most embarrassing things that Negro Christians have to face today is the fact that people of our race are admitted to Denominational [sic] schools as well as State [sic] schools, but cannot enter a Christian (?) school operated by members of the church of Christ."[28] He did not merely make abstract claims; he called the guilty parties by name. Hogan's comments allow one to understand his perception of segregation as a moral issue, not simply as a social one.

Many white member of Churches of Christ remained aloof or even antagonistic toward the Civil Rights Movement, reasoning that racism and segregation were social issues and therefore beyond the purview of the church. The lawlessness of many civil rights activists was another reason many whites stood in opposition to the movement. Many white conservatives had for years hidden behind the "law of the land" argument in their support of Jim Crow segregation. The law of the land, in the minds of many southerners, allowed them to maintain the hierarchic order of their southern, organic society by keeping African Americans in their place. Hogan criticized his white denominational counterparts for their practice of hiding behind the "law of the land," and he further admonished them to take note of a new law they had decided to ignore, namely the mandate to desegregate schools.[29] Turning the tables on some white editors, he highlighted the fact that by ignoring the *Brown v. Board of Education* decision, "we yet have a few out-laws [sic] who are refusing to obey God or man."[30]

In spite of Hogan's protest against white denominational colleges, every school but Pepperdine College in California remained segregated into the 1960s. In their reluctance to desegregate, these Churches of Christ colleges were similar to other southern private schools. Belhaven College in Jackson, Mississippi, a college associated with the PCUS, did not desegregate until 1967 and only then to ensure the school would continue to receive student loan money from the federal government. Die-hard segregationists protested the decision at the 1967 Synod of Mississippi.[31] Another school, Tulane University in New Orleans, desegregated in 1961. *Brown v. Board of Education* nullified the "separate but equal" clause in public schools of all levels. Some private institutions, however, used their private status as a shield to protect them from having to challenge southern racism and the segregated system it built. Nevertheless, a Supreme Court decision just four years after *Brown v. Board of Education*, *Cooper v. Aaron* (1958), warned that private institutions receiving any funds from the state also fell under the demands of the Fourteenth Amendment.[32] Though a private institution, Tulane also accepted some federal funds; therefore, its segregated status placed it in opposition to the law. Despite its legal violation, however, the Tulane administration needed the prodding of a lawsuit filed by John Nelson to force its compliance.

The administrators of private Churches of Christ colleges also refused to comply with the law, aligning themselves with Jim Crow instead of the Supreme Court. In addition to hiding behind their private school status, these administrators took seriously the Court's decision in 1955, in a case commonly referred to as Brown II, which ordered district courts to carry out the desegregation mandate "with all deliberate speed." Abilene Christian College, David Lipscomb College, Harding College, and other Churches of Christ institutions took great liberty with this clause.

Evidence bears witness that the administrations of these schools lagged not only behind other denominational schools but also behind the desires of their student bodies. Calls from the student body of ACC for integration began as early as 1948 in the school's paper, the *Optimist*; and the number of similar editorials skyrocketed in 1954.[33] A long list of students, including Bob Barnhill, Phil Bradshaw, Bruce Branscome Jr., Howard Norton, and Joe Schubert registered their positions to the administration through the *Optimist*.[34] In May of 1954, the paper's editor released a staggering statistic to the ACC community, revealing that more than 80 percent of the student body favored immediate integration of the school.[35] In spite of this spirit among the young white students, the school did not begin the process of desegregation until the early 1960s.

When William Floyd was student body president of Harding College in 1957, he circulated a petition throughout the student body. The statement articulated the students' desire for Harding to desegregate and encouraged the administration of the university to make their desire a reality. In a humble tone, Floyd said his letter was "by no means an attempt to precipitate action by the Administration or Board of Trustees of Harding College." He sought only to express to the governing bodies of the college the "internal readiness of the Harding community" for integration.[36] In all, forty-nine members of faculty, forty-two staff members, and eight executive directors signed the letter. The total number of signatures totaled 946, and the student body of Harding College in 1957 totaled 986. In reaction to the petition, then president of the college, George Benson, made a public denunciation of the effort in a special announcement during the daily chapel service. During his

Pictured here from left to right, Don Morris, George Benson, Athens Pullias, and Norvel Young served as presidents of Abilene Christian College, Harding College, David Lipscomb College, and George Pepperdine College in the mid-twentieth century. From their posts, they helped steer Churches of Christ in areas related to theology and race relationships.

comments, he reportedly told the student body: "The redbirds, the bluebirds, the blackbirds, they don't mix and mingle together, young people!" Some witnesses state that the next morning, those first to rise found an interesting sign hanging from the bird bath in the central courtyard of Harding College. The sign read: "White only."[37]

The reaction of many white students and faculty members of white denominational colleges coupled with the rejection of white-imposed segregation by many African Americans reveals an important truth concerning Churches of Christ in the 1950s and 1960s. Many members, African American and white, recognized the great chasm separating these two racial factions; yet, the most influential theological mediators of the denomination (journals, colleges, and lectureships) failed to address the issue. The white leaders were functioning as whites in the larger southern society and simply brought into Churches of Christ the ideology of white skin privilege. Even if many members were ready to admit division, key leaders and entities were content to perpetuate racism and the illusion of unity.

Hogan may not have changed the minds of many white leaders, but he certainly spoke loudly against white racism in the 1950s and 1960s. Throughout the period of the Civil Rights Movement, Hogan was the chief African American opponent to white leaders in Churches of Christ, consistently urging them to recognize the separation between African Americans and whites in the denomination and to take steps to bridge the divide. Hogan, however, did not act alone; other African Americans joined his mission from the pages of the *Christian Echo* during the 1960s. A man who would become a prominent leader in African American Churches of Christ in the second half of the twentieth century, Andrew J. Hairston, presented a clear picture of the growing animosity between the two racial factions. He wrote: "The race issue is no more social and to be divorced from the life and preaching of the true church today than it was when Christ died for the demolition of that wall separating man from man."[38] James Maxwell, another African American leader, wrote a three-part series on the sociological impact of the race issue, discussing such matters as education, voting, housing, and public accommodations.[39]

One of the most vivid illustrations that a new era had arrived in Churches of Christ arose from the pen of Norman R. Adamson. Unlike his white counterparts who viewed the Civil Rights Movement with suspicion, Adamson, an African American, participated in the Selma March and wrote his reflections on the event in the *Christian Echo*. Believing "the march and the whole Civil Rights Movement is a success," Adamson encouraged his African American peers to join hands in their direct, non-violent confrontation of white members of the denomination. Writing "Now is the time for us to let our white brothers who have bigoted and segregated hearts filled with hatred know that they stand condemned before God," Adamson signaled an end of one era and the beginning of a new one.[40] He along with many other African American members of Churches of Christ no longer were willing to keep their resentment of white racism a secret. The days when white paternalism represented the most common form of public interaction between African Americans and whites in the denomination were over. The days of passive accommodationism were over. The days of the Keeble stream had passed, and Bowser's stream had come of age.

Though a student of Keeble, the individual who most epitomized the rejection of white-imposed segregation, paternalism, and racism by African American members of Churches of Christ during the Civil Rights Movement era was acclaimed civil rights attorney Fred D. Gray. During his Alabama career, Gray served as the primary lawyer for the Montgomery Improvement Association, which initiated and led the Montgomery bus boycott, an event that, in many people's minds, sparked the American Civil Rights Movement.[41] During that period, he also served as primary counsel for both Rosa Parks and Martin Luther King Jr. In 1956, with *Gomillion v. Lightfoot* (a case he eventually argued before the United States Supreme Court), he challenged the Alabama Legislature's gerrymandering of Tuskegee for the purpose of denying African Americans the right to vote. That case helped set the precedent of "one man, one vote." Nearly a decade later, in 1965, Gray filed *Hosea Williams v. George C. Wallace*, which forced the Alabama Governor to provide protection for African Americans marching from Selma to Montgomery. Gray believes that demonstration led to the eventual passing of the Voting Rights Act of 1965.[42]

In light of his numerous accomplishments in the courtroom, Gray has received many honors throughout his legal career. He became the first African American elected as president of the Alabama State Bar Association (2002); but before that, he served as president of the National Bar Association from 1985-1986. In 1996, the American Bar Association awarded Gray the "Spirit of Excellence Award"; and, in 2004, that same organization presented him with the coveted Thurgood Marshall Award, which "recognizes long-term contributions to the advancement of civil rights, civil liberties, and human rights in the United States."[43] Perhaps one of the greatest accolades accorded Gray came from the foremost icon of the Civil Rights Movement. Speaking to a crowded auditorium at the Holt Street Baptist Church in 1956, Gray's long-time friend and co-worker in the Civil Rights Movement, Martin Luther King Jr., referred to Gray as "a brilliant young attorney."[44] Gray's lists of accomplishments related to his ability as a civil rights attorney are too many to mention, but he discusses many of them in his 1995 autobiography, *Bus Ride to Justice*.

Gray not only participated in the American Civil Rights Movement, he helped initiate it. As evidence of this fact, one has only to consider the events of December 1, 1955, the day Rosa Parks was arrested for disorderly conduct. On that evening, Gray met with two other African Americans in the home of Jo Ann Robinson to lay the foundation for the Montgomery bus boycott.[45] If Gray had never met with Parks and Robinson to plan the Montgomery protest or if he had never filed *Browder v. Gale* in the months that followed their meeting, the Montgomery bus boycott and the Civil Rights Movement certainly would have occurred without his efforts. Robert Glennon correctly surmised that "No system of law can resist forever the force of an idea whose time has come."[46] Nevertheless, Gray did help plan the protest, and he did file the lawsuit the led to the eventual desegregation of Montgomery buses. Gray existed at the center of the American Civil Rights Movement. His story, however, did not begin in Jo Ann Robinson's living room; but it did begin in Montgomery.

Born on December 14, 1930 in the Washington Park section of Montgomery, Gray spent his early childhood in poverty. African American mothers were not even permitted to give birth to their children in city hospitals, so a midwife delivered the son of Nancy Gray. Interestingly, as Gray described his early childhood in his autobiography, he almost immediately mentioned the influence of Holt Street Church of Christ, the congregation his parents attended at the time of his birth and the same congregation that Gray would later serve as assistant minister when he returned to Montgomery following law school in Cleveland.[47]

Shortly following Gray's second birthday, his father died. Despite her meager income as a single mother who worked as a domestic for white families, Gray's mother found the money to send her son to Nashville Christian Institute after he finished the seventh grade. As a student in Nashville from

Marshall Keeble provided education and guidance to countless African American young men at Nashville Christian Institute, including Fred Gray, pictured here seated next to his mentor.

Fred Gray grew up to become one of the foremost leaders in the Civil Rights Movement, serving as attorney for both Martin Luther King Jr. and Rosa Parks.

1943-1947, Gray became a prized student of Keeble, who took the future civil rights attorney on many fundraising and preaching tours across the nation. Early in his life, Gray wanted to become a preacher; and, throughout his career as a lawyer, he continued to work as a minister at various Churches of Christ, including the Holt Street and Newtown congregations in Montgomery and the Tuskegee Institute congregation in Tuskegee.

Though Gray certainly held different perspectives on race relations than the publicly accommodative Keeble, the former described the latter as a mentor and described him as "a pioneer preacher in Churches of Christ."[48] Years later, after Gray became the chief attorney for the Montgomery bus boycott, an NCI student commented to Keeble, "Fred Gray is smart. He is involved in the Civil Rights Movement." Keeble responded, "He's too smart."[49] Gray understood Keeble's comment as his disapproval of Gray's choice to fight white-imposed segregation in such a public forum. Keeble never chose to publicly protest white racism either in Churches of Christ or in the South; nevertheless, many of his students, including Gray, did not fit the mold created by their teacher.

Gray stood in the tradition of another influential African American, namely G. P. Bowser. Instead of perpetuating the illusion of racial unity in Churches of Christ like Keeble, Gray never masked the separation between white and African American members; and he also worked diligently to bridge that great divide. Speaking of the involvement of Churches of Christ in the Montgomery bus boycott, Gray discussed his own role as well as the roles played by other African Americans. When asked how white congregations responded to the boycott, he said, "We had no contact with white congregations at that time."[50] In 1956, Keeble provided a regular column to the *Gospel Advocate*; and, in the same era, he was a regular speaker at the Abilene Christian College, David Lipscomb College, Harding College, and Lubbock Christian College lectureships.[51] In 1956, white congregations welcomed students from NCI into their congregations to preach, recite scripture, and raise money for their school. In the 1940s and 1950s, white audiences packed into the War Memorial Auditorium of Nashville to see NCI students display the fruits of white financial contributions. Of the same years that numerous white leaders and Keeble used NCI to perpetuate the illusion of racial unity in Churches of Christ, Gray said, "We had no contact with white congregations at that time." Evidently, African Americans and whites within Churches of

Christ viewed their relationship differently. Where whites saw racial unity, African Americans saw racial disparity.

In addition to his efforts in the courtroom to destroy everything segregated he could find, Gray also combated segregation in Churches of Christ. The clearest example of his work in this arena centers on the Tuskegee Church of Christ. In 1973, Gray moved to Tuskegee. While maintaining his law practice, he also became the preacher for the Tuskegee Church of Christ, an African American congregation. Located in the same town was the East End Church of Christ, a white congregation. Shortly after his arrival in Tuskegee, Gray worked in cooperation with James Allen Parker, the minister of the East End congregation, to merge the two groups. On the first Sunday in November of 1974, the Tuskegee Church of Christ, a racially united congregation, held their first services.[52] At the end of the twentieth century, Gray continued leading that congregation as an elder.

In a 2008 interview, Gray was asked to reflect on other members of his denomination who have labored for African American civil rights since the mid-twentieth century. Though he did not provide his interviewer with the names of unsung heroes, he said, "When I hear people talk about the church not being completely involved in the Civil Rights Movement, I know that isn't the truth. I was involved. Most of the members in our church were involved. I think the Lord played a major role in bringing about civil rights."[53] The *Gospel Advocate, Firm Foundation,* and various white Churches of Christ lectureships failed to address the existence of the social and moral revolution taking place in the American South in the 1950s and 1960s; nevertheless, Fred Gray and "most of the members of his church" were actively involved. Even though the white mediators of theology in Churches of Christ chose to ignore the Civil Rights Movement, African American members in Alabama chose to protest.

Gray and his African American Churches of Christ peers in Montgomery and Tuskegee joined other African Americans from predominantly white denominations in their protest against white racism in the 1950s and 1960s. Gayraud Wilmore, an African American minister, professor, and author from the predominantly white PCUSA, has written on the subject of African American religion for nearly half a century. In his 1973 work, *Black Religion and Black Radicalism,* Wilmore traced the legacy of African American protest from the period of American colonization to the present. In his 1983 book, *Black and Presbyterian,* Wilmore helped his readers take a closer look at his denomination from an African American perspective. From the midst of a racist denomination, wrote Wilmore, African Americans have historically "united for concerted action."[54] For example, as early as 1893, African American Presbyterian leaders such as Francis Grimke, Matthew Anderson, and John Reeves formed the Afro-Presbyterian Council as a forum for black Presbyterians to maintain fellowship with one another and also to voice their concerns before the denomination. African American Presbyterians, including Wilmore himself, along with Gray and other African American members of Churches of Christ continued to challenge southern white racism through books, articles, and sermons throughout the twentieth century.

As a southern African American minister and community leader, Gray interacted with many other African American civil rights activists from other denominations. In fact, Gray shared office space with Solomon S. Seay Sr., a minister and the secretary-treasurer of the Home Mission Department of the AME Zion Church. In his autobiography, Gray wrote that Seay advised him on many matters and over time "became like a father to me."[55] Seay was no bystander to the Civil Rights Movement. He served on the executive board of the Montgomery Improvement Association along with King, and helped sustain the boycott for a year. Even after the boycott concluded, Seay continued his activism by allowing freedom riders to stay in his house as they passed through Montgomery. In 1964 Seay's name appeared alongside the names of King, Ralph Abernathy, Fred Shuttlesworth, and Joseph Lowery as defendants in *New York Times Co. v. Sullivan.* In that case, L. B. Sullivan sued the New York Times Company for libel after an advertisement in their paper accused Alabama state and local officials of harassing civil rights activists and repeatedly arresting King without cause. The names of four African American ministers (Abernathy, King, Seay, and Shuttlesworth) also appeared on the advertisement, so they were included in the suit. The case eventually made it to the United States Supreme Court, which ruled in favor of the New York Times Company. Seay's inclusion in this landmark case indicates not only his frustration with state and local officials, but also his leadership in the Civil Rights Movement. Eventually, Gray invited Seay's son, Solomon Seay Jr., to join his law practice as a partner. They worked together in that capacity for over thirty years. Seay Sr. published an autobiography in 1990 entitled *There by the Grace of God* which recounted his career as a civil rights activist in Montgomery. In sum, in his protest against racism, Gray worked alongside not only his Churches of Christ peers in Montgomery and Tuskegee, but also interacted with and was influenced by African American Methodists and Baptists.

A closer look indicates that African American members of Churches of Christ in Montgomery and Tuskegee were not the only ones affected by the Civil Rights Movement. By the late 1960s, African American members of Churches of Christ in Texas were allowing their resentment towards white-imposed segregation and racism to rise to the surface. Given the identity of Churches of Christ as primarily a southern Christian denomination, the silence of white lectureships comes as little surprise; but what may surprise some is the silence of their African American counterparts during the same period. The SWCC Bible Lectures began in 1952 and continue to be held each year from the fourth Sunday in November until Thanksgiving Day. Despite the college's identity as an African American institution, its lectures did not include a racial theme until 1967. That year, the lectureship director named "Christ for the Crises" as the annual theme, and Zebedee Bishop taught a three-day class on "Improving Race Relations." At the same meeting, a white speaker, John Allen Chalk, presented a series entitled "Christ for the Crisis in Race Relations."[56] Until that time, the Southwestern Lectures offered themes similar to those of white lectureships, including "Enlightening the Whole Man," "Proclaiming God's Good News," and "The Restoration Plea."[57]

The tardiness of African American Churches of Christ in addressing the issue demands a closer look. Carroll Pitts Jr. discussed at length the reasons African Americans did not offer a critique of America's race problem until 1967, positing finally that African Americans born into the southern system of racial segregation accepted their social inferiority out of habit. The abandonment of their true feelings "became part of the Negro's whole existence."[58] His assessment agrees with Hans A. Baer and Merrill Singer's analysis of white paternalism. They assert that African American slaves over time "internalized portions of the slaveowners' ideology," an ideology that found its basis in white superiority.[59] The acceptance of white paternalism stymied the growth of an independent identity among African Americans, causing them instead to identify themselves in relation to the white community. Only when African Americans rejected white paternalism publicly were they able to fully create and sustain an independent African American identity, one not dependent upon the white community. Understanding these undercurrents of paternalism allows one to begin to comprehend why African American members of Churches of Christ failed to address racial injustice for so long.

Nevertheless, neither Pitts' analysis nor that of Baer and Singer can be accepted without reservation. Though they offer some helpful insight into the African American community, they fail to acknowledge that African Americans held positions of leadership and operated out from underneath white control long before the Civil Rights Movement period, especially in the Black Church. Gordon W. Allport described a phenomenon known as passive acquiescence. He wrote: "By agreeing with his adversary he [oppressed person] escapes being conspicuous, has no cause for fear, and quietly leads his life in two compartments: one (more active) among his own kind, one (more passive) in the outer world."[60] In other words, the leaders of the Southwestern Lectureship did not address the racial crisis until 1967 because their identity had become one of nonconfrontation. Even if they abhorred the practice of segregation in their own racially defined communities, they refrained from challenging the status quo in public out of fear or strategy. Keeble's calculated passive acquiescence allowed him to raise money for NCI and support his own ministry for decades. One must be careful to acknowledge the agency and leadership of African Americans within their own communities long before the 1950s and 1960s. African Americans may have adopted an accommodationist position publicly, but privately they thrived apart from white control. During the Civil Rights Movement era, their private world spilled over into their public world.

The SWCC presidency of Jack Evans helped move African American activism into the public arena. Evans became the first African American president of SWCC in 1967. The first year under African American leadership, the SWCC Lectureship centered on the theme of racial crisis; and its speakers orchestrated a frontal attack on the segregated system of the American South. An independent African American identity began to publicly manifest itself in Churches of Christ.

When asked about his decision in 1967 to center the college's lectureship on racism within the church, Evans said, "1967 was the beginning of a new definition for the school."[61] Until Evans' presidency in 1967, white school presidents had forced the school to conform into the mold of many other southern institutions. During Hogan's protest against segregated white denominational schools in the late 1950s and early 1960s, the white president of SWCC pulled the *Christian Echo* off the shelves of the school's library. That same president also refused to attend daily chapel with his African American faculty, staff, and student body.[62] In 1967, however, Evans, an African American, took control of the school. From that time forward, Evans set out to create "a new definition for the school."

In these events, African American members of Churches of Christ joined other southern African Americans in their public protest against white racism, a movement of protest that began over a decade before Evans' SWCC presidency. Aldon D. Morris chronicles the mass protest movement, beginning with the bus boycott that took place in June of 1953 in Baton Rouge, Louisiana. Two years prior to the more famous Montgomery bus boycott, the Baton Rouge campaign, argues Morris, laid the foundation for a decade-long attack against southern segregation by African Americans.[63] The Baton Rouge effort was followed in close succession by the Montgomery boycott in 1955 and the Tallahassee boycott in 1956. The American Civil Rights Movement signaled a change in the relationship between African Americans and whites. Even though African American individuals always had protested white racism, beginning in the late 1940s and early 1950s, African Americans in large numbers "directly confronted and effectively disrupted the normal functioning of groups and institutions thought to be responsible for their oppression."[64] Mass African American activism already was stirring in the southern states by the 1950s. In the 1960s, African Americans in large numbers within Churches of Christ joined a public protest movement already in full swing, because, in addition to their membership in Churches of Christ, they were integral parts of protesting black communities.

The overt attack on racial prejudice during the 1967 SWCC Lectureship signaled a new era of race relationships in Churches of Christ. No longer did many African Americans publicly acquiesce to white paternalism or second-class citizenship; instead, the only remaining African American college of the denomination, under the new leadership of an African American president, set a new course, a course that would become increasingly distant from the path followed by white members of Churches of Christ. Nevertheless, not everyone recognized the new course in the late 1960s.

White Responses to the Civil Rights Movement

By examining white journals, on the one hand, and African American journals, on the other, one notices an obvious difference between the two.

Mainstream white denominational journals remained silent on the issue of racial civil rights, condemned civil rights activists as lawbreakers, and discouraged Christians from getting involved in social concerns, which they believed lay beyond the scope of the church's jurisdiction. Articles written by African Americans in the *Christian Echo,* however, reflected a sense of urgency toward change and consistently viewed segregation as an immoral and sinful institution in America, especially among Christians. As African Americans allowed their resentment to spill over into the public arena, these differing viewpoints allowed the chasm between white and African American Christians to widen.

The most common position taken by white journals concerning the Civil Rights Movement in the 1960s was silence. The *Gospel Advocate* maintained its silence until 1968, ignoring the events of Montgomery, Alabama, in 1963, the March in Washington the same year, and even the death of King. Only the death of Keeble ended their deafening silence on the issue of race, and many writers in that special tribute edition took opportunity to criticize those African Americans who chose not to follow in the footsteps of the more accommodative Keeble.[65] The *Firm Foundation,* another influential white journal, likewise, virtually ignored the Civil Rights Movement, abandoning that position only sporadically to condemn the lawlessness of "organizations whose express business it is to create tensions."[66] Indeed, longtime editor of the journal, Reuel Lemmons, acknowledged the *Firm Foundation*'s premeditated intent to remain silent on the subject.[67]

Considering the Churches of Christ's southern context, the silence of denominational journals may not come as a surprise, unless one considers that their regional counterparts wrote prolifically on the subject in the 1950s and 1960s. For example, PCUS members who supported and disapproved of the Civil Rights Movement debated their positions regularly in the *Presbyterian Outlook* and the *Southern Presbyterian Journal* (also referred to as the *Presbyterian Journal.*)[68] Southern Baptists, likewise, filled the pages of the *Royal Service, Light, Baptist Standard,* and *Baptist Message* with articles concerning racial tension and civil unrest.[69] One reason for on-going discussions of civil rights issues in white journals of other southern denominations is that their centralized bodies encouraged that discussion by their official pronouncements. As various southern Christians proposed the establishment of private segregated schools in churches (to avoid sending their children to desegregated schools), many presbyteries, synods, as well as the General Assembly of the PCUSA made statements opposing this idea.[70] The Southern Baptist Convention passed a resolution in 1965 supporting the Civil Rights Act of 1964. In 1968 it adopted the "Statement Concerning the Crisis in Our Nation," which called for an end to segregation and encouraged Southern Baptists to work toward "equal opportunities in public services, education and employment."[71] Each of these pronouncements encouraged discussions of race relations by inviting either support or criticism from denominational journals. For example, when the Southern Baptist Convention passed its resolution in support of the Civil Rights Act of 1964, even some Baptist segregationists made their change of heart apparent through denominational journals. Mrs. S. A. Williams of Arkansas, a former segregationist, wrote in 1964, "I no longer believe in race superiority as I once did."[72] Williams' letter to the editors of the *Royal Service* joined many other articles in the *Biblical Recorder*, the *Florida Baptist Witness*, *Baptist Press*, *Baptist History and Heritage*, and other Baptist journals debating the Convention's declaration.[73] Lacking any official body to incite such conversation, the private owners of the *Gospel Advocate* and the *Firm Foundation* refrained from using their journals to discuss the matter.

Lemmons momentarily broke his silence in January of 1968 when he encouraged his readers to reflect on the "long hot summer" of previous months. Tying the events of that time to Communist plots, he admonished Churches of Christ to resist the efforts of America's enemies to gain a foothold. People would know when this type of anarchy had arrived, according to Lemmons, when "agitators, anarchists, rioters, looters, and hate peddlers" would become the idols of individuals and the press.[74] Lemmons postulated that the only hope for defeating those Communist plots would not arise with protests or other acts of lawlessness but instead when the nation returned to "the principles of Jesus Christ."[75]

On at least one occasion, Lemmons stepped away from his public platform as editor of the *Firm Foundation* and engaged in a private correspondence with John Allen Chalk. Chalk had written a letter to Lemmons earlier, requesting that the editor include a tribute to King in the *Firm Foundation*. Lemmons' response to Chalk's request speaks volumes to the former's view of civil rights activists. Referring to King as a Communist, an outsider to the communities he disrupted, and a notorious liar, Lemmons' chief complaint about King concerned his "disobedience to law and order."[76] Lemmons, like many other southern leaders, made it his goal to protect the hierarchic order of the southern, organic culture.

In these statements, Lemmons resembled other southern racial conservatives like Jerry Falwell. Falwell expressed similar sentiments in 1965, referring to King as a "Communist" and accusing him and other civil rights activists of "exploiting every incident to bring about violence and bloodshed."[77] This same skepticism toward "lawbreakers" dominated the white press in Churches of Christ during this period. Racial conservatives, though they did not advocate physical violence against African Americans, used rhetoric to keep African Americans in their white-relegated place in society. Understandably, African Americans would begin to distance themselves from a group of people who viewed their work toward civil rights akin to common criminal activity.

Most white members in Churches of Christ who wrote on the subject of the Civil Rights Movement called attention to its distance from the real purpose of the Christian life, namely the conversion of lost souls. Much like the white power structures of their regional contemporaries, the white power structures in Churches of Christ viewed the issue of racial prejudice as a social problem, not a spiritual one. As a social issue, many leaders of the denomination encouraged their constituents not to bother themselves with such a peripheral matter. Echoing the countercultural views of Lipscomb two generations earlier, Lemmons wrote: "Christianity and church were neither planned in heaven nor commissioned on earth to revolutionize existing governments nor to uproot social structures."[78]

Hugo McCord openly criticized one African American member of Churches of Christ, Franklin Florence, for his involvement in a civil rights dispute with the Eastman Kodak Company. An acquaintance of Malcolm X, Florence and his organization, FIGHT (Freedom, Integration, God, Honor, Today), challenged the company for its alleged discriminatory hiring practices.[79] Responding to such activism, McCord wrote: "One wonders if the apostle Paul, probably in the ghetto of Corinth, was 'the leader of FIGHT, an organization which operates a tent-making factory.'"[80] Continuing, McCord stated that "the chief problem of our day, as it was in Jesus' day, is sin."[81]

Other racial conservatives such as Alan E. Highers, Dale Simpson, and Rex A. Turner viewed the efforts of civil rights leaders beyond the scope of the church's responsibility in the world.[82] Many of those who even believed in the mission of the Civil Rights Movement and the equality of all people, found it difficult to accept the activist and sometimes militant tactics of civil rights workers.[83] Each of these white leaders found themselves increasingly distant from their African American counterparts.

Only two denominational periodicals, the *Christian Chronicle* and *20th Century Christian,* took seriously the Civil Rights Movement; and neither of these had a fraction of the following enjoyed by the *Gospel Advocate* or *Firm Foundation* in the 1960s. Following an ACC Lectureship speech delivered by Carl Spain in 1960 in which he challenged white colleges to desegregate their campuses, the *Christian Chronicle* was the first white publication to end its silence by calling for a dialogue on the subject of race. This publication provides the best window into the rank and file of Churches of Christ from this period because of its open call for letters to the editor on the subject of racial prejudice. Years following that event, letters continued to flow from the pages of this religious newspaper both praising and ridiculing Spain's boldness.[84]

M. Norvel Young and William S. Banowsky, editors of the *20th Century Christian,* devoted the entire July 1968 issue of their journal to the subject of race relations. In that issue white and African American leaders wrote on the subjects of "racism in the church," "tearing down the walls," and "total equality in Christ." Such boldness on their parts would seem to suggest a changing climate in the denomination. Much like the *Christian Chronicle,* however, *20th Century Christian* was a small publication with only a fraction of the readership enjoyed by the *Gospel Advocate* and *Firm Foundation.* Further indicating the unchanging attitudes of many white members of the denomination, some estimate that the total readership of *20th Century Christian* was cut in half following the release of their July 1968 issue.[85]

The efforts of the *Christian Chronicle,* the single edition posted by *20th Century Christian,* and even the sporadic mentioning of racial unrest in the *Firm Foundation* and *Gospel Advocate* represented the exceptions rather than the rule. The silence of white periodicals in Churches of Christ reflected the most damaging sentiment to race relations in this era. Many, and perhaps most, white members did not perceive any real problem in their relationships with African Americans. In a classic statement in 1964, the influential editor of the *Firm Foundation* wrote: "We do not believe that segregation has ever been a problem with the Lord's church. . . . The kingdom of heaven is the most completely integrated institution we know, and all the brethren accept all the

As editor of the *Firm Foundation* from 1955 to 1983, Reuel Lemmons wielded considerable influence upon Churches of Christ, offering his commentary on such pivotal issues as the Holy Spirit, religious legalism, the social gospel, and the Vietnam War. Nevertheless, he ignored the Civil Rights Movement and suggested segregation had never been a problem in the Lord's church.

brethren as brethren. We have never had a problem here."[86] In his attempt to protect the order of his southern society, Lemmons ignored the revolution taking place around him. Problems arose in the denomination when African Americans challenged the illusion of racial unity created and perpetuated by Lemmons and other white editors.

White lectureship directors also worked to perpetuate the illusion. As with denominational journals, however, there were exceptions to the general rule. In 1955 Abilene Christian College used its annual lectureship to address the issue of race in the church. In a four-person panel format, L. M. Graves, Leon Locke, J. W. Treat, and J. Roy Willingham Jr., discussed briefly the biblical and ecclesiastical implications of integration and segregation.[87] Though each speaker offered a different perspective on the issue, they all favored the path of least resistance by rejecting an immediate end of segregation in the South, arguing instead for a gradual change of individuals through their encounter with the Christian message.

Willingham, the speaker most sympathetic to equal rights, rested his argument on Jesus' response (or lack of a response) toward slavery. Citing Jesus' refusal to openly attack the system of slavery (even though he believed Jesus rejected the idea of slavery), Willingham stated: "For this reason we should not be overzealous in attempting to produce immediate changes in social and political structures."[88] Students of the denomination hear echoes of Willingham's words throughout the pages of Churches of Christ journals and speeches in the late 1950s and 1960s.

Following the 1955 panel, the ACC Lectureship remained silent on race relations until Spain's speech in 1960. It was the most dramatic white challenge to the racial status quo in Churches of Christ up until that time. In a speech William Banowsky referred to as "the most spectacular speech ever delivered in Abilene," Carl Spain challenged the segregated status of Churches of Christ colleges.[89] Spain could have attacked racial segregation through many avenues (a radio address, a sermon from a large pulpit, etc.), yet he chose to mount a frontal attack on the system at the 1960 ACC Bible Lectureship. No other platform provided such a wide audience and possibility for rapid change. In

Carl Spain delivered a shocking keynote address during the 1960 ACC Lectureship that challenged racism in Churches of Christ colleges, including the school at which he was speaking.

Churches of Christ, church leaders mediated their theology through these lectureships.

In the days following World War II, when American nationalism had considerable influence on American culture and churches, Churches of Christ followed suit. A movement once dedicated to pacifism stood directly in line with most other Protestant American denominations in their glorification of America's triumphant return from foreign lands and their denunciation of Communism. In this milieu, Spain said before thousands of people at the ACC Lectureship in 1960: "There is little to be gained by preaching against the immoral actions of Communists, unless we as Christians are willing to repent of our own idolatry and murder."[90] Spain not only attacked segregation from the stage of an institution that had not yet complied with *Brown v. Board of Education*, he also equated racial discrimination with Communism and Nazism. In doing so, he sought to redraw racial boundary lines within the denomination.

Of all white efforts to challenge white-imposed segregation within Churches of Christ, Spain's effort had the most dramatic effect. Early in 1960, the ACC Board of Trustees, like so many southern institutions, found itself divided on the issue of segregation and integration. At that time, the board appointed a special Integration Committee to examine the issue closely and report back with a recommendation. The committee made long-range plans to desegregate the college, but Spain's speech seems to have increased the speed of those plans. Following the event, Spain's employer desegregated its graduate school, leading to the desegregation of the entire student body the following year.[91] Just months after the lectureship, the *Christian Chronicle* began publishing letters and editorials on the subject of race relationships, which effectively ended the near silence on the subject among denominational journals.[92] Spain forced the denomination to acknowledge the reality of the social revolution at its doorstep. In spite of Spain's ability to end the deafening silence on the subject of racial prejudice, however, his efforts at the 1960 Lectureship were incapable of changing the racist status quo that had come to dominate Churches of Christ.

The sporadic events in Abilene in 1955 and again in 1960 were the exceptions rather than the rule. Aside from a few intermittent events, Churches of Christ lectureships followed the lead of denominational journals in their nearly utter silence on the race issue. Carroll Pitts provided insightful discussion of the lectureships in his 1969 master's thesis. He recorded the themes among some prominent lectureships from 1954, the year of *Brown v. the Board of Education*, and 1966.[93] Boycotts, riots, sit-ins, marches, and intense racial confrontation characterized these years; nevertheless, Churches of Christ lectureships continued with only the slightest hint of any national crisis. Some of the themes from those years were: "The Restoration Principle," "The Christian and Morality," "Biblical Doctrine of the Last Things," and "Christ in the Space Age," but not once did a lectureship planning committee choose to devote their meeting to the racial situation of the 1950s and 1960s. Even when the committees did make an attempt to address their social context, as when Harding College's 1959 committee chose "Some Current Problems and Opportunities Facing the Church" as its theme, not one of the speeches from the meeting addressed the racial unrest of the nation. Instead of addressing one of the most pressing issues of the day, the Civil Rights Movement, Churches of Christ lectureships focused instead on church growth, missions, and morality, which included drinking and dancing, but not racial prejudice.

A United Effort: The Race Relations Workshops

In addition to sporadic efforts among whites and more widespread efforts among African Americans to challenge the white-imposed segregated system of Churches of Christ, both groups joined in 1968 in a series of Race Relations Workshops designed to promote communication and lasting change. The Race Relations Workshops functioned much like other lectureships in Churches of Christ. Speakers presented papers and articulated their opinions to fellow members in an attempt to mediate the denomination's position on race relations. Members from across the globe gathered at a central location to renew or perhaps establish for the first time relationships with one another. A final analysis of these race meetings reveals that they not only created some new relationships between individuals but that the meetings also led to a greater division within the denomination.

The Race Relations Workshops consisted of three separate meetings that took place over a period of three years: January 1966, March 1968, and June 1968. The first one took place in Nashville. A private, by-invitation-only meeting, this gathering was orchestrated by key white leaders: Walter Burch (public relations consultant in Abilene), George Gurganus (professor at Harding Graduate School), Ira North (pulpit minister at Madison Church of Christ),

Dwain Evans (minister of a congregation in West Islip, New York), and John Allen Chalk (regular speaker of the Herald of Truth radio program). Unlike many of their racial conservative peers, these men constituted the racial liberal element in Churches of Christ. These white men took bold steps in the 1960s to reconcile African Americans and whites. During this first meeting, these prominent white leaders, unbeknownst to their peers, met to discuss the importance of healing racial wounds. The secrecy surrounding that gathering has prohibited future generations from gaining much knowledge of its outcome; however, a meeting also held in Nashville two years later has become an open book to denominational historians.

In March of 1968, the leaders of Schrader Lane Church of Christ in Nashville (an African American congregation) hosted a meeting on the subject of race relations at their new building. David Jones Jr., African American minister of Schrader Lane Church of Christ, seems most responsible for initiating

David Jones Jr. has served as the preaching minister at the Schrader Lane Church of Christ in Nashville, Tennessee for over fifty years, offering considerable leadership not only to his congregation but also to the city of Nashville and African American Churches of Christ nationally.

the assembly. Jones attended NCI in the 1950s before he became the preacher of Schrader Lane in 1963 (a position he continues to hold in 2012). His congregation continues to be one of the largest African American congregations in Churches of Christ with a membership well over a thousand. At the time of the Race Relations Workshops he already provided a significant voice from within the African American membership of Churches of Christ.

This meeting increased in significance when the *Christian Chronicle* decided to include a complete report of the workshop in a supplemental issue of May 10, 1968. This biracial meeting, which took place between March 4 and March 8, 1968, provided a forum for approximately 550 African American and white speakers and attendees[94] to come together for five consecutive nights to address the "the most critical domestic problem facing our nation today."[95]

Exemplifying the new era dawning in Churches of Christ, Jones began the conference by asserting his independence from white-imposed segregation. He bemoaned the ill effects of white paternalism, because, in his estimation, most southern whites were "unaware of the deep psychological and sociological effects paternalism has had upon the Negro." Regardless of their public acquiescence to paternalism, Jones said many African Americans privately discussed their disdain for the dominant pattern of race relationships in 1960s southern America, a pattern they viewed as sin.[96] Signaling a new era of African American independence in Churches of Christ, Jones joined African American activists in other denominations from Baton Rouge, Montgomery, and Tallahassee in his public call for an end to white paternalism in the denomination.

The biracial attendance and excitement surrounding this meeting would seem to point to improved race relations in Churches of Christ. Joining this African American minister in his condemnation of paternalism were white ministers and leaders such as Lawrence L. Stumbaugh, Don Finto, and Burch. On the final night of the meeting, over seven hundred people squeezed together to witness the dawning of a new era.[97] Pointed messages from seasoned veterans encouraged whites to resist the temptation of being driven by image consciousness, and equally challenging addresses from college students lamented the cowardice of white Churches of Christ preachers to discuss the race issue. These speeches led many bystanders and participants to expect improved relationships within the denomination; nevertheless, in spite of the calls for change inside the Schrader Lane church building, white picketers protested the meeting outside the building.

A final meeting, held in June of the same year, in Atlanta, provided a bittersweet moment in Churches of Christ race relationships. Organized by a biracial committee consisting of white leaders Burch, Evans, and Jimmy Allen in conjunction with African American leaders Roosevelt Wells and Eugene Lawton, the meeting brought together fifty prominent members of Churches of Christ at the Simpson Street congregation to "discuss ways and means to eliminate the sinful existence of racial discrimination in the Church of Our Lord."[98] At the conclusion of the conference, many of the delegates signed a statement acknowledging racial prejudice in Churches of Christ and their proposals for improving race relations.[99] The document encouraged congregations, schools, publishing houses, media outlets, and Christian-owned businesses to take public steps to both acknowledge their past sins of racial segregation and also to work toward greater meaningful contact and dialogue between whites and African Americans.

In the days following the workshop, noticeable changes did occur. Chalk found so much energy from the meetings that he presented a series of sermons entitled "Three American Revolutions" on the nationally broadcast Herald of Truth radio and television show. The sermons brought to fore the significance of the race problem into countless living rooms among members of Churches of Christ. In June of 1968, the *Firm Foundation* published a hard-hitting article by Walter Burch, wherein he accused the church of spending too much time addressing issues like evolution, school-sponsored dances, and gambling while refraining to address "the single most pervasive moral issue of our age."[100] In the months following the meetings, the *20th Century Christian* published its special issue entitled "Christ and Race Relations."

In a final analysis, however, the Race Relations Workshops failed to bridge the gap between African American and white members of the denomination. The failure of the conferences may be attributed to many things. First, the events never received widespread support. Although white racial liberals worked with African American leaders to confess past sins and lay out plans for the future, one must remember that white racial conservatives held the power in Churches of Christ of the 1960s. Absent from these meetings were key leaders such as white college presidents or white journal editors. A second reason for their failure was the absence of involvement by key mediating influences. Though many white leaders were involved in the meetings, only the *Christian Chronicle* took an interest in them. Other, more influential mediators of the denomination's theology, including the *Gospel Advocate, Firm Foundation*, Abilene Christian College, and David Lipscomb College failed even to acknowledge the meetings.

The "successes" of 1968 proved to be short-lived. The sentiment of the workshops did not move far beyond the walls of the Simpson Street Church of Christ, and some failure even crept into the meeting room itself. Though a large contingent of African American and white leaders signed the document, many others refused the opportunity. In addition to those, many individuals who did not attend the meeting took great exception to the gathering. Glenn L. Wallace, writing in the *First Century Christian*, lamented the actions of so many denominational leaders. He denied that any great racial problem existed in Churches of Christ and encouraged schools, papers, radio programs, and television programs to stay far away from the "social gospel agenda."[101] The next year, in 1969, Harding College invited an African American, Roosevelt Wells, to speak at their lectureship (seemingly as an effort to follow one of the proposals from the Atlanta Conference Statement); but, upon receiving a transcript of his speech, "The Case for the Black Revolution," the institution rescinded the invitation, saying his speech "did not fit the assigned topic."[102]

In spite of the attempts by many leaders within Churches of Christ to bridge the division between African Americans and whites through lectureships, these meetings proved incapable of completing the task laid before them. By the end of the 1960s, the picture was coming into focus: in Churches of Christ there existed two distinct racially defined factions, and they were continuing to move farther apart from each other.

Conclusion

In 1960, a prominent white professor at Abilene Christian College delivered a stirring address at the school's annual lectureship, thereby opening a public debate on race relations within the denomination. In 1966, the most prolific white benefactor to African American congregations, A. M. Burton, died. In 1967, a significant bridge between the factions, Marshall Keeble, also died. In the same year, the white-controlled Board of Directors of NCI closed the school; and a bitter court case ensued, publicly pitting African American members of Churches of Christ against their white counterparts. The Race

Conferences that took place in 1968, which seemed like an overwhelming success to so many, led to increased bitterness in the African American community when white congregations boycotted and picketed the meeting and when many white participants refused to sign the statement acknowledging racial injustice at the conclusion of the meeting. After all of the major denominational colleges finally abided by the decade-old Supreme Court mandate to desegregate their student bodies, many African Americans believed their actions resulted more from financial necessity than moral convictions.[103] Much like the racial revolution taking place in America, these events created a racial crisis in Churches of Christ.

Other denominations experienced similar racial confrontations during this period. Indeed, the Civil Rights Movement turned many denominations into racial battlegrounds. African American journals across denominations addressed the race issue, and many more white journals completely ignored the Civil Rights Movement.

The significance of this period for Churches of Christ lay not only in its conflicts over race, but also in the refusal of the most influential leaders and organizations to either address the conflicts or work toward a solution. When the *Presbyterian Outlook* and the *Southern Presbyterian Journal* disagreed about how to handle the race issue within their denomination in the 1950s, the General Assembly served as the final arbiter.[104] Though Southern Baptists and the journals tied to that denomination held varying opinions on how to address southern segregation, the Southern Baptist Convention issued denominational statements in response to the Civil Rights Movement. Lacking any such centralized authority to force the issue into the public arena, most white Churches of Christ leaders ignored the Civil Rights Movement. When African Americans publicly declared their independence from the white-imposed segregated system of the past, most white leaders ignored them still. As a result, following the Civil Rights Movement, the two racial factions in Churches of Christ became increasingly estranged from each other.

By 1969, G. P. Holt could proclaim that "there are two Churches of Christ on earth today—a white church and a black church. They are growing farther apart each day."[105] Following this turbulent decade, African Americans mediated their theology and framed their identity from their own institutions, virtually losing all contact with the white constituency of Churches of Christ. Future generations would send their children to Southwestern Christian

College, read the *Christian Echo,* and attend the National Lectureship, the Annual Youth Conference, and the annual Thanksgiving lectureship held at SWCC. By 1967, a new denomination was forming.

CHAPTER IV

THE CLOSING OF NASHVILLE CHRISTIAN INSTITUTE

Race matters. In 1967, white members of Churches of Christ learned how much race mattered when African American members of their own denomination brought them to court, refusing any longer to passively acquiesce to white racism and finally exposing decades of separation. One year before the deaths of Martin Luther King Jr. and Marshall Keeble, the white-controlled Board of Directors of Nashville Christian Institute decided to close the doors of the school and place its remaining assets in a scholarship fund for African American students at the recently desegregated David Lipscomb College. Outraged at their decision, NCI alumni and other African American members of Churches of Christ filed suit in federal court, seeking an injunction against the actions of the board.

The events surrounding the closing of NCI revealed the secret that had remained hidden by journals, colleges, and lectureships for decades, namely that within Churches of Christ there existed two racially defined factions with their own customs, identities, and views concerning race relations. Regardless of their assertions to the contrary, African American and white members of Churches of Christ were separated. From the end of the nineteenth century until the late 1960s, most African Americans in the denomination acquiesced to white-imposed segregation, paternalism, and racism out of necessity, but the actions of NCI's board brought their feelings of resentment to the surface. The public spectacle which pitted two racial factions of the same denomination against one another shattered the illusion of unity in Churches of Christ and stirred even greater estrangement between African Americans and whites.

Nashville Christian Institute: Concealing the Secret

From its foundation in 1941 until its close in 1967, NCI afforded white members of Churches of Christ a vehicle to conceal their racism. Through the *Gospel Advocate,* white leaders encouraged their peers to send money to help the African American students at NCI; and, for nearly thirty years, white preachers invited students from NCI to their local congregations to recite scripture from memory, preach sermons, and provide visual evidence for the racial unity in Churches of Christ. Their exposure to NCI students gave whites a feeling of satisfaction, a sense that they had indeed accomplished their God-ordained responsibility toward African Americans.

As was the case in other southern denominations, white-led Churches of Christ initially engaged African Americans through paternalism. In this respect, NCI resembled many other southern schools established by predominantly white denominations for African Americans. For example, white Presbyterians in Tuscaloosa, Alabama founded Stillman College in 1876 as a training school for African American male ministers. Though a school for African Americans, Stillman College did not have an African American president until 1967.[1] Until that time, white Presbyterian leaders maintained control of Stillman in much the same way white leaders in Churches of Christ maintained control over NCI.

One window into the similarities between Stillman College and NCI arises from an examination of a fund-raising effort led by the General Assembly of the PCUS in 1952. The denomination attempted to raise two million dollars to be split evenly between the Negro Work Program and Stillman College. Much like efforts among whites in Churches of Christ, white Presbyterian leaders began their effort by petitioning white denominational journals such as the *Presbyterian Outlook* and the *Southern Presbyterian Journal* for financial pledges.

Initially, these journals were successful in their efforts; but, by 1954, a significant event changed the course of race relations in America and stalled the fund-raising effort by white Presbyterians. Joel Alvis reported that following *Brown v. Board of Education* in 1954 and the statement of the General Assembly in the same year that declared segregation incompatible with Christianity many white members of the PCUS began withdrawing their pledges in fear that their money would be used to promote civil rights causes.[2] As long as whites believed they could help African Americans without allowing them to move out of their place in society, money flowed into the campaign. The prospect of significant African American uplift, however, forced white racism into the open. Alvis rightly stated: "The issues involved in the incorporation of black and white Presbyterians into one church were frequently the issues all Southerners faced, regardless of their religious label."[3]

One of the significant "issues" faced by all southerners, including Presbyterians and members of Churches of Christ, surfaced as African Americans began to publicly reject white paternalism in mass in the 1950s and 1960s. Even in the era of American slavery, white southerners, ironically, viewed themselves as the protectors of African Americans. In the years and decades that followed, white Christians believed it their responsibility not only to protect, but also to evangelize and to educate African Americans. Describing the southern white ideology, David Reimers wrote: "The Negro, ran the argument, was in need of self-discipline, character building, and training in the habits enshrined by the Protestant ethic."[4] A problem certainly existed in the South; but the problem, believed many white southerners, lay not in segregation or racism, but instead in the inability of African Americans to lift themselves up from their innate inadequacies.[5] In the minds of many white southerners, white-led African American education was the necessary tool to lift these intellectually inferior citizens.

Bishop Atticus G. Haygood of the Methodist Episcopal Church, South was a strong advocate for African American education. He did not believe in African American equality nor did he believe schools or churches should be integrated or desegregated; nevertheless, he spent most of his life working to teach African Americans.[6] Haygood spent many years as director of the John Slater Fund, a group that raised money and created awareness for African American education. The Slater Fund was not the only organization designed to aid in this process. The northern Methodists established the Freedman's Aid Society in 1866;

and, by 1880, that organization had collected and distributed nearly a million dollars for the cause.[7] Other denominations, including Baptists, Presbyterians, Episcopalians, Lutherans, and Quakers, also started organizations to raise money for African American education in the post-bellum period.[8]

Though Churches of Christ lacked such official agencies, a perusal of the *Gospel Advocate* in the 1940s and 1950s indicates that white paternalism significantly influenced support for NCI. In an effort to raise money for the school, W. E. Brightwell, "News and Notes" editor for the *Gospel Advocate,* compared NCI to "an orphan upon our doorstep."[9] Another writer to the journal wrote, "It is up to the white man to teach him [the African American] the way of the Lord more perfectly."[10] Underlying these statements were two important premises. First was the belief that African Americans were the responsibility of whites, the childlike Sambo figure who first appeared in the last decades of slavery.[11] Even if northern reconstructionists thrust slaves toward freedom before they were ready and even if racial radicals threatened the lives of freed persons, the true protectors of African Americans, reasoned conservative whites, would lift their children up with white-controlled education.

A second important premise underlying white paternalism in Churches of Christ centered on the belief in African American inferiority. White leaders gave their money and time to educate African Americans because they fully believed them incapable of accomplishing such a task on their own. Wendell Clipp, a professor from David Lipscomb College, boasted that he had seen the potential of the school and agreed to "teach a course in chemistry—gratis, *of course*" (italics added).[12] One wonders why Clipp included the last two words of this sentence. Why would anyone assume he would teach his NCI course free of charge? A reasonable assumption is that Clipp viewed NCI as a poor, African American school, incapable of paying for his services.

Likewise noting the distinctions between African Americans and whites was an article written in the *Gospel Advocate* in 1947. Sister Lambert Campbell, a white preaching teacher at NCI, was praised for her ability to write sermons for her African American students that were "strikingly adapted to the psychology of the Negro race."[13] Not only did this author suggest a distinction between the psychological abilities of African Americans and whites, he or she also argued that one needed special gifts to teach African Americans to preach.

Consistent with racial conservatives of the early and mid-twentieth century, the author, though an advocate for African American education, downplayed the accomplishments and abilities of African Americans. The article supposedly advertised the upcoming program of NCI students, but only two paragraphs of the six were devoted to them. The other four paragraphs sang the praises of Lambert, whom the author referred to as "Sister Lambert Campbell (white)."[14] Instead of lauding the accomplishments of the young preachers who would present their material at the upcoming program, the author reminded readers that many of the "scripturally sound" sermons were written by Campbell, a white woman whose "teaching, influence, and suggestions are carried through the country by the preachers, young and old, trained by her."[15] According to this author, the real accomplishment came through Campbell, not her African American students.

In addition to providing a vehicle for white paternalism in Churches of Christ, NCI also functioned to boost white confidence in their mission to African Americans. Whites took pride in NCI. Thurman Sensing, a white member, wrote: "The people of the church of Christ may well be proud of the Nashville Christian Institute."[16] NCI administrators scheduled an annual program at the War Memorial Building in Nashville as a fundraiser for the school, but these events served the secondary function of displaying to whites the success of their African American mission. Each year, NCI students preached sermons, sang songs, and recited scripture before a full auditorium.[17] Whites in attendance were encouraged to give more money; but, throughout the program, they were given proof that their finances had been used wisely. In other words, through their contributions to NCI, they met their responsibility to African Americans.

More prevalent than the annual programs in Nashville were the preaching trips NCI students took across the United States, often in the company of Marshall Keeble. Keeble and "his boys," as they often were called, traveled to congregations to preach, raised money for the school, and displayed the success of NCI before white members.[18] Fred Gray became one of Keeble's most outstanding students. In fact, Gray routinely traveled with Keeble on preaching tours across the South..[19] In addition to displaying the success of NCI, these trips, as well as the *Gospel Advocate* articles written about them, gave the false impression of racial unity in Churches of Christ. Keeble and "his boys" became the picture of the denomination's African American constituency to whites.

In the pre-Civil Rights Movement period, white southerners expected African Americans to play the role of Sambo, that childlike personality given life in the last generation of slavery. In one telling comment, Brightwell wrote of African Americans:

> These conditions would have discouraged most groups. The colored race is not easily discouraged. When asked why colored people never commit suicide, a member of the race deposed: "Oh, they have things to worry about, and sometimes a colored person will contemplate suicide; but when he sits down to figure out his plans, he usually drops off to sleep, and that is the last of it!"[20]

In the mind of Brightwell and many other white members of Churches of Christ, African Americans were passive, childlike figures who never rocked the boat or protested their place in life. Instead, this leading member of the denomination describes African Americans as unfocused and incapable of even devising an effective suicide plan. In the minds of many whites, African Americans would never challenge the childlike mold created for them by whites; and, as long as African Americans played the role of the Sambo, whites either did not notice or chose to ignore the race problem in Churches of Christ.

The fiction of racial unity received reinforcement from the foremost African American evangelist in twentieth-century Churches of Christ. Keeble regularly wrote columns for the *Gospel Advocate* in which he routinely referred to African Americans and whites as members of the same body with the same ultimate goal.[21] In 1948, he wrote, "For a number of years, brethren, both white and colored, have looked for an opportunity to contribute to the preparation of colored people for better service in the kingdom of God." Again, in the same article, he explained that, by sending money to NCI, everyone (African American and white) would help develop men and women for Christian service.[22] Keeble gave the impression of perfect harmony and racial unity, and he certainly ignored, or chose not to mention, the fact that African Americans and whites had been divided for many decades.

Keeble also gave the false impression of racial unity by his habit of praising the generous white members of Churches of Christ. In a short 1949 article advertising the NCI commencement, Keeble took the opportunity to praise no less than ten white leaders, a white college, and four white journals for their help in supporting his school.[23] Sister Campbell had African Americans well prepared for their annual program. A. M. Burton offered his "great wisdom" to the administration of NCI. S. H. Hall, a white board member, arranged for the city to run a bus line in front of NCI. The Gospel Advocate Company, the *Firm Foundation*, the *Christian Chronicle*, and the *Apostolic Times* all had given generously to the school.[24] If an outsider were to read Keeble's words, he or she would get the impression that whites worked hand in hand with African Americans to build and sustain an exemplary school for members of their denomination.

In spite of efforts of both whites and Africans to convince their readers otherwise, however, African Americans and whites were not united. They were divided, and sometimes their own rhetoric revealed the secret. In his attempt to convince white members to support NCI, Brightwell indicated the real state of Churches of Christ. Encouraging white members to spend their resources on African American missions (like NCI) rather than sending their money overseas to foreign missions, he wrote: "They [African Americans] understand our language, traditions, and way of life. . . . These expanding millions are our responsibility."[25] Contrary to Keeble's inclusion of African Americans in the denomination of Burton, Goodpasture, and the *Gospel Advocate*, Brightwell's words reveal the hidden truth. Whites had their own language, traditions, and way of life. African Americans, likewise, had their own language, traditions, and way of life. Though they shared a common church label, African American and white members of Churches of Christ were divided.

Though hidden in white journals, the separation became more evident in the *Christian Echo* during the 1950s and 1960s. The public confrontation between African Americans and whites within Churches of Christ began with R. N. Hogan's decade long attack against white segregated Churches of Christ colleges. Undaunted by Hogan's appeals, those schools remained segregated up to ten years following *Brown v. Board of Education*. Throughout the Civil Rights Movement period, white members remained largely unsympathetic to African American cries for freedom and equality. Certainly, a few courageous souls such as Carl Spain and Dwain Evans went against the grain, but they were the exceptions rather than the rule. Content with white-imposed segregation and paternalism, whites must have been shocked at the events surrounding the closing of NCI.

The Aftermath of NCI's Closing

In February of 1967, citing decreased enrollment and dire financial problems, NCI's board decided to close the school and to liquidate its assets. The board discussed several possibilities for disposition of the assets, including ministerial training, an orphan's home, a day care facility for children of working mothers, and/or use of the funds for the purpose of educating African Americans in other institutions.[26] Finally, the board chose to transfer the assets into a scholarship fund for African American students at the recently desegregated David Lipscomb College. The board further named the new scholarship the "Burton-Keeble Scholarship Fund," honoring two men, one white and one African American, who helped maintain NCI for nearly three decades.

The decision of the NCI board to place its remaining assets into another institution bears resemblance to a decision in 1901 by the administration of Maryville College in Tennessee. Following the enactment of a 1901 Tennessee law barring interracial education, Maryville College, a predominantly white Presbyterian institution which had admitted a limited number of African American students, was forced to close its doors to African Americans altogether. Maryville's board, in response to the new law, transferred $25,000 from its endowment into Swift Memorial College, a Presbyterian school for African Americans.[27] Instead of challenging the racist status quo of the South, denominational officials chose instead to support Jim Crow segregation by building up the only southern Presbyterian school for African Americans, thereby alienating further African American and white members of the PCUS.

In 1967, the white board of directors of NCI contributed to the alienation of African American and white members of Churches of Christ in another way. By placing the assets of NCI into a school only recently and reluctantly desegregated, Pullias and other white board members enraged African American church members, finally forcing their long-time resentment onto the surface.

Following their decision to close the school, the board charged Keeble with the task of informing the churches of their decision through the *Gospel Advocate*. Citing accreditation problems, lack of land for a new building, low teacher salaries, and decreasing enrollment following the desegregation of other "finer schools" as reasons for the board's decision, Keeble urged African Americans to send money to the Burton-Keeble Scholarship Fund to further the cause of African American education.[28]

If the board of NCI and other white leaders expected Keeble's words in the *Gospel Advocate* to ameliorate a potentially negative response by African American members of Churches of Christ, they grossly underestimated the built-up resentment caused by a century of white-imposed segregation, paternalism, and racism. The African American response to the board's decision was swift and shocking.

Just weeks after the board's decision, a large group of NCI alumni and other African American members of Churches of Christ filed suit in federal court, seeking an injunction against the actions of NCI's board.[29] Their lead attorney was none other than famed civil rights litigator and NCI alumnus, Fred Gray. The United States Court of Appeals record lists the plaintiffs as "Negro members of the Church of Christ and alumni, patrons, and students of NCI."[30] This designation is important. Not only a few disgruntled former students filed suit; a large number of African Americans sought to block the actions of the NCI board.

The plaintiffs had two principal criticisms. First, the Burton-Keeble Scholarship Fund, being limited to college students, would not meet the need for high school educated African American ministers in Churches of Christ. Second, the plaintiffs argued that most African American students would be reluctant to attend David Lipscomb College due to its long history of segregation and its present status: "only tokenly integrated."[31] In light of their criticisms, the plaintiffs alleged three grounds for injunctive relief. First, they alleged that the board of NCI "abused their fiduciary duty in undertaking the transfer of assets." Second, "the transfer constituted an illegal diversion of corporate property under Tennessee law." Third, "the dissolution and transfer constituted a violation of the due process and equal protection clause of the Fourteenth Amendment."[32]

The District Court of Tennessee ruled in favor of the NCI board, and the U. S. District Court upheld its decision. The final judgment rendered that there was no evidence of fraud, unfairness, or self-dealing by the NCI board of directors.[33] A historical footnote has been added to this story by Jack Evans, who attended the court proceedings in Tennessee. According to Evans, the federal judge of the case, Frank Gray, routinely turned his back on Fred Gray during the trial and also refused to address the civil rights attorney as "Mr." Judge Gray, commented Evans, was also a long-time friend of Athens Clay Pullias (President of David Lipscomb College, the NCI Board of Directors, and the named defendant in the case).[34] This evidence suggests that, at the least, the federal judge was sympathetic toward Pullias and the NCI board. More likely, the court held the same racist beliefs that brought the case to trial in the first place. In spite of that racism, the assets from the sale of NCI did indeed go into the Burton-Keeble Scholarship Fund. The problems created by the board's decision, however, were far from settled.

The closing of NCI and the ensuing court case pushed the resentment of African American members of Churches of Christ into the open. No longer content to passively acquiesce to white-imposed segregation, paternalism, and racism, African Americans openly challenged their white denominational counterparts. R. N. Hogan published an article entitled "The Grab of the Century" in the *Christian Echo* in which he accused whites of prejudice and robbery.[35] He did not, however, reserve his comments to the NCI incident. His article began by recounting the closing of two other African American schools, the Silver Point School and the Southern Practical Institute. First, he wrote that Burton "persuaded" Bowser to "give up" the Silver Point School and go to work for him at a new school, the Southern Practical Institute. The new school, however, quickly failed because of white racism. He wrote of that event: "They made the mistake of placing a prejudiced white man over the school by the name of C. E. W. Doris who soon insisted that the Negro students enter the school by the back door because his office was in the front of the building."[36] Bowser quit. The racism persisted. The school closed.

In addition to presenting the facts of these events, Hogan provided helpful insight into the workings of the African American community in Churches of Christ in the early twentieth century. He wrote, "The action on the part of the white Brethren [sic] angered the Negro brethren to the extent that many of them met and decided to raise money and build their own school."[37] The white racism displayed at the Southern Practical Institute in 1920 caused African Americans to protest by taking proactive steps to open a new school, NCI.

From Hogan's words, two important historical artifacts emerge. First, contrary to the picture of the black Sambo displayed in the pages of the *Gospel Advocate,* many African American members of Churches of Christ resisted white paternalism and racism, even in the 1920s. Second, NCI began as an African American effort, and it was built by African American dollars. The messages from the *Gospel Advocate* gave the impression that the school could not function apart from white aid. Never once did the editors or authors of the *Gospel Advocate* write about the African American ingenuity and finances that helped establish NCI.

Perhaps more alarming is that fact that this information never surfaced in the *Christian Echo* until 1968. Never once did editors or authors of the

Following the closing of NCI and the ensuing court case, R. N. Hogan encouraged African American members of Churches of Christ to support African American initiated and led institutions, including Southwestern Christian College and the *Christian Echo.*

Christian Echo lament the way in which whites took control of the NCI board; but, in 1968, Hogan wrote: "Under the guise of wanting to help the Negro, some white brethren, who claimed to be Christians, became members of the Board of Directors of this Negro school."[38] Until the closing of NCI and the ensuing court case, many African American leaders chose not to confront publicly white leaders of the denomination; but, following those events, African Americans revealed the secret they had been carrying for many decades: they passionately resented white-imposed segregation, paternalism, and racism. In the words of Hogan, "Negroes have decided to fight for their rights."[39]

Churches of Christ had been racially divided from the beginning, but only in the late Civil Rights Movement period did African Americans fully reveal and acknowledge the degree of their separation. Hogan continued his article by urging African Americans and their congregations to take up special collections and to send money to support the court case, which would cost approximately six thousand dollars.[40] Anticipating that some may have difficulty with the prospect of violating the New Testament admonition to refrain from taking a brother or sister to court, Hogan defended the case by writing: "Certainly we should not and if we were dealing with Christians instead of those who pretend to be it would not be necessary to go to law."[41] Hogan's statement further supports the argument that African American and white Churches of Christ were divided, for he refused to even count them as Christians, much less members of his denomination.

Following the NCI court case, African American and white members of Churches of Christ continued to drift further apart. Many of the leaders of the case, including Gray and Hogan, poured their time and energy into the only remaining African American school in Churches of Christ, Southwestern Christian College. Appearing opposite Hogan's "Grab of the Century" article in the *Christian Echo* was an article by the new president of Southwestern Christian College, Jack Evans. His article was entitled "Remember N. C. I.," and he urged his readers to use that slogan in much the same way Texans used the slogan "Remember the Alamo," as a reminder of the past. Evans argued that NCI "fell" because it was "inadequately supported."[42] He urged African Americans not to make the same mistake twice. "Southwestern Christian College," wrote Evans, "is the last surviving Christian institution that we say is 'ours,' and for which we have assumed responsibility."[43] Through Evans' language, one witnesses the separation between African Americans and whites. He calls Southwestern "ours," and he even put the word in quotation marks, emphasizing that the school belonged to African Americans, not white members. Southwestern Christian College was independent, and so were African American members of Churches of Christ.

As evidence of their independence and their resentment of the newly established Burton-Keeble Scholarship Fund at David Lipscomb College, some African Americans established a new scholarship fund at Southwestern Christian College, the "Bowser Memorial Scholarship Fund."[44] Those who established the scholarship undoubtedly had the David Lipscomb College scholarship and the NCI case in mind. The author of a *Christian Echo* article wrote that Gray insisted to the board that such a charter should be incorporated in the state of Texas.[45] The charter would "protect all monies contributed and held by the Bowser Memorial Scholarship Fund in the event the School (SWCC) should ever cease to exist."[46] Gray, a leader in the NCI case, wanted to avoid another situation wherein the hard-earned money of African Americans would be lost. Another step they took to avoid such a situation was their construction of an all-African American executive board of the scholarship fund: Levi Kennedy, Robert Woods, G. E. Steward, R. N. Hogan, Mattie Jackson,

Thelma Holt, Noveline Kennedy, and Anna Woods. From 1967 onward, Southwestern Christian College and the Bowser Memorial Scholarship Fund remained African American efforts.

In contrast to the response of the African American community to the closing of NCI in the late 1960s, the *Gospel Advocate,* the *Christian Chronicle,* the *Firm Foundation,* and other white journals never mentioned the case or the growing distance between African American and white members of the denomination. In 2003, NCI alumni worked to make the NCI site a historical site. The editors of the *Christian Chronicle* included an article about the event in their newspaper, but never once did the author mention the events surrounding its closing.

Douglas A. Foster, who served as an assistant professor of church history at David Lipscomb University in the 1980s, served on the Teacher Education Committee. Part of the committee's task involved designating the student who would receive the annual Burton-Keeble scholarship. Foster recalls that each year he was amazed at what he called the "puzzling apathy by black preachers and congregational leaders" concerning their students' attendance at David Lipscomb University. In 1999, after Foster had joined the faculty of Abilene Christian University, that institution held the One in Christ Conference, which sought to heal some of the racial wounds of the past half century. During that gathering, Foster finally came to understand the resentment the Burton-Keeble Scholarship invited from African Americans. He recounts a statement made to him by an African American attendee at the conference:

> For all those years you refused to allow any of us to attend your school, then you took by force and against our will one of the only rallying points we had, let it be swallowed up in your multi-million dollar operation and then you say to us, "You can come over here and be like us now. We still don't particularly value your culture and history and the way you live, and act, and worship, but you can come over here with us, as long as you just do like we do." Can you understand the resentment expressed at this act?[47]

The board's decision to close NCI and the subsequent lawsuit created a deep wound in Churches of Christ that has festered for over forty years, but it also pushed African American resentment into the open.

Carroll Pitts, African American preacher in Churches of Christ, made an important statement in 1969: "I am an American, a Christian, and I happen to be black. I am proud to be all three."[48] Pitts joined countless other African Americans of the late 1960s in asserting his pride in being black. The Black Power movement sprang up in America in the latter stages of the Civil Rights Movement. Both Richard Wright (author) and Adam Clayton Powell (Congressman) used the term before Stokely Carmichael; but, the latter popularized the slogan "Black Power" in various speeches and writings, beginning in 1966.[49] Carmichael challenged the notion of black inferiority and encouraged African Americans to take pride in the color of their skin. James Cone, however, most fully articulated a definition of Black Power in his 1969 classic, *Black Theology and Black Power.* At the core of his definition is the sense of "black freedom, black self-determination, wherein black people no longer view themselves as without human dignity but as men, human beings with the ability to carve out their own destiny."[50] The Black Power movement gained influence in America, especially among younger African Americans, in the late 1960s.

As the Civil Rights Movement waned, many African Americans became convinced they would never gain equality with whites in America without first separating from them. In an unprecedented series of events during a 1967 gathering of the National Council of Churches' (NCC) Division of Christian Life and Work in Washington, D. C., African American delegates demanded that the conference be divided into two groups: African American and white. For two of the three days of the conference, the two racial factions met separately from one another, each attempting to draft their position on race relations within the NCC. At the conclusion of the meeting, both factions agreed to the establishment of African American caucuses in all predominantly white churches and greater involvement of all denominations in the problems of the cities.[51] More important to this study than the final resolutions of the 1967 gathering were the actions of the African American delegates. Instead of succumbing to the white leadership of the NCC, African Americans asserted their equality and demanded that their voices be heard. In this gathering, African Americans turned a deaf ear to the rhetoric of black inferiority by declaring their independence.

African American members of Churches of Christ seem to have been affected by the Black Power movement as well. Pitts' words stood in direct opposition to the African American Sambo figure. Speaking of the power of the Civil Rights Movement, Joel Williamson wrote, "Most of all it accomplished the nearly total destruction of neo-Sambo."[52] Pitts refused any longer to pacify white members of the denomination; instead, he chose to assert his independence. He challenged the long-held southern cultural lie that asserted the superiority of "whiteness" over "blackness." Echoing the 1960s slogan, Pitts agreed that black is beautiful. Indeed, the Civil Rights Movement played a formative role in Pitts' life, for his article is filled with references to Martin Luther King Jr. and other iconic symbols of the movement. He wrote: "It [the Civil Rights Movement] has forced white Americans to face up to the sad plight of black people, as they have been ignored for a century."[53] Though white members of the denomination ignored the Civil Rights Movement, Pitts and other African American leaders not only recognized its presence but were greatly influenced by it.

In the last years of the Civil Rights Movement and in the years following the NCI court case, many African American members of Churches of Christ challenged white racism, but none more pointedly than G. P. Holt. In a 1969 issue of the *Christian Echo*, Holt boldly declared: "Brethren, I do not believe God is happy or pleased with two churches, and believe me there are two Churches of Christ on earth today—a white church and black church. They are growing farther apart each day."[54] In his short article, Holt, more than any other African American leader, revealed the full extent of the secret which had been hidden for nearly a century. He argued that a strong tension had existed between the two racial factions of the denomination for decades, but most members failed to acknowledge its presence.[55]

Holt believed the tension had three principle causes. First, the tension arose as a result of failed communication. Whites had treated African Americans as children (building them church buildings and paying their preacher's salaries) without ever stopping to ask what they really needed.[56] He encouraged whites to stop long enough to listen to African Americans instead of assuming their racial counterparts needed or appreciated their help. Instead, Holt said their history of paternalism was offensive to most.

The second thing responsible for the tension was that fact that "only one black man has been permitted to speak for all black Christians."[57] Holt, obviously referring to Keeble, wrote:

G. P. Holt poignantly articulated the anger and frustration many African Americans had felt toward their white counterparts in his 1969 article entitled, "Tension between the Black and White Church."

> There is no white man that can speak for you, and likewise there is no one black man that can speak for us. Brethren, we are tired of hearing Brother *Blank* said you folk did not want to attend—Brother So and So said this or that was all right—That Brother So and So said that, quote "You Colored Folk would be happy to print your Church News on the back pages of the *Gospel Advocate*—That you folk want your own Church building, one man speaking for all of us—one man saying what you wanted to hear.[58]

This rhetoric of Holt indicates that he and others had long been offended by Keeble's articles in the *Gospel Advocate* and his regular appearances at white lectureships. Not many African Americans were willing to accept the back page of the *Gospel Advocate,* and not many African Americans were content with segregated congregations. Until 1969, however, even Holt had remained silent, allowing the illusion of racial unity to persist in Churches of Christ.

The third reason for the tension in Churches of Christ, argued Holt, was the dishonesty of African Americans. He wrote: "We smiled, went behind the rope and told you how we enjoyed ourselves, and the minute you turned your back, we talked about how unchristian you were."[59] This assertion by Holt offers strong support for the primary contention of this study, namely that African Americans and whites in Churches of Christ have always been divided; but the full measure of their separation has been shielded from view by their journals, colleges, and lectureships. Regardless of Keeble's words in the *Gospel Advocate*, regardless of his regular appearances at white lectureships, regardless of the paternalistic cooperation of African Americans and whites with NCI, and regardless of the denial of nearly every white leader, African American members of Churches of Christ never welcomed or accepted white-imposed segregation. Their protests came early, but only after the NCI court case did most of them become public.

When Holt opened his protests up to the public, he unleashed decades of resentment. After revealing the fact that African Americans had been dishonest with their white counterparts, Holt turned over a new leaf. He began several paragraphs with the words, "Let's be honest with one another." He then proceeded to list those actions most offensive to African Americans, including the habit of whites of calling special attention to African Americans' presence in white worship services, the consistent mispronunciation of "Negro" by whites, the way in which whites routinely accepted invitations to preach and teach at African American congregations even though African American preachers and teachers were never asked to visit white congregations, and the repeated characterization of Martin Luther King Jr. as a Communist.[60] Far from being a Communist, Holt wrote that "to a black man he is a Moses."[61]

Conclusion

African American and white members of Churches of Christ disagreed on much more than the character of King. As African Americans assaulted the racism of white members, most white leaders continued to ignore the social upheaval around them. White ambivalence further estranged them from their African American denominational counterparts; and, throughout the remainder of the twentieth century, African Americans gravitated toward Southwestern Christian College, their annual lectureship, and the *Christian Echo*. During the same period, whites continued to mediate their identity through their own colleges, lectureships, and journals. By the end of the 1960s, African American members of Churches of Christ had declared and were enjoying their independence.

CHAPTER V

GREATER SEPARATION COMING

Race matters. During the 1950s and 1960s, as large numbers of African Americans traded passive acquiescence for active protest, the southern, organic society created by white racial conservatives met its most formidable challenge. Churches of Christ, a denomination brought into existence and maturity in the American South, encountered the challenges of the Civil Rights Movement as much as southern Baptists, southern Methodists, or southern Presbyterians; nevertheless, lacking official denominational bodies to compel white leaders to acknowledge and work toward the dissolution of racism, white leaders in Churches of Christ virtually ignored the social and moral revolution of the mid- twentieth century. Emboldened by the Civil Rights Movement and the ideology of Black Power, African American leaders of the denomination declared their independence by taking white leaders to court in 1967 and finally turning their attention toward their own mediators of theology in the late twentieth century, namely SWCC, the annual SWCC Bible Lectureship, and the *Christian Echo*. Once African American members of Churches of Christ declared their independence in the late 1960s, they accelerated their estrangement from white members of Churches of Christ in the final three decades of the twentieth century, possibly foreshadowing an official separation in the future.

African American Churches of Christ

In their journey from segregation to independence, African American members of Churches of Christ have relied upon the leadership of influential churchmen. Marshall Keeble modeled public accommodation in the 1930s and 1940s. G. P. Bowser, R. N. Hogan, and Fred Gray moved African Americans toward independence at mid-century. In the latter decades of the century, Jack Evans, President of SWCC, provided leadership to an independent African American faction within Churches of Christ that moved closer and closer toward independence. Churches of Christ have always been a racially divided denomination; but, as the twentieth century drew to a close, their separation no longer resulted from white-imposed segregation. Instead, African Americans perpetuated that separation through their own agency and independent spirit.

Jack Evans

Evans has provided a prominent voice in the pantheon of African American leadership in Churches of Christ for the last half century. He has authored several books, spoken at numerous lectureships, and currently serves as publisher of the *Christian Echo*. His positions of influence have allowed him a considerable voice before the approximately 169,000 members of African American congregations and make him among the most recognized faces within that faction of the denomination.[1]

Unlike Bowser, Keeble, Hogan, or Gray, Evans did not spend his earliest years in the deep South, but he did spend four formidable years there. As an early adolescent in Houston, Texas (the city of his birth), Evans attended a church meeting led by Keeble and his NCI students. Encouraged and motivated by the prospect of attending such a school himself, Evans left Houston in 1954 at the age of sixteen to become a resident of Nashville and a student at NCI.

Despite their differing philosophies on race relations, Evans continues to praise the ministry and legacy of Keeble and considers Keeble one of the greatest influences on his own life.[2] As one example of their differing philosophies, Evans recounted a conversation he had with Keeble during Evans' eleventh-grade year at NCI. As the Montgomery bus boycott continued in Alabama, the two were discussing Martin Luther King Jr. and his role in the emerging Civil Rights Movement. Though Evans expressed his interest and support for King's activist leadership, Keeble acknowledged his disapproval of King's public protest against segregation.[3]

Several years later, during the early days of the NCI court case, Keeble remarked to Evans, "Son, are you in this case of former students against *us*?" (italics added).[4] Instead of aligning himself with African American members of Churches of Christ, Keeble aligned himself with the white board of directors. Evans, however, vehemently disagreed with his mentor on that issue and many others. Keeble represented a previous generation of African Americans in Churches of Christ, one more comfortable with passive acquiescence. Evans followed more in the line of Bowser: both men publicly confronted white racism.

Another aspect of their differing philosophies comes into view by visiting Evans' present office at SWCC. Whereas Keeble passively acquiesced to white-imposed segregation and paternalism throughout his term as president of NCI, the walls of Evans' SWCC presidential office reveal his rejection of both. Hanging on the wall of his office is a picture of Frederick Douglass, the great African American abolitionist. Next to Douglass is a picture of influential African American leaders in Churches of Christ, including Bowser and R. N. Hogan, the two most vocal proponents of African American independence in the early and mid-twentieth century. Hanging next to his door is a picture of John F. Kennedy shaking the hand of Martin Luther King Jr, a picture Evans' former mentor certainly would not have displayed in his office.[5]

Despite their differences, however, Evans acknowledges the influence of Keeble upon his life. When asked to explain the influence of Bowser and Keeble upon him, Evans said, "I consider myself a combination of Bowser and Keeble."[6] From Keeble, Evans' inherited a passion for bold and confrontational preaching. Keeble routinely challenged his audiences with the "errors of denominationalism" and consistently referred them to the pattern of New Testament Christianity. For example, in a sermon entitled "The Great Physician," Keeble discussed Baptists who had heard the plain message of the New Testament and left their denomination "to become Christian."[7] Evans, likewise, has spent years preaching against sectarian denominations, urging his audiences to accept the plain message of the New Testament.

Evans became president of SWCC in 1967, and he continued to hold that post in 2008. During his long tenure at the only African American college associated with Churches of Christ, Evans has exerted a considerable influence on African American members and congregations. One particular episode reveals the extent of this influence. The "Gulf Coast Restoration Forum" took place on April 29-30, 1986, in Miami. The title given to this meeting does not accurately describe its purpose or its proceedings; this spring 1986 meeting represented the heresy trial of Ivory James Jr.

David Shanks, elder and minister of the Overtown Church of Christ in Miami, began contacting James, preaching minister of the Riviera, Florida-based "S" Avenue Church of Christ, in the spring of 1985 regarding the latter's recognition of those outside Churches of Christ as "Christians."[8] Shanks, like many other members of Churches of Christ, viewed members of other Christian fellowships as outside the will of God and, therefore, not true Christians. The fact that James welcomed those outside Churches of Christ as "Christian brothers and sisters" amounted to heresy in Shanks' mind. Following a series of letters, the two agreed to make their positions public in April of 1986 at a Miami Holiday Inn. On that occasion, approximately two hundred people listened to numerous African American preachers present their challenges to James' alleged "liberalism." This large gathering of Churches of Christ ministers and leaders at a meeting dubbed "a momentous event" by one denominational periodical, included only one white speaker, Leroy Garrett.[9] He assumed the task of defending James at the trial.

At the conclusion of the forum, the time for decision, African American leaders called the president of SWCC to the platform for the concluding address. During his speech, he all but called for James' banishment with his use of 1 John 2:18-19, saying certain ones "went out from us; for if they had been of us, they would no doubt have continued with us."[10] Evans blamed white Churches of Christ for polluting James. Indicating both his criticism of James and the existence of two racially defined factions within Churches of Christ, Evans said, "It will be up to the black churches to call the white churches back to the Bible. They [the white churches] pushed away, and we are still holding to the book."[11]

A week later, from his office in Terrell, Texas, Evans removed all ambiguity by writing a letter to "Brethren Yeldell, Lawton, Wells, Washington, Shanks, Rice, and Miller" (key African American leaders) recommending the immediate withdrawal of fellowship from James.[12] Lacking any centralized control or official authority as head of the church, Evans' recommendation did not amount to a unilateral edict; but the fact that, immediately following receipt of his letter, several African American congregations and preachers chose to follow his advice signals his unofficial authority within African American Churches of Christ.[13]

The Gold Coast Restoration Forum sparked further racial tension when Garrett wrote about the event under the title "The Underbelly of the Black Church of Christ" in his journal, *Restoration Review*. Recognizing the influence and power of Evans and SWCC in the Gulf Coast proceedings, Garrett wrote: "This story reveals how far we have gone toward hierarchical government. . . . Since when does an *ad hoc* forum of preachers have the right to exclude a fellow minister from the fellowship?"[14] In his critique of the Gold Coast Forum, one also notices his emphasis on congregational autonomy. From the days of Alexander Campbell, members of Churches of Christ have rejected any form of governance beyond that offered by congregational leaders. Their congregational autonomy has also aided, perhaps inadvertently, in their racial estrangement. In other words, white racial conservatives could use congregational autonomy for an excuse to ignore African American members and congregations of the denomination.

Garrett believed Evans held considerable power over African American Churches of Christ, which he described as a separate entity from white Churches of Christ. He wrote in 1986: "There is almost no contract at all between white and black Churches of Christ, whether in a given locality or at a national level. The black churches have their own leadership, their own college, their own journals, and their own 'lectureship.'"[15]

Garrett's criticisms of the proceedings incited the reaction of Evans, who responded to Garrett's article in the *Christian Echo*. Though Evans did not disagree with Garrett's recognition of two racially defined entities, he laid the blame at the feet of white members of the denomination, writing, "The racism reflected in the attitudes of the so-called 'white church of Christ' drove black people together and thus created the 'black church.'"[16] Once again, Evans' modeled the independent, confrontational spirit of Bowser. These men never hesitated in calling attention to the racism that dominated Churches of Christ. Following the 1960s, the public denunciation of denominational racism by Evans helped increase the distance between white and African American members.

Southwestern Christian College

SWCC, the institution led by Evans for half a century, also helped model an independent spirit and increase the distance between African Americans and whites in Churches of Christ. SWCC did not suddenly arrive on the scene in 1968; the events that set that school in motion began at the turn of the twentieth century when Bowser established a small school for African Americans at Jackson Street Church of Christ in Nashville. The legacy of SWCC may be traced through various efforts toward educating African Americans in Churches of Christ: the Jackson Street Church of Christ school, Silver Point Institute, the Bowser Christian Institute, and finally, the Southern Bible Institute. Each of these institutions helped facilitate Bowser's dream for Christian education among African Americans.

When Bowser's Christian Institute failed in 1946, he moved from Ft. Smith, Arkansas, to Detroit, Michigan, and opened a similar school under the same name in the educational building of the Jos Campau Church of Christ.

Though he never served as an administrator or teacher at Southwester Christian College, G. P. Bowser saw the site of the new school just months before he passed away. His students give Bowser's vision credit for the establishment of the sole predominantly African American college in Churches of Christ.

During his time in Michigan, J. S. Winston worked diligently to secure the funds and property to build a new school in Texas. In 1945, Winston and George Edward Steward held a meeting with a prominent white member of Churches of Christ, D. B. Rambo of Huntsville, Texas, to discuss their vision of an African American school in that state.[17] Catching the vision of his two African American denominational counterparts, Rambo met with then president of Abilene Christian College, Don Morris. Morris, along with Walter Adams, then dean of ACC, scheduled meetings with influential white leaders to discuss the possibility of establishing a school for African Americans in Texas. The result of these meetings was the formation of a bi-racial committee to make the vision a reality. John G. Young, a white doctor from Dallas, served as the committee's chairperson, and Adams served as its secretary.[18] That committee purchased an army barrack, moved it to Fort Worth, divided it into classrooms and a dormitory, and opened the Southern Bible Institute in 1948. The bi-racial committee appointed Winston, an African American, as the school's president. As one of Winston's first acts of business, he called Bowser from Detroit to head the Bible Department.[19]

The Southern Bible Institute quickly outgrew its property in Fort Worth, and the school's board began to raise money to purchase new property on the east side of Fort Worth. During this fundraising campaign, however, another property, the former home of the Texas Military School, became available in Terrell, Texas. The Board of Directors raised money from both African Americans and whites of the denomination and purchased this property for $75,000.[20] The school closed for one school year (1949-1950), relocated to Terrell, and reopened in 1950 under a new charter as SWCC. Though Bowser died of cancer shortly before the opening of SWCC, many view him as a primary reason for the school's establishment.[21] This honor only seems fitting when one considers the path eventually taken by SWCC in the late 1960s. The school began much like other such efforts in Churches of Christ history: African Americans perceived the need for better educational opportunities and then petitioned their white counterparts for help in securing funds for the project.[22] When the Board of Directors of SWCC opened the school under its new charter in 1950, they appointed a white president, E. W. McMillan.

History has born witness to the fact that virtually all colleges established for African Americans in the South by southern denominations between Reconstruction and the mid twentieth century had white presidents.

Colleges such as Bethune Cookman in Florida or Tennessee State University in Tennessee provide exceptions to this general rule: these schools have had African American presidents since their establishments. A few African American colleges began appointing African American presidents following the Great Depression. As economic hardships caused many white northerners to reduce or cut off completely their support from these ventures, the futures of many of these institutions was in doubt. In this climate, resistance to the selection of African American administrators waned, allowing many of these colleges to hire their first African American presidents. One scholar has suggested that some institutions hired African American presidents in the 1930s to set up "a convenient scapegoat if the institution were to fail."[23]

Most African American colleges in the South did not hire an African American president until the mid-twentieth century. Paine College, a Methodist institution, though established in 1882, did not hire an African American president until 1971. Spellman College in Atlanta, Georgia, was established by Baptists in 1881, but did not hire its first African American president until 1953. Xavier University in Louisiana hired its first African American president in 1968 even though the school began in 1915. To this list may be added SWCC. Even though white and African American members of Churches of Christ established the school in 1950, Evans was hired as the first African American president in 1967.

Evans described a "plantation mentality" that existed on the campus of SWCC in its earliest years.[24] White racial conservatives who controlled the board of SWCC viewed the college as their outlet to help poor, uneducated African Americans. In the words of Evans, the white chairman of the board simply wanted to "teach negras English and Bible."[25] His regular mispronunciation of "Negro" only reiterated his lack of genuine concern for African American education. Edward Robinson, an African American church historian in Churches of Christ, said that E. V. Isbell, the last white president of SWCC, also had the habit of referring to his students and administrators as "negras."[26] Until 1967, the white-led board of directors and white president of SWCC, in the minds of some African Americans, failed to view the college as a credible academic institution. Instead, their involvement with the school originated from a need to satisfy their perceived paternalistic obligation to African Americans. In the days following the NCI court case, African Americans relieved white members of the denomination of their perceived obligation.

Evans became dean of SWCC in 1963, and he served in that role until 1967 when the board of directors named him president. An examination of the school's lectureships and board's racial make-up clearly indicates that Evans led the school in a different direction than that of his predecessors. Less clear, however, are the circumstances surrounding Evans' appointment as the school's president. Robinson suggested that "racial tension" led to the ousting of the last white president, E. V. Isbell, in 1967.[27] He also suggested that the board of directors may have named Evans president of the school, hoping to satisfy African Americans who grew increasingly angered by Isbell's racism.[28] Robinson's deduction seems probable, especially considering the time of Evans' appointment. In 1967, as the Civil Rights Movement waned, many African Americans became more vocal in their resentment of white-imposed

Jack Evans has served as president of Southwestern Christian College since 1967. His position at SCC as well as his debating ability has afforded him considerable influence among African American Churches of Christ.

segregation, paternalism, and racism. In such a racial climate, the white board of directors of SWCC replaced Isbell with Evans. One also wonders if the board anticipated that Evans would follow the lead of Keeble at NCI by publicly accommodating to white authority.

Beginning in 1967, however, the school charted a new path in race relationships within Churches of Christ, a path more in line with the independently minded Bowser. After Evans' selection as president, the committee for the school's annual lectureship chose the theme: "Christ for the Crisis in Race Relations," the first theme ever to address the topic of race relations in the event's seventeen-year history.[29] Just as Bowser eventually rejected white paternalism, SWCC also became the most independent educational effort among African Americans in Churches of Christ. For nearly half a century, SWCC has provided leadership for African Americans in Churches of Christ, apart from whites. In addition to its training of ministers, the school also has hosted an annual lectureship on its campus. At the beginning of the twenty-first century, the once white-led board of directors had only one white member.

African American Lectureships and Journal

Each year SWCC hosts between 1500-2000 people on its campus on the week prior to Thanksgiving for a series of lectures given by leading African American preachers and teachers of Churches of Christ. As is the case with white lectureships, these African Americans offer no official voice of authority for the church; however, lacking any such official platform, lectureships function to mediate the denomination's theology on a wide array of ecclesiastical issues.

Many of these lectureships predate the late 1960s; however, one will notice a stark shift in their direction in the late 1960s. As has already been mentioned about the SWCC Lectureship, the first time that gathering addressed the race issue was 1967, the inaugural year of its first African American president. Likewise, the other lectureships led by African American members of Churches of Christ, though they existed much earlier than the late 1960s, did not steer their constituents in an altogether different direction from whites until that time. Indeed, theologically speaking, the messages heard at the Annual National Lectureship (a large African American lectureship) in 1950 were quite similar to those heard in the Moody Coliseum at ACC of the same year.

The Annual National Lectureship began in Oklahoma City in 1945.[30] The gathering continues into the twenty-first century with the same purpose: to aid in the teaching programs of individual congregations. G. E. Steward, the lectureship's founder, said the lectureship began to "teach God's word on various subjects, and give Bible answers to Bible questions, and enjoy good fellowship among ourselves."[31] In its more than half a century history, the Annual National Lectureship has been held all across America in Texas, California, Illinois, Pennsylvania, Ohio, Michigan, Indiana, Kansas, Alabama, New York, Tennessee, and Colorado. This gathering had become one of the largest gatherings of African American members of Churches of Christ by the end of the twentieth century, hosting thousands of people each year.

SWCC and its president presently provide unofficial authority to African American Churches of Christ, and the two continue to challenge perceived false teachers of the denomination.[32] African American lectureships, likewise, have helped members mediate their theology apart from white lectureships, colleges, and journals. Also from the campus of SWCC arises another important voice of the African American denomination, the *Christian Echo*. Following the death of Hogan in 1997, the editorship of the journal passed to Bethel Smith; but in 2000, Smith handed over the duties to SWCC. At present, Evans serves as *Christian Echo*'s publisher; and his administrative assistant, Tracy Gray, serves as managing editor.

The *Christian Echo* first appeared in 1902 under the editorship of Bowser near Nashville. One year before his death in 1950, Bowser turned the paper over to his protégé, R. N. Hogan. As we have seen in an earlier chapter, Hogan used the *Christian Echo* to stridently attack segregation within Churches of Christ, most notably the refusal of denominational colleges to follow the Supreme Court's mandate to desegregate. The *Christian Echo* has helped build African American solidarity not only through challenging racism and encouraging support of SWCC but also through its advertisement of African American events, including lectureships.[33]

One window into the *Christian Echo*'s ability to steer African Americans in a different direction from white members comes from a June 1967 issue. Written in the same year as the NCI court case and the establishment of the Burton-Keeble Scholarship Fund at David Lipscomb College, the *Christian Echo* editors encouraged African Americans to pour their money into a different scholarship fund, the "Bowser Memorial Scholarship Fund," which would benefit African American students at SWCC.[34] A primary grievance of the African Americans who sued the NCI Board of Directors centered on that board's refusal to place the money earned from the school's assets into SWCC. Understanding the history of NCI helps one recognize the way in which those who established the Bowser fund were influenced by the tension surrounding the Burton-Keeble Scholarship. Fred Gray, the African American attorney in the NCI case, advised the Executive Board of the Bowser Memorial Scholarship Fund that a charter for the organization should be incorporated in Texas by a Texas lawyer. One of the primary stated purposes of such a charter was its ability to protect the fund's money in the event of SWCC's closing. Nine individuals, all African American, comprised the newly established Executive Board of the fund.

The *Christian Echo* reported the establishment of this fund in 1967.[35] In this article, one witnesses African Americans in Churches of Christ cutting ties with whites and uniting instead around independent African American ventures. The sole African American denominational journal encouraged African Americans to send their money, not to the David Lipscomb College scholarship fund, but instead to a scholarship fund benefiting students of SWCC. The symbolic nature of this episode should not go unnoticed. Instead of supporting the fund established in the names of Keeble and Burton, two icons of the accepted African American accommodationism and white paternalism of an earlier era, the *Christian Echo* encouraged African American members to support a scholarship fund whose namesake stood for African American independence.

African American self reliance was a central theme of the *Christian Echo* in the post-civil rights era. In 1974, G. E. Steward provided a history of the Annual National Lectureship. In his report, one witnesses his perception of African American autonomy. Steward wrote that when he established the Annual National Lectureship, he had no intention of doing so. Nevertheless, "the brethren decided i [sic] would be difficult for the few strong preachers which we had at that time to spread themselves over the brotherhood each year speaking on different lectureship programs, so it was decided that all who could and would meet in some section of the brotherhood each year and have one big lectureship."[36] Steward viewed African Americans as members of their own "brotherhood," a group of people with a "few strong preachers" and in need of one central lectureship. Nowhere in his statement is any mention made of white lectureships, such as those held on the campus of ACU. The "brotherhood" described by Steward included only African Americans.

The *Christian Echo* also emphasized a rejection of white paternalism in the late 1960s. As leaders of both factions attempted to reconcile their differences through race conferences and special journal issues dedicated to race relationships, the *Christian Echo* invited several white leaders to submit articles. The reaction to one such author, John Waddey, signaled the end of the Keeble era. In November of 1969, Waddey wrote an article entitled "A Plea to My Black Brethren," celebrating the imminent end of racial tension in Churches of Christ; but, several statements from his article reminded Roosevelt Wells, a leading African American preacher, of a previous generation characterized by white paternalism. Waddey made the statement: "Today we stand at the gateway of a new era. Across the land, white brethren have realized their Christian responsibility to extend the hand of congregational fellowship *to men of any race who want to worship with them*. For this we should thank God." (italics added)[37] Waddey believed whites had a parental responsibility to African Americans, the responsibility to welcome them into their houses of worship. No mention is made, however, of whites visiting African American congregations. As in the early twentieth century, these comments reflected white superiority and white agency. African Americans, on the other hand, were consistently the ones being acted upon and were perceived to have no agency. Referring to such a sentiment as "the Father knoweth best approach," Wells expressed his disgust and accused Waddey of joining the throngs of "self-appointed experts who are always advising Black brothers."[38]

Even more offensive to Wells, Waddey also encouraged his "black brethren" to refrain from getting involved with "social and political issues," as some already had done.[39] Such a path, Waddey believed, tore one away from the most important thing, the Bible. Waddey failed to mention that involvement in "social and political issues" also challenged the white-established southern, organic society by moving African Americans out of their place. Contrarily, Wells suggested that the spirit overtaking the nation in the late 1960s and early 1970s, a spirit that encouraged individuals to challenge injustices and inequalities toward African Americans, should be adopted by all African Americans and "indeed all Christians."[40]

To this exchange between Waddey and Wells could be added scores of other articles from the *Christian Echo* from the late 1960s to the end of the twentieth century, articles lamenting the relationship between African Americans and whites and encouraging a new path for the future.[41] Some of these articles, like Waddey's, attempted to narrow the gap between African Americans and whites in Churches of Christ; but, in the end, Wells correctly judged the effect of these words, saying, "Such articles do not narrow the gaps; they only succeed in broadening them."[42] Certainly estrangement continued and increased in the post-Civil Rights Movement era, and the *Christian Echo* helped African Americans mediate their theology and articulate their concerns.

The degree of that estrangement was exemplified to readers of Churches of Christ journals and hearers of Churches of Christ sermons in the last half of the twentieth century. Through those mediums, African American and white leaders began to separate not only physically but also, and more importantly, theologically. As one window into that theological separation, this study now addresses an issue of paramount concern to members of the Stone-Campbell Movement, namely biblical hermeneutics.

Denominational Estrangement Viewed Through Biblical Hermeneutics

This study does not primarily concern biblical hermeneutics, and the following paragraphs may seem like an illogical break from the issue of race relations in Churches of Christ; nevertheless, the following pages play an important role in exemplifying the vast theological distance created by thirty years of physical distance between African American and white members. Biblical hermeneutics have stood at the center of Churches of Christ identity since their beginnings. The writings and sermons of African Americans and whites in Churches of Christ throughout the twentieth century indicate that, for most of their history, these two factions shared key components of a common biblical hermeneutic. In the closing years of the twentieth century, however, African American and white members had adopted two differing interpretive methods. By recognizing these differing hermeneutics, one must question whether or not these two factions share a common identity any longer.

The Historic Stone-Campbell Hermeneutic

The rules governing biblical interpretation in Churches of Christ have played a significant role in their identity since the days of Alexander Campbell and Barton W. Stone. Eugene Boring describes well the centrality of biblical interpretation to Stone-Campbell Movement theology: "Examine the role the Bible has played in Disciples [sic] thought, and you have your hand on the pulse of the denomination's theology."[43]

The biblical hermeneutic that dominated Churches of Christ throughout the twentieth century owes much to Campbell's nineteenth-century *Christian Baptist*. In that early publication, Campbell outlined his vision of biblical restorationism or primitivism. E. Brooks Holifield has argued that many nineteenth-century American religious leaders desired to "restore the Christianity of the first century," believing that such an endeavor would rid Christian theology of its "human inventions."[44] Abandoning long-standing Christian creeds and the developed theologies of elitist scholars and clergy, Campbell joined his peers in urging Christians to focus on the simple message of primitive Christianity found in the pages of the New Testament. In his mind, the completion of such a task would result in the unity of all Christians. Toward the accomplishment of this goal, Campbell published a thirty-two-part series entitled "A Restoration of the Ancient Order of Things" between 1824 and 1830 in the *Christian Baptist* that outlined his view of primitive Christianity.

Two important themes surface from a perusal of Campbell's writings on biblical hermeneutics: dispensationalism and what Theodore Dwight Bozeman has labeled "Christian Baconianism."[45] Campbell developed the first of these principles, dispensationalism, by building upon the covenant (federal) theology of Hugo Grotius and Johannes Cocceius. Campbell believed the Bible recorded the history of God's people through three dispensations (Patriarchal, Mosaic, and Christian), with each period presenting the world a fuller portrait of God and providing more authority for the community of God.[46] Campbell's biblical dispensationalism had the practical effect of granting supremacy to the New Testament, an exegetical decision he inherited from his father. Father and son believed the New Testament, as a revelation of the final and most complete dispensation, overshadowed the Old Testament in its authority for Christians. In the fourth proposition of his *Declaration and Address*, Alexander's father, Thomas, wrote that the New Testament provided governance for Christians the same way the Old Testament provided governance for Israel.[47] Alexander, like his father, believed the New Testament provided the basis for Christian understanding and practice.

Alexander fully articulated his understanding of the relationship between the two testaments in his "Sermon on the Law" (1816), which he delivered before the Regular Baptist Association Meeting in Moss Creek, Virginia, and later published in the *Millennial Harbinger.*[48] Speaking of the Old Testament as "law" and the New Testament as "gospel," Campbell stated: "In respect of existence or duration, the former [law] is denominated 'that which is done away'—the latter [gospel], 'that which remaineth'—the former was faulty, the latter faultless—the former demanded, this bestows righteousness—that gendered bondage, this liberty—that begat bond-slaves, this freemen."[49] The purpose of the Old Testament, for Campbell, lay in its foreshadowing of the Christian dispensation. The great lawgiver, Moses, existed simply as a type for the great savior, Christ. Though the Old Testament provided guidance and instruction for the Jews, perfection, fullness, and completion arrived with the New Testament.

The second principle of Campbell's biblical hermeneutic, Christian Baconianism, allowed him to view the Bible as a sourcebook of facts. According to this view, one simply collected all the facts on a given topic and then drew an informed and proper conclusion. In 1850, Campbell wrote that the "inductive style of inquiring and reasoning is to be rigidly carried out in reading and teaching the Bible facts and documents, as in the analysis and synthesis of physical nature."[50] Hughes rightly compares this method of biblical interpretation to the scientific method.[51] The Bible, for Campbell, was not so much a book of theology as it was a blueprint for church governance and practice, which helps one understand Campbell's insistence on referring to the Bible as "the constitution of the church."[52] Just as the constitution provided the blueprint for the new nation, the Bible, or more specifically, the New Testament, provided the blueprint for the restored church.

Building upon Campbell's earlier hermeneutic, second generation leaders such as Moses E. Lard, solidified the emerging Churches of Christ biblical hermeneutic. Echoing the Baconian ideology of the denomination's founder, Lard argued that all Christians are able to interpret the Bible identically, writing, "It is a humiliating fact that they will not see alike, and a grand lie that they cannot."[53] In other words, there is no excuse for misinterpreting scripture or, rather, for interpreting scripture differently than Lard. He wrote in 1863 that a biblical doctrine or practice may be established in one of two ways: "by being actually asserted" or "by being necessarily implied."[54] Lard's two-part formula for biblical interpretation developed quickly into a tripartite formula, adding the authority of biblical examples. Accordingly, readers of the text seek commands, examples, and necessary inferences to guide them in their task of restoring the patterns of the first century church. On the one hand, members of Churches of Christ regularly conform their ecclesiastical practices to those things commanded (baptism or communion), those things exemplified (the appointment of elders in every congregation or the partaking of communion), and those things necessarily inferred (adult-only baptism or the partaking of communion every first day of the week). One the other hand, they reject from their practices those things not commanded, exemplified, or inferred from the New Testament, such as the use of instrumental music in worship or infant baptism.

Twentieth-century leaders established the tripartite formula as the centerpiece of Churches of Christ hermeneutics. J. D. Thomas' 1958 book, *We Be Brethren*, posited that examples and inferences found in the New Testament bear just as much weight as clear commands.[55] In one telling comment, he suggested that the tripartite formula had been accepted by the entire denomination since the beginning of the Stone-Campbell Movement.[56] Thomas' estimation may not be far off the mark as one considers the words of Thomas Campbell's *Declaration and Address*. Writing in 1809, the elder Campbell discussed the authority of examples, commands, and "inferential truths."[57] Though he did not view the latter category as equally authoritative as the former two, his discussion of these three categories indicates the longevity of the tripartite formula in the Stone-Campbell Movement.

By the end of the nineteenth century, a distinct biblical hermeneutic had developed among members of Churches of Christ, both African American and white. This hermeneutic stressed the restoration of first-century Christian practices as revealed from the perceived pattern of the New Testament. In matters of scriptural silence, denominational leaders (through sermons and articles) encouraged prohibition. From the turn of the twentieth century until the Civil Rights Movement, one notices a strict allegiance to this biblical hermeneutic by members of Churches of Christ.

This quest to find the New Testament pattern for Christian practice was not limited to the white community in the first half of the twentieth century; African Americans also sought the pattern. In recognizing their affinity with whites, however, one also must acknowledge that African Americans in Churches of Christ shared much in common with African Americans in other denominations.

In *Stony the Road We Trod,* Cain Hope Felder compiled a series of essays devoted to African American biblical interpretation. One of the chief characteristics of African American sermons throughout time has been the theme of suffering. Not only do African Americans share in the suffering of all human beings (sickness, broken homes, death, wars), but they also carry an additional level of suffering through slavery, racism, and discrimination.[58] Like African American sermons from the AME Church, the PCUS, and the United Methodist Church, those from Churches of Christ also emphasized suffering and the Christian response to it. In a 1964 sermon, reprinted in the *Christian Echo,* James Maxwell rehearsed the suffering of African Americans throughout history until the period of the Civil Rights Movement. Toward the end of his sermon, Maxwell encouraged Christians to "use your handicaps and sufferings as spurs to success." A Christian, argued Maxwell, had the gift of Jesus that alleviated any suffering.[59]

Storytelling has been another consistent theme among African American sermons, and the most popular story used in those sermons was the biblical account of the Exodus. American slaves not only compared themselves to the Israelites in slavery, but they also looked forward to their own exodus from bondage.[60] Albert Raboteau has well chronicled the place of the Exodus story in slave religion, but one also should recognize the narrative's place in the post-bellum period.[61] In the years following the Civil War, the Exodus narrative dominated African Americans sermons; and, in their retelling of the story, the journey of the Israelites became their own. Just as Moses led Hebrew slaves from Egypt, God would sometime soon lead African Americans from their bonds of racism, prejudice, and segregation.

Martin Luther King Jr. wrote *The Strength to Love* a century following the Civil War, and his language continued to reflect the African American appropriation of the Exodus narrative. He chastised his contemporaries for preferring the "land of Egypt" to the freedom offered to them in the civil rights struggle.[62] Just four years later in *Where Do We Go from Here,* King compared his present age with the Exodus: "the present struggle in the United States is a later chapter in the same story."[63]

African Americans in Churches of Christ mirrored this emphasis on the Exodus. Indeed, in a 1965 issue of the *Christian Echo,* Norman Adamson intertwined the story of ancient Israel and his own story. Comparing his involvement in the March to Selma, Adamson wrote concerning his experience, "I feel that my road has been made straighter to the Promised Land."[64]

One of the most prominent African American preachers in early twentieth-century Churches of Christ to appropriate the Exodus narrative was Samuel Robert Cassius. A pioneer preacher in Oklahoma and California, Cassius helped establish the first African American Churches of Christ in those states. In addition to his congregational ministries, Cassius also operated a school for African Americans, the Tohee Industrial School. Unlike many of his African American peers in Churches of Christ, Cassius openly discussed the topics of racism and prejudice within and outside of the church; and, unlike many of his white denominational counterparts, he drew upon the story of the Exodus as if he had experienced deliverance himself. In response to the monetary aid sent to him by many Christians in 1901, he wrote, "Then I cried unto God and he heard me, and has put it into the hearts of his children to deliver me."[65] "Deliverance" was a common theme in Cassius' writings and sermons: on certain occasions he experienced deliverance; and, on other occasions, he assumed the role of the deliverer. For example, two years after comparing himself to a rescued Israelite, he compared himself to Moses, writing, "When the children of Israel fought against Amelek, they could only prevail when Moses had his arms stretched out. So in order that they might prevail, Aaron and Hur built two pillars under Moses' arms, so that they could keep them up. If I succeed, it may be that my arms will have to be held up once more."[66]

To white Christians who read Cassius' words, his statement seemed harmless enough: God supplied Cassius to help bring the gospel to African Americans, and those who offered financial assistance to his ministry aided that cause. In recognition of Cassius' abhorrence of racism in Churches of Christ and his routine statements against it, however, his words offered a dual meaning to his African American readers. Cassius' ministry not only worked toward spiritual freedom but also toward freedom from oppression and discrimination. Will Coleman argues that many African Americans throughout history have engaged in "tribal talk" or "multivoiced configurations" that can be found in their speeches and writings.[67] In other words, Cassius' routine discussions of deliverance and the Exodus had more than one meaning--one meaning for his white audience and another for his African American audience. Cassius could ask white members for support, using biblical language they welcomed and with which they were comfortable; and, simultaneously, he could offer hope of a better future to his African American peers.

In Cassius' appropriation of the Exodus story, another dissonant with the historic white biblical hermeneutic should come into focus, namely his use of the Old Testament. Unlike Campbell, Lard, or other white denominational leaders of his time, Cassius drew freely from the Old Testament prophets,

Samuel Robert Cassius challenged white racism in his sermons by drawing upon common African American preaching themes, such as the Exodus.

Psalms, and Genesis. As Cassius migrated west from Oklahoma to California by train, he discussed the possibilities before him. Notice the distinct Old Testament allusions used by this African American leader:

> "Shut down the windows!" is the next command, and then our train plunged in the mountain. All was heat, smoke and darkness. I said, "Surely this is the valley of the shadow of death," but while I thought on these things a small ray of light caught my eye; then suddenly I burst forth into the full sunlight of God's day, and I felt that I was alive again from the dead. Then came a chain of mountains, monuments of God's power. I thought of Noah resting in the ark upon the mount, and of Abraham alone with God upon the mount, with living sacrifice in hand. I thought of Jacob and his dream upon Mount Moriah, of his wrestling with the angel. I thought of Moses fleeing into the desert, and of the burning bush. I thought of his trip up Mount Sinai to meet God, and at last of his going up in the mount to die before the Lord.[68]

Cassius here utilizes no fewer than ten separate Old Testament allusions; and, once again, he could be accused of using tribal talk, for underlying his discourse on mountains lies the theme of freedom. Cassius set out on a new mission, heading west without the inhibitions of the South impeding him any longer.

In their use of the Bible, African American members of Churches of Christ resembled their black peers in other denominations, but one should not overlook their affinity with white members of their own denomination. Edward Robinson, Cassius' biographer, highlights the tension apparent in his subject's biblical hermeneutic. On the one hand, Cassius' "transition from a piece of property as a slave to a free citizen in the United States doubtlessly influenced his reading of Scripture," causing him, for example, to identify with Old Testament stories, such as the Exodus narrative.[69] On the other hand, Cassius exemplified many of the biblical hermeneutical characteristics common among white members of Churches of Christ. For example, even though Cassius drew heavily from the Old Testament, he adhered to Campbell's dispensationalist ideology, granting supremacy to the New Testament. In 1912, Cassius came under attack from members of his denomination. In response to their criticisms, he insisted that their charges arose because "he preached to people that do not follow teaching of the Scripture as they are taught in the New Testament."[70] Instead of referring to the entire Bible, Cassius singled out the authority of the New Testament, a common practice of many white members of Churches of Christ.

Cassius also adhered to the tripartite formula so common among white members of Churches of Christ. In 1918, he denounced those religious groups who believed a "sinner's prayer" would bring about salvation. Instead, he wrote, "At no time and in no place in God's word has any part of the world ever been granted eternal life because someone prayed for it."[71] Cassius based his argument on the *example* of John 17:9. Another example to which he often referred was the "five essential steps of salvation: hearing, believing, repenting, confessing, and being baptized," a list commonly recited by white members of the denomination, dating back to the days of Walter Scott in the early nineteenth century. In 1901, Cassius wrote a pamphlet "Faith, Repentance, Confession and Baptism" in which he evidenced his allegiance to Scott's "five finger exercise."[72]

Cassius' biblical hermeneutic, and indeed the hermeneutic adopted by many African American members of Churches of Christ in the twentieth century, may be viewed as a fusion of two great influences: their African American heritage and their denominational heritage. Cassius and his African American peers in Churches of Christ certainly shared much in common with members of the AME, AME Zion, and several black Baptist denominations; but they also adhered to many of the rules governing biblical hermeneutics among their white denominational counterparts. For most of the twentieth century, this biblical hermeneutic fusion remained strong; but, as the Civil Rights Movement approached, the connection between African Americans and whites in Churches of Christ began to splinter.

A Hermeneutical Shift

Following a series of events in the 1960s, the distance already existent between African Americans and whites within Churches of Christ widened. As African Americans moved closer to independence, differences were allowed to grow. Following the Civil Rights Movement, the physical distance created between these factions led to theological differences.

At mid-century, a shift began to take place within white Churches of Christ. With the establishment of a graduate school of Bible at Abilene

Christian College and the exposure of many faculty members to theological education outside of Churches of Christ, many white leaders in Churches of Christ began to challenge the long-held denominational biblical hermeneutic. Over the next half century, a significant element of white Churches of Christ began to shift toward a new hermeneutic.[73] African Americans did not experience the shift with their white counterparts; consequently, at the dawn of the twenty-first century, as African Americans and whites once again sought communication, they noticed the results of their estrangement.[74]

The hermeneutic that began to emerge in scholarly Churches of Christ circles in the 1950s and 1960s continues to develop and change into the twenty-first century. Regardless of its amorphous shape, some features of the new method become increasingly clearer. Richard Hughes has provided perhaps the best description of this shift in his 1996 history of Churches of Christ. In his lengthy discussion of the "hermeneutical crisis" of the late twentieth century, he refers to the change as a "paradigm shift—a shift from a patternistic version of Christian primitivism filtered through the grid of Lockean empiricism and Scottish Common Sense rationalism to an emphasis on the relational dimensions of the Christian religion."[75] This new hermeneutic places the emphasis less on the New Testament as a blueprint and more on the person of Jesus Christ: it is Christocentric rather than bibliocentric. Along with this change in the driving force of the hermeneutic, other alterations to the historic method of interpretation within Churches of Christ have occurred, including a renewed interest in the Old Testament, increased interaction with higher biblical criticism, and an almost complete rejection of the tripartite formula.

One could trace the birth of this new hermeneutic to Abilene, Texas. ACC began offering graduate courses in religion during the 1950s; in that period, the school produced world-renowned scholars such as Everett Ferguson, Abraham Malherbe, William Martin, and J. J. M. Roberts. These scholars left their alma mater to attend Harvard University, with two returning a decade later to teach in the Bible department in Abilene. Additionally, many Abilene scholars, most notably Malherbe, joined together to establish the first scholarly journal in Churches of Christ. *Restoration Quarterly* began publication in 1957 with the express purpose of passing on high quality scholarship to preachers, teachers, and students within the denomination.[76] In its half century of existence, the editing responsibilities of the journal have been passed down to newer generations of scholars, including Everett Ferguson, Thomas

Olbricht, Carl Holladay, Douglas Foster, Jack Reese, and James Thompson. The graduate program in Abilene, coupled with the *Restoration Quarterly,* have provided a forum for scholarship and have encouraged preachers, teachers, and students within Churches of Christ to rethink, challenge, and alter their traditional biblical hermeneutic.

The new hermeneutic fermented and developed in the 1960s and 1970s among college faculty, but it found a wider hearing among preachers, editors, and authors in the two decades that followed. In recent years, considerable attention has been given to the "hermeneutical crisis" in Churches of Christ. In 1988, *Restoration Quarterly* published a lightening rod essay by Russ Dudrey entitled "Restorationist Hermeneutics among the Churches of Christ: Why Are We at an Impasse?" in which he challenged many of the long-held staples of the traditional hermeneutic, most notably patternism.[77] Dudrey became one of the first members of Churches of Christ to blatantly call for a "hermeneutic revolution," saying, "We cannot equate restoration with the process of recovering biblical patterns; the formalistic approach has shown itself spiritually unequal to the task.[78] The literary model he advocated encouraged readers to take into account the historical context of biblical literature, to appreciate the missionary context in which the authors of the New Testament wrote, and to consider the theological implications of the writings.[79] Dudrey devoted a great deal of space to describing the problem of biblical hermeneutics in Churches of Christ but little time providing the tools to build a new method of interpretation; however, his essay sparked widespread conversation that led to a meeting two years later among white denominational leaders to address the issue.[80]

The 1990 Christian Scholars' Conference rallied professors, teachers, and preachers to Abilene for a conference on the subject of biblical hermeneutics. Individuals presented papers on topics ranging from prophetic hermeneutics to Old Testament hermeneutics to the tripartite formula to apologetics. The development of a new denominational hermeneutic provided a consistent theme for each address. Several issues stand out from the conference. First, Michael Houston challenged the contention that the Hebrew Bible existed simply as "prolegomenon to the New Testament." Standing on the heels of other recent Old Testament scholars within Churches of Christ, such as Tony Ash, Jack Lewis, Rick Marrs, Rodney Plunkett, and John Willis, he lamented the fact that since the beginning of the Stone-Campbell Movement, the Old

Testament had been viewed as either irrelevant, the holder of New Testament prophecies, or simply a catalog of illustrations.[81] He argued instead that Christians should view the Old Testament as an authoritative text.

Second, Larry James, a Dallas area preacher, offered ten principles for biblical interpretation. In one telling statement, James said, "We overlook the fact that the Bible does not call us to pursue a patternistic regimen in our practice of interpretation of its contents."[82] His words not only challenged the historic hermeneutic but, more importantly, showed that the emerging hermeneutic in Churches of Christ reached beyond scholarly circles and into congregations. Along with James, other preachers, including Don Jackson and Rubel Shelly, also attended the conference and presented papers that challenged the historic Churches of Christ hermeneutic.[83]

A third significant development from the conference surfaced in a paper delivered by J. Paul Pollard. He traced recent trends in the world of biblical hermeneutics outside Churches of Christ and then encouraged church members to learn from the methods of others. For a denomination historically dedicated to isolation and sectarianism, Pollard's comments signaled quite a shift. In particular, by lauding the work of biblical scholars who had written on the subject of "pre-understanding," the recognition of one's own biases brought to the table of interpretation, Pollard called into question the flat reading of the text that had become common in Churches of Christ by the late twentieth century.[84] He posited that readers bring to interpretation their own worldviews that affect their understanding of the Bible. In other words, two people reading the same text read it and interpret it differently.

In the same year that ACU hosted the Christian Scholars' Conference, that university's press published a book by C. Leonard Allen that helped articulate the hermeneutical shift to non-scholars. *The Cruciform Church: Becoming a Cross-Shaped People in a Secular Word* expanded the position Allen set out in his earlier work, *The Worldly Church,* by challenging the historic Churches of Christ hermeneutic and also offering suggestions for improvement. In *The Cruciform Church,* Allen encouraged members of the denomination to "recognize the remoteness of the text" and commit themselves to historical study, "enlarge their functional canon" by making the Old Testament along with the Gospels more central to their identity, appreciate the various genres of biblical literature instead of treating it as a "collection of facts," and distinguish the "central story" of scripture from secondary material.[85] Much like members of the Christian Scholars' Conference, Allen discouraged readers from seeking a pattern from the New Testament or reading scripture as if neither the text nor the reader had a history.

From the opening of the graduate school in Abilene until the turn of the twentieth-first century, biblical hermeneutics in Churches of Christ changed considerably. Hughes offered a helpful tool in understanding this shift by labeling Rubel Shelly as a "microcosm of the hermeneutical changes" that took place.[86] As the Civil Rights Movement raged in the 1960s, Shelly stood in line as the next great champion of the most conservative wing of the denomination. Shelly completed a PhD in philosophy from Vanderbilt and co-founded with Thomas Warren the *Spiritual Sword*, a conservative journal among Churches of Christ that promoted New Testament patternism and exclusivism.

Despite the seemingly obvious trajectory of Shelly's career, however, by the mid-1980s he was viewed by many as the foremost leader of Churches of Christ reformers who championed the idea of grace and openness. His 1984 book, *I Just Want to Be a Christian*, functioned as his "declaration of independence from sectarian orthodoxies."[87] A few years later, he co-authored a book with Randy Harris entitled *The Second Incarnation: A Theology for the Twenty-First Century Church* in which he challenged the long-held belief within Churches of Christ that they had finally restored the Kingdom of God on earth. Instead, he called for a new ecclesiology that viewed the church as the "second incarnation" of God in the world. In other words, the goal of the church did not lie in the restoration of first-century forms but rather in the ongoing ministry of Christ in the present age.

Shelly shared this message through various books into the twenty-first century, spoke at numerous lectureships, and communicated this new biblical hermeneutic each week for over twenty years from the pulpit of his home congregation, Woodmont Hills Church of Christ in Nashville, one of the largest congregations among Churches of Christ. In 1992, Shelly, along with Mike Cope and Philip Morrison, founded *Wineskins*, a denominational magazine which ensured that their ideals would continue to disseminate for years to come.

In attempting to capture the salient elements of this new hermeneutic, at least four points surface above the others. First, through the scholarship of leaders such as Houston, Lewis, Marrs, Plunkett, Roberts, and Willis, Churches of Christ have a renewed interest in the Old Testament. The New Testament certainly remains the primary canon, but the Hebrew Bible continues to gain

Rubel Shelly helped usher in a new hermeneutic to white Churches of Christ in the late twentieth century as an author, preacher, and regular lectureship speaker.

attention through denominational colleges and pulpits. Second, the tripartite formula that has defined biblical hermeneutics in Churches of Christ since the days of the Campbells is rapidly losing appeal. Scholars and preachers alike continue to challenge its adequacy as a tool for biblical interpretation.[88] Third, Churches of Christ as a whole value the fruit of biblical scholarship more now than in the past. Specifically, denominational colleges have trained more than one generation of preachers to engage scripture through historical critical and literary analysis methods. Fourth, and most importantly, the driving force of Churches of Christ biblical hermeneutics has moved from an attempt to restore the pattern of the first-century church to an attempt to conform the church to the image of Jesus Christ. In the words of the founding editors of *Wineskins*, a primary goal of Christians should be the "Christocentric study of scripture that can challenge the church to act out the meaning of Christ in this age."[89]

As one window into the far-reaching effects of this new hermeneutic, this study turns its attention to the final ACU Lectureship of the century.

In addition to numerous classes and sermons presented by professors and preachers of Churches of Christ, seven prominent speakers presented plenary addresses on that occasion: Royce Money (president of ACU), Monte Cox (director of missions at Harding University), Jack Reese (dean of the College of Biblical Studies at ACU), Harold Hazelip (chancellor of Lipscomb University), Mike Cope (preacher at the Highland Church of Christ in Abilene, Texas), Mark LaValley (preacher at the North Street Church of Christ in Fayetteville, Arkansas), and Ervin Seamster (the lone African American speaker and special assistant to the president of ACU). From these addresses, one notices a shift in biblical interpretation away from the historic Churches of Christ hermeneutic. These sermons reflected an increased use of the Old Testament, a virtual absence of the tripartite formula, evidence of critical biblical studies, and a new driving force, namely the attempt to conform the church to the image of Jesus Christ.

Though nearly every keynote address employed the New Testament more than the Old, two speakers in particular, Monte Cox and Mark LaValley, relied significantly on the Old Testament. In encouraging the lectureship audience to engage more intentionally in worldwide missions, Cox used Isaiah 49:6 as his primary text. He said by keeping its attention on the needs of other Christians, the church casts too small a vision.[90] He spoke at length about the vision of such Old Testament prophets as Isaiah and Jonah. Drawing from Isaiah, Job, and Psalms, LaValley pointed out the way the Old Testament formed the memory of many New Testament characters, thus uniting the Christian age to the Jewish age. He posited that for any people to move forward and make progress, they first must have a firm grasp of their history.[91] Other speakers, including Jack Reese and Ervin Seamster, made mention of Old Testament texts but relied most heavily on the New Testament. Curiously absent from the slate of keynote addresses was a single sermon centering on the book of Acts, the centerpiece of the Churches of Christ canon for nearly a century. At the end of the twentieth century, the New Testament still took precedence in Churches of Christ biblical hermeneutics, but the Old Testament continued to increase in importance.

A second noticeable trait in these keynote addresses arises through their absolute disregard of a historic hallmark of the Churches of Christ biblical hermeneutic, the tripartite formula. Not one address admonished its hearers to follow the commands, examples, or necessary inferences of scripture.

Instead of calling church members to find the pattern for Christian existence and practice in scripture, Cope encouraged his hearers to notice the way the diverse Christian community represented in Romans 16 found unity, not uniformity.[92] Instead of relying solely on the examples and commands of scripture, Harold Hazelip used various theologians, artists, and Christian bodies, such as Soren Kierkegaard, Augustine, John Calvin, John Wesley, Dwight Moody, Handel, Mozart, Thomas Edison, Albert Einstein, Annie Dillard, and the World Council of Churches in addition to scripture in his address.[93] Perhaps more striking than any of these individuals or bodies used by Hazelip, however, was the central admonition of his message in which he encouraged Christians to follow the Trinitarian formula of Ephesians 1:3-14. For a tradition that had historically discounted any discussion of theology, favoring instead clear biblical mandates, Hazelip's use of Trinitarian theology signals a significant shift in focus.

As a third sign of the changing Churches of Christ biblical hermeneutic, one notices the fruits of biblical scholarship throughout the keynote addresses. In previous generations, members of the denomination accepted a flat reading of the text, ignoring the historical context or literary devices employed by biblical authors. These late twentieth-century leaders, all educators within or educated by Churches of Christ colleges, provided examples of their biblical scholarship. Cox spent a large portion of his time discussing the background of Isaiah, commenting at length on the exilic and post-exilic periods of both Israel and Judah.[94] Reese encouraged his hearers to consider the context of every passage of scripture, take into account the genre of each biblical book, and notice that not all teachings of scripture bear the same weight.[95] In other words, said Reese, "All scripture is inspired, but not everything is at the center."[96] Reese's words not only help one appreciate the increased level of attention given to biblical genre and biblical criticism, they also open up a window to the most startling aspect of the hermeneutical shift.

Whereas the driving force of Churches of Christ had for nearly two centuries focused on the goal of restoring the pattern of first-century New Testament Christianity, by the end of the twentieth century, many leaders encouraged their hearers to conform the church into the image of Jesus Christ. Not one speaker encouraged his audience to find and model the perceived pattern of the New Testament. In fact, Money, Cox, Reese, Cope, and LaValley spoke directly or indirectly against that former dominant aspect of the Churches of

Christ biblical hermeneutic. In contrast to following the pattern of the New Testament, on the first night of the lectureship, Money told his audience that Jesus, not doctrine, good deeds, or perfect obedience, had to become the "central focus of our faith."[97] Cox said, "It's all about Jesus, the focal point of all who believe."[98] Speaking of the current state of affairs among Churches of Christ and echoing the statement of Reese, Cox went on to say: "Some call it an identity crisis; I call it a reorientation—a reorientation away from the boundaries, toward the center."[99] Speaking against the traditional desire to restore a pattern from the New Testament and focusing on the new center, Cope said, "We are built on the truth of Jesus Christ—not because we agree on everything, not because we are alike in everything, but because there is truth in Jesus Christ."[100] Previous Churches of Christ lectureships centered on restoring the pattern of New Testament Christianity or following the five steps toward salvation (as perceived from the pages of the New Testament). The final ACU lectureship of the century focused instead on a new driving force.

Ervin Seamster delivered the seventh and final keynote address of the 2000 lectureship. The only African American to deliver a keynote address, his invitation undoubtedly arose from an attempt to faithfully carry out the pledge of Money, who promised only three months prior to the ACU Lectureship, during the SWCC Lectureship, that the former institution would work to heal the wounds caused by decades of separation. In his introduction, Seamster acknowledged the distance between African American and white Churches of Christ; and, though his use of scripture in his sermon did not separate him from his white counterparts as much as his delivery style, one paying close attention to his hermeneutic notices some differences between it and that of his peers. For example, instead of focusing on a single primary passage or discussing the context of the scriptures he employed, Seamster referred to over twenty different texts without once describing for his audience the historical background, genre, or authorial intent of any passage. Also, unlike the white speakers at the lectureship, Seamster ended his sermon with a reference to baptism, a common conclusion to most white sermons in previous decades and contemporary African American sermons. As this study has shown, the distance between African American and white members of Churches of Christ since the 1960s has manifested itself in more ways than physical proximity; increased estrangement also has allowed theological differences to flourish.

An increased use of the Old Testament, a virtual abandonment of the tripartite formula, an increased emphasis on biblical scholarship, and a new driving force had radically changed the shape of Churches of Christ biblical hermeneutics—that is, *white* Churches of Christ hermeneutics. The same cannot be said of African American congregations. Separated from the white colleges, journals, and lectureships in which this transformation occurred, African Americans remained more committed to key components of the biblical hermeneutic articulated generations earlier by Campbell and Lard. In place of ACC, the *Gospel Advocate, Wineskins,* or numerous white lectureships, African American members of Churches of Christ increasingly found their identity through SWCC, the *Christian Echo,* the SWCC Bible Lectures, and the Annual National Lectureship. African American members of Churches of Christ, in short, did not embrace the hermeneutical shift that took place among their white counterparts during the last decades of the twentieth century.

As another window into this phenomenon, this study now turns to a lectureship gathering of African American members of Churches of Christ that took place a few months after the 2000 ACU Lectureship. Instead of providing proof of a hermeneutical shift, an examination of these sermons provides proof of their maintenance of key components of the biblical hermeneutic followed by Campbell, Lard, and Cassius.

The 2000 SWCC Lectureship brought together dozens of the most prominent African American preachers from Churches of Christ to address the topic "Standing at the Crossroads." Through a careful examination of these addresses, one notices the important role played by SWCC among African American congregations: the president presented what amounted to a state of the union address on the final evening of the meeting, attendees of the lectureship showed their support of the gathering by presenting nearly $70,000 to cover expenses, and the chairman of the board of directors for SWCC used the venue to encourage support for both the *Christian Echo* and the college that hosted the lectureship. At this particular lectureship, the final meeting of the millennium, preachers assessed many issues confronting Churches of Christ, including ecclesiastical leadership, broken marriages, and the dangers of liberalism in the church.

The sermons presented at the lectureship not only provide insight into the theological positions of the denomination on a variety of issues; they also provide a window into the biblical hermeneutic of African American Churches of Christ, a hermeneutic consistent with earlier generations. The themes that defined the biblical hermeneutic of earlier generations (an almost complete disregard for the Old Testament, the tripartite formula, and patternism) dominated the sermons presented at the 2000 SWCC gathering.

Peter Martin, speaking on the topic "Standing at the Crossroads of Biblical Knowledge and the Knowledge of Men" provided one example of this historic hermeneutic. Though Martin did reference a text from Hosea, he garnered most support from various Pauline texts in his attempt to move his audience to follow the "commands of God" in scripture.[101] He lamented the inroads of "liberalism" in the church, which he believed came about when "feeling" and "experience" replaced "following the clear commands of God" as the chief aim of Christianity.[102] He viewed the Bible as a pattern for Christians, a guide or blueprint that presented followers of God with a clear path to follow. Those who questioned the authenticity or absolute truth of the pattern were guilty, according to Martin, of following the knowledge of men over the knowledge of God.

Orpheus Heyward provided another window into the hermeneutic with his sermon, "Standing at the Crossroads of Accepting a Contaminated Gospel." He urged the preachers in his audience to "preach Jesus," which he defined as preaching the five steps of salvation (hearing, believing, repenting, confessing, and being baptized).[103] For Heyward, the New Testament presented a pattern for unbelievers to follow that would lead toward eternal salvation with Christ. In fact, the pattern proved so important to his theology that he equated that pattern with Jesus himself.

The speaker who exemplified the patternistic aspect of the hermeneutic most obviously was Harold Redd. In his attempt to present to his listeners "The Nuts and Bolts of Spiritual and Numerical Church Growth," Redd utilized the perceived pattern found in the New Testament letter of Titus.[104] From this text, Redd concluded that Titus had given every generation of Christians a pattern to follow that would lead to "spiritual and numerical church growth," especially in spiritually deprived regions such as Crete. First, the church should set up a strong leadership. Second, the preacher should articulate sound doctrine to the congregation. Third, the congregation should engage in good works. Based upon his patternistic biblical hermeneutic, Redd treated these three steps practiced by the first-century Cretan congregation as normative for church growth in all generations.

If Redd best exemplified the patternistic aspect of the hermeneutic, Lawrence Gilmore provided the best glimpse of the tripartite formula from the lectureship. Gilmore primarily sought to warn his listeners of "denominational influences."[105] Viewing members of Churches of Christ as the only members of the true church, Gilmore believed influences from the "religious sector" of the world were beginning to affect negatively the only true Christians. From a plethora of New Testament passages, Gilmore provided "proof" that God ordained certain activities and rejected others. God rejected open membership, female leadership, and various charismatic activities because the Bible never mentioned such activities. Additionally, the Bible never used the title "pastor" for the local preacher; therefore, congregations should avoid the label. He also pointed out the absence of clerical robes and choirs in the New Testament. Lacking any commands for such activities, Gilmore encouraged Christians to abstain from them. He also encouraged Christians to follow the example of taking the Lord's Supper only on the first day of the week as articulated in the New Testament book of Acts. In his discussion of these activities he asked the rhetorical question, "What are we to teach?" to which he answered, "Only what Jesus commanded."[106]

To these sermons could be added scores of others,[107] each one firmly attached to the hermeneutic that guided Churches of Christ for most of their history. Whereas many white leaders and congregations experienced a shift in their biblical hermeneutic in the late twentieth century, most African American leaders and congregations remained committed to key components of a biblical hermeneutic that had been dominant for most of their history. These theological differences between white and African American Churches of Christ at the end of the twentieth century reinforced the separation that the Civil Rights Movement precipitated.

The preceding discussion on biblical hermeneutics is an important one for a study involving Churches of Christ. In this biblicist denomination, biblical hermeneutics had become a matter of soteriology. Often disagreements on matters of biblical interpretation between members place one outside of the church, condemned. As one example, when the Churches of Christ and Disciples of Christ divided in the late nineteenth and early twentieth centuries, the division took place largely because members of Churches of Christ could not allow themselves to be bound to, in their minds, a group of heretics. In matters of biblical interpretation, they preferred division instead of compromise. As the twenty-first century begins, and as African American and white members of the denomination become more aware of their hermeneutical differences, one wonders whether division once again will prove more compelling than compromise.

Attempts at Reconciliation

Churches of Christ took the first steps in answering that question in the waning years of the twentieth century. Finally recognizing the vast separation within Churches of Christ, key white leaders attempted to close the gap between African American and white members and congregations. During a September 7, 1998 Lipscomb University chapel service, then university president Steve Flatt confessed that the school was guilty of "overt racism."[108] In October of 1999, ACU administrators and faculty went a step further by hosting nearly thirty leaders from predominantly African American Churches of Christ on their campus for the One in Christ Conference. According to Royce Money, then president of ACU, this gathering was designed to "re-establish lines of communication among various churches and between the churches and ACU."[109] Douglas Foster, an ACU faculty member and attendee of the gathering, said conversations throughout that weekend were often forthright and tense. Many African American leaders were denied admission to ACU in the 1950s and 1960s, and several of the leaders expressed their resentment toward white members, stemming from the NCI closing and ensuing court battle over three decades earlier.[110]

White and African American leaders from Churches of Christ closed the One in Christ conference on their knees together in prayer; and, as a final expression of their sincerity, Money and Don Crisp (chairperson of ACU's Board of Directors) offered to attend the SWCC lectures the following month and offer their public apology for ACU's past sins of racism and discrimination. Evans accepted their offer, and Money presented that apology before one of the largest annual gatherings of African Americans in Churches of Christ on November 22, 1999. In that statement, Money told his audience: "We are here today to confess the sins of racism and discrimination and to issue a formal apology to all of you, to express regret and to ask forgiveness."[111]

In addition to the One in Christ Conference and Money's apology at the SWCC Lectureship, ACU has taken some significant strides toward racial reconciliation. In recent years, the university has hired Jerry Taylor and Edward

Robinson, two African American graduates of SWCC, as members of their College of Biblical Studies and Ministry. ACU's annual lectureship, likewise, has invited numerous African American speakers since the turn of the century, including keynote speakers Ken Greene, Ervin Seamster , Jerry Taylor, and J. C. Thomas Jr. As the twenty-first century opens, one wonders what impact these reconciliation efforts will have within Churches of Christ. After generations of protecting an illusion of racial unity, the last half of the twentieth century has made one thing crystal clear: that illusion has been shattered.

Conclusion

Race matters. Though white editor bishops, influential preachers, and college representatives have downplayed the role of race in the history of Churches of Christ, this study has provided evidence of its overwhelming effect on the course this denomination has followed since the days of Campbell and Stone. Certainly, race has affected Churches of Christ as much as race affected other southern denominations, such as Presbyterians, Methodists, and Baptists. Lacking a formal structure to vote or mandate division, however, Churches of Christ journals, colleges, and lectureships created and perpetuated an illusion of racial unity. Division within Churches of Christ occurs through less formal means. Division does not take place formally through the vote of a synod but, instead, when two racial factions begin to set their own courses as they lose contact with each other. The different courses followed by African American and white members of Churches of Christ has resulted in physical, theological, and, perhaps, denominational estrangement.

EPILOGUE

Race matters. This study has shown how much race has mattered in Churches of Christ by examining their history through the window of white and African American relations. Though no governing body such as a synod, conference, or assembly officially divided Churches of Christ along the fault line separating African Americans and whites, these two racial factions, nonetheless, remained separated throughout the twentieth century. Events in the early years of the twenty-first century reveal the extent not only of their physical separation, but also of their theological separation. Given the soteriological function of biblical hermeneutics in Churches of Christ, this author wonders how long one can properly consider African American Churches of Christ and white Churches of Christ members of the same Christian body.

This query becomes more intriguing as one considers events that took place in the Stone-Campbell Movement a century earlier as Disciples of Christ and Churches of Christ divided from one another. Church historians have pointed to various causes for their division, including sectionalism, disagreements on worship practices (especially the use of instrumental music in worship assemblies), and socioeconomic disparity. Underlying these issues, however, was another. One reason the Disciples of Christ and the Churches of Christ drifted apart was that these segments of the movement had begun to view scripture differently.

In *Disciples and the Bible,* Eugene Boring discussed at length the shift in hermeneutics that took place in the "crucial third generation" of Disciples.[1] A major reason for this shift centered on education. In the third generation of the Stone-Campbell Movement, a great number of northern Disciples earned degrees from major graduate schools and theological seminaries, including Yale, Harvard, Princeton, and Chicago. Their interaction with higher biblical criticism and the broader world of Christendom gave birth to a new development in the Disciples' biblical hermeneutic.[2] Disciples such as L. L. Pinkerton, R. L. Cave, Hugh C. Garvin, Thomas Haley, George W. Longan, Allan Bailey Jones, Alexander Procter, and Herbert Lockwood Willett challenged the biblical hermeneutic of their heritage. Pinkerton emphasized the "saving power of Christ, not in doctrines."[3] Resembling the later classical liberals, Cave stressed the teaching role of Jesus but tended to downplay his divinity. Garvin challenged a centerpiece of the Stone-Campbell hermeneutic by questioning the idea of a New Testament pattern.[4]

The importance of this development for this study arises from its duplication a century later. One notices a similar shift in the mid twentieth century among members of Churches of Christ. As scholars such as Everett Ferguson, Carl Holladay, Abraham Malherbe, Thomas Olbricht, J. J. M. Roberts, and James Thompson attended major universities and seminaries such as Harvard, Vanderbilt, Cambridge, and Princeton, a new biblical hermeneutic began to develop within Churches of Christ. Similar to the shift in the mid-nineteenth century, those most closely aligned with these individuals and their schools moved in different theological directions than their predecessors from the early twentieth century. Those not connected to their schools, including African Americans, did not follow the hermeneutical shift. Just as the late nineteenth-century shift led to the formation of two distinct denominations, the mid twentieth-century shift may end with the same result.

The new hermeneutic of the nineteenth century manifested itself from the pages of denominational journals (as did the new hermeneutic of the twentieth century); therefore, consistent with their history and future, religious periodicals stood at the center of denominational debates. In fact, the events that led to the 1906 division began with a non-member of the Stone-Campbell

Movement reading pages from the *Gospel Advocate*. When S. N. D. North was put in charge of the United States Religious Census of 1906, he collected scores of religious periodicals from the nation, attempting to better understand his task at hand. As he read the *Gospel Advocate,* he noticed that sometimes the publication seemed to be aligned with the Disciples of Christ; and, at other times, it seemed to represent a separate denomination. He wrote a letter to David Lipscomb asking him if there existed a distinct body called "Churches of Christ" that should be listed separately from the Disciples of Christ. Lipscomb replied in the affirmative, and the "official" division took place.[5]

"Official," however, seems out of place in a discussion concerning Churches of Christ. Lacking an official denominational structure (conference, synod, assembly) to make such a decision for the entire body, that task fell to another entity: the United States Religious Census Bureau. Battles raged in Stone-Campbell Movement periodicals for half a century, and no one or nobody had the authority either to pull them together or pull them apart. The "official" division required the initiative and authority of an outside agency; and, even then, many denominational leaders reluctantly accepted the decision. When J. H. Garrison, editor of the *Christian Evangelist,* read of the division in the *Gospel Advocate,* he was shocked at Lipscomb's response to North. He claimed Lipsomb's recognition of two denominations was "news to us." He went on to ask, "By whose authority does Bro. L. make this important pronunciamento?"[6] Garrison asked a good question. The organizational structure failed to provide a governing body capable of making such an official decision. Left without such an option, the division between Churches of Christ and Disciples of Christ took place gradually, beginning with the conflict over slavery in the mid nineteenth century.

For nearly half a century, members of the eventual Disciples of Christ and Churches of Christ remained united under the same denominational umbrella; however, their differences grew more apparent year by year. Likewise, African American and white members of Churches of Christ in the opening days of the twenty-first century maintain the same denominational label, but evidence suggests that these two factions have little else in common.

The United States Religious Census ceased to exist after 1936; therefore, its director will never read for research purposes articles from the *Christian Echo,* the *Gospel Advocate,* or *Wineskins Magazine* and notice the existence of two separate, racially defined groups. No government agency likely will call an editor from a Churches of Christ periodical or a president of a Churches of Christ college, asking him or her to confirm the existence of such division. If the Religious Census had continued into the twenty-first century and the director did make those phone calls, one wonders whether or not an "official" division would take place once again.

NOTES

Introduction Notes

1 Jess O. Hale Jr. argued that slavery did not divide the Stone-Campbell Movement as it did other American denominations during the Civil War in "Ecclesiastical Politics on a Moral Powder Keg: Alexander Campbell and Slavery in the *Millennial Harbinger,* 1830-1860," *RQ* 39, no. 2 (Second Quarter 1997): 65–81.

2 The "encounter of black and white" has been described as one of three central themes of American religious history. David W. Wills, "The Central Themes of American Religious History: Pluralism, Puritanism, and the Encounter of Black and White," in *African American Religion: Interpretive Essays in History and Culture,* ed. Timothy E. Fulop and Albert J. Raboteau (New York: Routledge, 1997), 7-20.

3 C. R. Vaughan, "The Southern Assembly," *Presbyterian Quarterly* 1 (July 1887): 147.

4 Michael O. Emerson and Christian Smith, *Divided by Faith: Evangelical Religion and the Problem of Race in America* (New York: Oxford, 2000), 7.

5 Ibid.

6 Brad Braxton, *No Longer Slaves: Galatians and African American Experience* (Collegeville, MN: Liturgical Press, 2002), 8.

7 Winthrop D. Jordan, *White over Black: American Attitudes Toward the Negro, 1550-1812* (Chapel Hill, NC: University of North Carolina Press, 1968; New York: W. W. Norton & Company, 1977), 7. Citations are to the Norton Library edition.

8 Ibid., 9; George B. Harrison, *Shakespeare under Elizabeth* (New York: H. Holt and Company, 1933), 64–67, 310.

9 Jordan, *White over Black,* 11–13.

10 Ibid., 18.

11 Ibid., 24–28.

12 Ibid., 34.

13 Jean Bodin, *Method for Easy Comprehension of History* (1566; repr., New York: W. W. Norton and Company, 1969), 103–106, 143.

14 Oscar and Mary Handlin, "Origins of the Southern Labor System," *WMQ* 7 (April 1950): 206.

15 Jordan, *White over Black*, 219–228, 482–511.

16 Thomas Jefferson, *Notes on the State of Virginia*, ed. William Peden (Chapel Hill, NC: University of North Carolina Press, 1955), 139–140.

17 Ibid., 142–143.

18 Nathanial Shaler, "The Negro Problem," *Atlantic Monthly* 54 (November 1884): 703; Ibid., "Science and the African Problem," *Atlantic Monthly* 66 (July 1890): 42.

19 Joel Williamson, *The Crucible of Race: Black-White Relations in the American South Since Emancipation* (New York: Oxford, 1984), 2–7.

20 Ibid., 24.

21 Ibid.

22 Ibid., 32.

23 Albert Raboteau, *Slave Religion: The "Invisible Institution" in the Antebellum South* (New York Oxford, 1978); ibid., *Canaan Land: A Religious History of African Americans* (New York: Oxford, 1999).

24 Hans A. Baer and Merrill Singer, *African-American Religion in the Twentieth Century: Varieties of Protest and Accommodation* (Knoxville: University of Tennessee Press, 1992); Eugene Genovese, *Roll, Jordan, Roll: The World The Slaves Made* (New York: Vintage, 1972); Vincent Harding, "Resistance and Religion among Ante-Bellum Negroes," in *The Making of Black America*, ed. August Meier and Elliot Rudwick (Springfield, IL: Atheneum Press, 1969); Manning Marable, *Blackwater: Historical Studies in Race, Class Consciousness, and Revolution* (Dayton, OH: Black Praxis, 1981); Raboteau, *Slave Religion;* Gayraud Wilmore, *Black Religion and Black Radicalism*, 3rd ed. (Maryknoll, NY: Orbis, 1983).

25 W. E. B. DuBois, *The Souls of Black Folk* (Chicago: McClurg, 1903).

26 Benjamin Mays, *The Negro's God as Reflected in His Literature* (New York: Atheneum, 1968).

27 E. Franklin Frazier, *The Negro Church in America*, rev. ed. (1963; repr., New York: Schocken, 1974).

28 Carter Woodson, *The History of the Negro Church*, 2nd ed. (Washington: Associated Publishers, 1945), 278. (1945 edition)

29 Williamson, *The Crucible of Race*, 24.

30 Ibid., 23-24.

31 Ibid., 24.

32 For more information on John Woolman and the Quakers, see David M. Reimers, *White Protestantism and the Negro* (New York: Oxford, 1965), 4; H. Shelton Smith, *In His Image, But . . . . : Racism in Southern Religion, 1780-1910* (Durham, NC: Duke University Press, 1972), 24–32.

33 Samuel Willard, "Sermon CLXXIX [24 August 1703]," in *A Compleat Body of Divinity in Two Hundred and Fifty Expository Lectures on the Assembly's Shorter Catechism* (1726; repr., New York: Johnson Reprint Company, 1969), 613.

34 Cotton Mather, *The Negro Christianized: An Essay to Excite and Assist that Good Work, the Instruction of Negro-Servants in Christianity* (Boston: B. Green, 1706): 32.

35 Fleetwood, Unnamed Sermon, in *Anglican Humanitarianism in Colonial New York*, ed. Frank Joseph Klingberg, 197–212 (Salem, NH: Ayer Publishing, 1971), 205–206.

36 Whitefield, *George Whitefield's Journals* (1960; repr., London: Guildford and London, 1965).

37 Smith, *In His Image*, 24–35.

38 Henry Joel Cadbury, "Negro Membership in the Society of Friends," *Journal of Negro History* 21 (April 1936): 168.

39 Ibid.

40 Samuel Sewall, "The Selling of Joseph: A Memorial [Boston: 1700]," *Massachusetts Historical Society Proceedings, 1863-1864,* VII (Boston, 1864), 162, quoted in Smith, *In His Image,* 17.

41 Smith, *In His Image,* 127–128.

42 For a sampling of such arguments, see Smith, *In His Image,* 134–135.

43 Ibid., 135.

44 Dabney, quoted in Thomas Cary Johnson, *The Life and Letters of Robert Lewis Dabney* (Richmond: Presbyterian Committee of Publication, 1903), 129.

45 E. Brooks Holifield, *Theology in America: Christian Thought from the Age of the Puritans to the Civil War* (New Haven: CT: Yale University Press, 2003), 494–495.

46 Smith, *In His Image,* 264.

47 Henry Tucker, "Are We Orthodox on the Race Question," *Christian Index* (22 March 1883), quoted in Smith, *In His Image,* 265.

48 Ibid.

49 Rufus B. Spain, *At Ease in Zion: Social History of Southern Baptists, 1865-1900* (Nashville: Vanderbilt University Press, 1967), 113–119.

50 Charles Carroll, *The Negro a Beast* (St. Louis: American Book and Bible House, 1900); Richard Rivers, *Elements of Moral Philosophy* (Nashville: Publishing House of the Methodist Episcopal Church, South, 1887); William Brown, *The Crucial Race Question* (Little Rock: Arkansas Churchman's Publishing Company, 1907).

51 *Presbyterian of the South* 46 (8 November 1922): 1.

52 See, for example the *Annual of the Southern Baptist Convention* (Nashville: Bruce Company, 1903), 103.

53 Reimers, *White Protestantism and the Negro,* 99.

54 Peter Randolph, "Plantation Churches: Visible and Invisible," in *African American Religious History: A Documentary Witness,* edited by Milton C. Sernett, 63–68 (Durham, NC: Duke University Press, 1999), 64.

55 Mary Boykin Chesnut, *A Diary from Dixie,* quoted in Raboteau, *Slave Religion,* 221.

56 Raboteau, *Slave Religion,* 231–239.

57 Henry McNeal Turner, "God Is a Negro," *Voice of Missions* (February 1898); James H. Cone, "Black Theology and the Black Church: Where Do We Go from Here?" in *African American Religious History,* 573; Raboteau, *Canaan Land,* 76.

58 Turner, "Emigration to Africa," in *African American Religious History,* 292.

59 Manning Marable, *How Capitalism Underdeveloped Black America* (Boston: South End, 1983), 197.

60 Ibid.

61 Howard Thurman, *Jesus and the Disinherited* (Nashville: Abingdon, 1949; Boston: Beacon Press, 1996), 11–35. Citations are to the Beacon Press edition.

62 Lawrence Edward Carter, *Walking Integrity: Benjamin Elijah Mays, Mentor to Martin Luther King Jr.* (Macon, GA: Mercer University Press, 1998); Benjamin Mays, *Born to Rebel* (New York: Charles Scribner's Sons, 1971), 265.

Chapter 1 Notes

1 Joel L. Alvis, *Religion and Race: Southern Presbyterians, 1946-1983* (Tuscaloosa, AL: University of Alabama Press, 1994), 13; Kenneth K. Bailey, "Post Civil War Racial Separations in Southern Protestantism: Another Look," *Church History* 46 (December 1977): 453–473; Ernest Trice Thompson, *Presbyterian Missions in the Southern United States* (Richmond: Presbyterian Committee on Publication, 1934), 190–194; Willis D. Weatherford, *American Churches and the Negro* (Boston: Christopher Publishing House, 1957), 195.

2 Morris L. Davis, *The Methodist Unification: Christianity and the Politics of Race in the Jim Crow Era* (New York: New York University Press, 2008), 107.

3 Ibid., 1–2.

4 James S. Thomas, *Methodism's Racial Dilemma: The Story of the Central Jurisdiction* (Nashville: Abingdon, 1992), 42–44.

5 Presbyterian Church (USA), "Research and Statistics," n.p. [cited 1 August 2007]. Online: http://www.pcusa.org/research/statistics_faq.htm.

6 Karen L. Willoughby, "NAAF to Spotlight San Antonio Initiatives," *Baptist Press* (27 April 2007): n.p. Cited 1 August 2007. Online: http://sbcbaptistpress.net/bpnews.asp?id=25525.

7 Gilbert H. Caldwell, "Black Christians, White Church: At the Black Methodist Caucus," *Christian Century* (27 April 1994): 3. Cited 1 August 2007. Online: http://findarticles.com/p/articles/ mi_m1058/is_n14_v111_ai_15238625/pg_3.

8 Carl H. Royster, *Churches of Christ in the United States: 2006 Edition* (Nashville: 21st Century Christian, 2006), 19.

9 Shelly accepted a teaching position at Rochester College in 2005, thereby ending his more than two decades of service to Woodmont Hills Church of Christ in Nashville.

10 W. T. Moore, *Comprehensive History of the Disciples of Christ* (New York: Fleming H. Revell, 1909), 12.

11 One may question the necessity of exploring a nineteenth-century event to discern the character of Churches of Christ, a denomination born in the twentieth century. Richard Hughes, however, reminds his readers that the central ideal of Churches of Christ, the vision of primitive Christianity, arose in the nineteenth century in the works of Alexander Campbell and Barton W. Stone. He writes, "To ignore the nineteenth century would be to ignore the very heart and soul of the tradition and to render the twentieth century story of Churches of Christ essentially absurd." Hughes, *Reviving the Ancient Faith: The Story of Churches of Christ in America* (1996; reprint ed., Abilene, TX: Abilene Christian University Press, 2006), 9.

12 For an examination of Shannon's life, see Barry C. Poyner, *Bound to Slavery: James Shannon and the Restoration Movement* (Fort Worth: Star Bible Publications, 1999).

13 Boggs edited the *North-Western Christian Magazine*, an abolitionist journal, in Cincinnati, Ohio, from 1854-1858. The periodical became the *Christian Luminary* in 1858 and continued publication until 1863.

14 For an excellent, comprehensive study of Campbell's treatment of slavery from the pages of the *Millennial Harbinger* over this thirty-year period, see Hale, "Ecclesiastical Politics."

15 Alexander Campbell, "Our Position to American Slavery," *MH* 2, no. 2 (February 1845): 195.

16 Campbell, "Our Position to American Slavery," *MH* 2, no. 3 (March 1845): 108.

17 Campbell, "Our Position to American Slavery," *MH* 2, no. 5 (May 1845): 193.

18 Campbell's home in Bethany, which hosts Bethany College, became part of West Virginia with the state's annexation into the Union in 1863.

19 James D. Murch, *Christians Only: A History of the Restoration Movement* (Cincinnati: Standard Publishing, 1962), 80–81.

20 Campbell, "Prospectus," *MH* 1, no. 1 (January 1830): 1.

21 Campbell, "The Crisis," *MH* 3, no. 2 (February 1832): 86.

22 Williamson, *The Crucible of Race*, 2–7.

23 Campbell, "Our Position to American Slavery," *MH* 2, no. 2 (February 1845): 49.

24 Ibid., 88.

25 Martin R. Delany, "The Condition, Elevation, Emigration, and Destiny of the Colored People of the United States," in *African-American Social and Political Thought*

1850-1920, ed. Howard Brotz, rev. ed., 37–101 (1966; repr., New Brunswick, NJ: Transaction Publishers, 1995), 46–49; Edward W. Blyden, "The African Problem and the Method of Its Solution," in *African-American Social and Political Thought*, 126–139.

26 Hale, "Ecclesiastical Politics," 71.

27 Henry Noble Sherwood, "The Formation of the American Colonization Society," *Journal of Negro History* 2 (July 1917): 212–213.

28 Throughout *Reviving the Ancient Faith*, Hughes argued that Stone's premillennial worldview dramatically influenced those second and third generation members of the Stone-Campbell Movement who eventually constituted the Churches of Christ (even more than Campbell). Notwithstanding Stone's influence in the arena of millennial thought, however, Campbell's biblical hermeneutic certainly set the mold for future members of Churches of Christ. For this reason, he receives the most attention in this study as a pioneer in Churches of Christ ideology.

29 Holifield, *Theology in America*, 291.

30 Campbell, "Our Position to American Slavery," *MH* 2, no. 2 (February 1845): 51.

31 Hughes, *Reviving the Ancient Faith*, 22.

32 T. Brian Pendleton, "Alexander Campbell and Slavery: Gradualism and Anti-Slavery Rhetoric in the *Millennial Harbinger*," *RQ* 42, no. 3 (Third Quarter 2000): 149–154.

33 Moses E. Lard, "Can We Divide?" *LQ* 3 (April 1866): 336.

34 Winifred E. Garrison and Alfred T. DeGroot, *The Disciples of Christ: A History*, rev. ed. (1948; reprint, St. Louis: Bethany, 1958), 330, 468.

35 For an in-depth study of sectionalism's role in the division between Disciples of Christ and Churches of Christ, see David Edwin Harrell Jr., *Quest for a Christian America, 1800-1865: A Social History of the Disciples of Christ, Volume I*, rev. ed. (1966; repr., Tuscaloosa: University of Alabama Press, 2003).

36 Hale, "Ecclesiastical Politics," 80–81.

37 Gardiner H. Shattuck, *Episcopalians and Race: Civil War to Civil Rights* (Lexington: University of Kentucky Press, 2000).

38 Henry E. Webb, "*Christian Standard*," in *The Encyclopedia of the Stone-Campbell Movement*, ed. Douglas A. Foster, Paul M. Blowers, Anthony L. Dunnavant, and D. Newell Williams (Grand Rapids: Eerdmans, 2004), 197–198.

39 Hughes, *Reviving the Ancient Faith*, 128–132.

40 Lipscomb, "The Advocate and Sectionalism," *GA* 8 (1 May 1866): 273.

41 Ibid., 274.

42 Lipscomb, "A Visit to Chattanooga," *GA* 31 (3 April 1889): 214.

43 Lipscomb, "The South and the Freedmen," *GA* 10 (9 July 1868): 649–654.

44 Ibid., 652.

45 To view the distinct northern flavor of the *Christian Standard*, see, for example, Isaac Errett, "Slavery—Where Does the Blame Rest?" *CS* 2 (17 August 1867): 258; ibid., "Our Alleged Inconsistency," *CS* 5 (25 June 1870): 204.

46 For a closer look at the division of northern and southern Baptists, see Robert A. Baker *Relations Between Northern and Southern Baptists* (North Stratford, NH: Ayer Company Publishers, 1979); William Wright Barnes, *The Southern Baptist Convention, 1845-1953*, rev. ed. (1900; repr., Nashville: Broadman Press, 1954); Samuel S. Hill and Robert G. Torbet, *Baptists North and South* (Valley Forge, PA: Judson Press, 1964); Torbet, *A History of the Baptists*, 3rd ed. (1952; repr., Valley Forge, PA: Judson Press, 1973).

47 For a closer look at the division that led to the formation of the Methodist Episcopal Church, South, see Bailey, "The Post Civil War Racial Separations"; Emory S. Bucke, ed., *History of American Methodism in Three Volumes* (Nashville: Abingdon, 1964); Donald G. Mathews, *Slavery and Methodism: A Chapter in American Morality, 1780-1845* (Princeton: University Press, 1965).

48 Though the institution has been unofficially recognized as Lipscomb University since 1994, the legal change did not occur until the spring of 2006.

49 For additional information regarding Lipscomb University, see Robert E. Hooper, "Lipscomb University," in *Encyclopedia of the Stone-Campbell Movement*, 482–484; Hooper and G. David England, *A Century of Memories: Centennial Celebration, David Lipscomb University, 1891-1991* (Nashville: David Lipscomb University, 1992).

50 Douglas Foster, "Abilene Christian University," in *Encyclopedia of the Stone-Campbell Movement*, 1.

51 Michael Casey did significant work following the pacifistic roots in Churches of Christ. See, for example: "From Pacifism to Patriotism: The Emergence of Civil Religion in the Churches of Christ during World War I," in *The Stone-Campbell Movement: An International Religious Tradition*, ed. Michael Casey and Douglas Foster, 466–480 (Knoxville, TN: University of Tennessee Press, 2002).

52 William S. Banowsky, *The Mirror of a Movement: Churches of Christ as Seen Through the Abilene Christian College Lectureship* (Dallas: Christian Publishing Company, 1965).

53 For additional information regarding Harding University, see James Don Nichols, "A History of Harding College, 1924-1984," (EdD diss., University of Arkansas, 1985); John F. Wilson, "Harding University," in *Encyclopedia of the Stone-Campbell Movement*, 382–383.

54 For a detailed examination of the premillennial controversy within Churches of Christ and the role of Harding College in that controversy, see Hughes, *Reviving the Ancient Faith*, 151–153.

55 William Floyd, "Why I Could Not Be a Career Preacher," in *Voices of Concern: Critical Studies in Church of Christism*, edited by Robert Meyers, 155–174 (Saint Louis: Mission Messenger, 1966), 164–165.

56 Brian Bethel, "Local Universities Took Their Own Paths toward Desegregation," *Abilene Reporter News*, 16 February 2008.

57 Ibid.

58 Ibid.

59 Ibid.; Douglas Foster, "An Angry Peace," *ACU Today* (Spring 2000). Cited 13 July 2000. Online: http://www.acu.edu/acu-today/spring2000/cover02b.html; Carl Spain, "Modern Challenges to Christian Morals," in *Christian Faith in the Modern World—Abilene Christian College Bible Lectures1960*, 199–231 (Abilene: ACC Student Exchange, 1960), 217.

60 G. Michael Payton, "Civil Rights Panel Is Fair, Balanced," *Toledo Blade*, 7 February 2008.

61 See, for example, R. N. Hogan, "The Sin of Being a Respecter of Persons, "*CE* 54 (June 1959): 2, 5; ibid., "Is It the Law or Down-Right Prejudice," *CE* 58 (June 1963): 3.

62 R. N. Hogan, "The Grab of the Century," *CE* 63, no. 11 (November 1968): 1.

63 Ibid.; J. E. Choate, *Roll Jordan Roll: A Biography of Marshall Keeble* (Nashville: Gospel Advocate Company, 1974), 110.

64 Choate, *Roll Jordan Roll*, 110.

65 Ibid., 112; Hogan, "Grab of the Century," 1. Historical records provide two possibilities for this amount. Choate reports the number at $11, 500, but Hogan records that the city gave the Board of Trustees the new property plus $15,000.

66 Choate, *Roll Jordan Roll*, 31.

67 *Obie Elie et al. v. Athens Clay Pullias et al.*, 407 F. 2d 615 (6th Cir. 1969), 616.

68 Hogan, "The Grab of the Century," 2.

69 Choate, *Roll Jordan Roll*, 114.

70 Holt actually held the title "superintendent"; but, until Keeble, the school had no president.

71 Keeble spent years soliciting funds for NCI from the pages of the *Gospel Advocate*. For a sampling of his requests see: "A Great Opportunity," *GA* 86 (18 May 1944): 341;

"Nashville Christian Institute," *GA* 89 (26 June 1947): 452; "Nashville Christian Institute Commencement," *GA* 91 (30 June 1949): 402–03; "Nashville Christian Institute Has Many Friends," *GA* 94 (24 July 1952): 486; "Nashville Christian Institute Lectures," *GA* 98 (24 May 1956): 503.

72 A Teacher, "Interesting Facts about the Negro School," *GA* 90 (9 December 1948): 1187.

73 Ibid., 1186.

74 Robert J. Norell, *Reaping the Whirlwind: The Civil Rights Movement in Tuskegee* (New York: Alfred A. Knopf, 1985; Chapel Hill, NC: University of North Carolina Press, 1998), 13. All citations are to the University of North Carolina Press version.

75 Ibid., 14; Eugene E. Genovese, *Roll, Jordan, Roll,* 91.

76 W. E. Brightwell, "The Ripest Opportunity," *GA* 90 (9 December 1948): 1189–1190; Wendell V. Clipp, "Teacher Invests Time," *GA* (9 December 1948): 1189; Philip Hunton, "Keeble and His Boys at Albany, GA," *GA* 89 (5 June 1947): 398.

77 Marshall Keeble, "The Church among the Colored," in *Abilene Christian College Bible Lectures 1950* (Austin: Firm Foundation Publishing House, 1950), 142–156. Cited 27 July 2006. Online: http://www.mun.ca/rels/restmov/texts/mkeeble/keeble1.html; ibid., "Keeble's Speech," in *Lubbock Christian College Lectures 1958: Workers Together with God,* 37–46 (Jackson, TN: Nichols Brothers Publishing Company, 1958).

78 "Nashville Christian Institute Lectureship," *GA* 98 (1 March 1956): 213.

79 Jack Evans (president of Southwestern Christian College), in an interview with the author, 12 February 2008.

80 Hogan, "Grab of the Century."

81 Ibid.

82 Benjamin Franklin, "Our Position Defined," *ACR* 10 (12 March 1867): 84.

83 Douglas Foster, *Will the Cycle Be Unbroken? Churches of Christ Face the 21st Century* (Abilene, TX: ACU Press, 1994), 73.

84 Bobby Ross, "Unity Discussion Takes Center Stage at Freed-Hardeman," *CC* 63 (1 November 2006): 1.

85 Rick Atchley and Bob Russell, *Together Again: Restoring Unity in Christ after a Century of Separation* (Abilene, TX: Leafwood Publishers; Cincinnati: Standard Publishing, 2006).

86 Spain, "Modern Challenges to Christian Morals."

87 Hogan, "Grab of the Century," 2; Evans, interview with the author, 12 February 2008.CHAPTER II

Chapter 2 Notes

1 Hap C. S. Lyda, "African Americans in the Movement, Nineteenth Century," in *Encyclopedia of the Stone-Campbell Movement*, 11.

2 Williamson, *The Crucible of Race*, 151.

3 Ibid., 47.

4 Ibid., 49.

5 S. E. Harris, E. A. Elam, and Lipscomb, "The Negro in Worship," *GA* 49 (4 July 1907): 425.

6 David Lipscomb, "Noah's Curse upon Ham, &c," *GA* 10 (14 May 1868): 462.

7 Ibid.

8 H. Shelton Smith, *In His Image,* 130–131.

9 Lipscomb, "Noah's Curse upon Ham," 462.

10 Elam, Harris, and Lipscomb, "The Negro in Worship," 425.

11 Jordan, *White over Black,* 33–34.

12 Lipscomb, "The Freedmen—Their Condition," *GA* 10 (13 February 1868): 147.

13 Ibid.

14 Lipscomb, "Are the Negroes Neglected?" *GA* 68 (14 June 1906): 377.

15 Ibid.

16 Harris, Elam, and Lipscomb, "The Negro in Worship—A Correspondence," *GA* 49 (4 July 1907): 424–425; ibid. (1 August 1907): 488–489; ibid. (15 August 1907): 521; also available online: "The Negro in Worship," [Cited 14 June 2006]. Online: http://www.mun.ca/resl/restmov/ /texts/race/negro.html.

17 Harris, Elam, and Lipscomb, "The Negro in Worship," 425.

18 Ibid.

19 Ibid., 489.

20 Ibid., 489.

21 Evans, "Dwain Evans: Lipscomb Is Quoted on Racial Prejudice," *CC* 23 (5 August 1966): 3, 6; Don Haymes, Eugene Randall, and Douglas Foster, "Race Relations," in *Encyclopedia of the Stone-Campbell Movement*, 620; R. N. Hogan, "Brother David Lipscomb Stood with God on Race Prejudice in the Church of Christ," *CE* 55 (June 1960): 2–3.

22 Atticus Haygood, *Our Brother in Black, His Freedom and His Future* (New York: Philips, 1881).

23 Smith, *In His Image*, 278.

24 Haygood, *Our Brother in Black*, 45. See also ibid., "The South and the School Problem," *Harper's New Monthly Magazine* 79 (July 1889): 226.

25 Williamson, *The Crucible of Race*, 88-93.

26 Harris, Elam, Lipscomb, "The Negro in Worship," 425.

27 Nathanial Shaler, "Science and the African Problem"; Phillip A. Bruce, *The Plantation Negro as a Freeman* (New York: Putnam, 1889).

28 Foy E. Wallace, "Negro Meetings for White People," *BB* (March 1941): 7.

29 Ibid.

30 Ibid., "From M. Keeble," *BB* (April 1941): 5.

31 Wallace, "Negro Meetings for White People," 7.

32 Wallace, "From M. Keeble."

33 Williamson, *The Crucible of Race*, 259.

34 Andrew Sledd, "The Negro: Another View," *Atlantic Monthly* 90 (July 1902): 65-73.

35 Williamson, *The Crucible of Race*, 259.

36 John Spencer Bassett, "Stirring up the Fires of Race Antipathy," *SAQ* 2 (October 1903): 297–305.

37 Williamson, *The Crucible of Race*, 266.

38 Earl Ervin West, *The Search for the Ancient Order: Volume IV* (Nashville: Gospel Advocate Company, 1979; Germantown, Tennessee: Religious Book Service, 1987), 68. Citations are to the Religious Book Service edition.

39 Ibid.

40 A. M. Burton, "The Prospects and Needs of the Putnam County Industrial School for Negroes," *GA* 58 (10 February 1916): 132.

41 Ervin C. Jackson, "Silver Point School," in *Encyclopedia of the Stone-Campbell Movement*, 685; Choate, *Roll Jordan Roll*, 28; Darrell Broking, "Marshall Keeble and the Implementation of a Grand Strategy: Erasing the Color Line in the Church of Christ" (master's thesis, East Tennessee State University, 2002), 42.

42 *Elie v.* Pullias, 616.

43 Vernon Boyd, *Undying Dedication: The Story of G. P. Bowser* (Nashville: Gospel Advocate Company, 1985), 67.

44 Williamson, *The Crucible of Race*, 74.

45 August Meier, *Negro Thought in America 1880-1915: Racial Ideologies in the Age of Booker T. Washington* (Ann Arbor, MI: University of Michigan Press, 1963), 169.

46 W. E. B. DuBois, *The Souls of Black Folk* (Chicago: A. C. McClurg Company, 1903; Mineola, NY: Dover, 1994), 2. Citations are to the Dover edition.

47 In order to avoid confusion between Marshall Keeble, John Bell Keeble, and Major Horace Pickney Keeble, this paragraph will avoid using "Keeble" as their primary designation. Even this technique fails to remove the ambiguity between Marshall Keeble, his grandfather, and his uncle. They each shared not only a surname, but also a first name.

48 Choate, *Roll Jordan Roll*, 15-16.

49 Ibid., xiv, 125.

50 Ibid., xii, 95, 126.

51 *GA* 60 (18 July 1968); Reuel Lemmons, "Marshall Keeble," *FF* 85 (14 May 1968): 306.

52 Karl Pettus, "The Memorial to Marshall Keeble," *GA* 60 (18 July 1968): 449.

53 Choate, *Roll Jordan Roll*, 93.

54 Ibid.

55 J. W. Brents, "Brother Brents' Letter," *GA* 83 (15 October 1931): 1289.

56 Marshall Keeble, "Mission Work among Negroes," *GA* 63 (20 January 1921): 78.

57 A. B. Lipscomb, "It's Not Keeble, But the Bible Is Right," *CL* 45 (25 August 1931): 6.

58 Choate, *Roll Jordan Roll*, 54.

59 Wallace, "Negro Meetings for White People," 7.

60 Ibid.

61 Ibid.

62 Wallace, "From M. Keeble," 5.

63 Ibid.

64 John Mark Tucker, in discussion with the author, June 2007. Tucker also recounted this story in his essay "Six Black Women Who Influenced My Life: A Journey in Spiritual and Intellectual Formation," in *Restoring the First-Century Church in the Twenty-first Century: Essays on the Stone-Campbell Movement in Honor of Don Haymes*, ed. Warren Lewis and Hans Rollmann, 323–334 (Eugene, OR: Wipf and Stock, 2005), 326–327.

65 Ibid.

66 Tim Tucker, "'Potsherds:' A Piece of Middle Tennessee Samizdat Literature" (working paper, Autobiography, Faculty of Columbia Christian University and Lipscomb University, 1994).

67 Harry Kellam, "A Tribute to the Two Dr. K's," *CE* 84 (January 1987): 5.

68 Ibid.

69 Ibid.

70 Booker T. Washington, *Up From Slavery* (Doubleday, 1901; Boston: Western Islands, 1965), 118–120. Citations are to the Western Islands edition.

71 Meier, *Negro Thought in America*, 114.

72 Ibid., 113.

73 Ibid., 111.

74 Booker T. Washington, "Is the Negro Having a Fair Chance?" *Century Magazine* 85 (November 1912): 51.

75 Evans, in interview with the author, 12 February 2008.

76 Dennis C. Dickerson, *Militant Mediator: Whitney M. Young Jr.* (Lexington, KY: University of Kentucky Press, 1998), 9.

77 Ibid., 19.

78 Benton Cordell Goodpasture, *Biography and Sermons of Marshall Keeble* (Nashville: Gospel Advocate Company, 1931); Choate, *Roll Jordan Roll*; Forrest N. Rhoads Sr, "A Study of the Sources of Marshall Keeble's Effectiveness as a Preacher" (PhD diss., Southern Illinois University, 1970); Paul D. Phillips, "The Interracial Impact of Marshall Keeble,

Black Evangelist, 1878-1968," in *The Stone-Campbell Movement: An International Religious Tradition*, 317–328.

79 Robert Hooper, *A Distinct People: A History of the Churches of Christ in the 20th Century* (Eugene, OR: Wipf and Stock Publishers, 1993), 255–280; Hughes, *Reviving the Ancient Faith*, 295–299.

80 Broking, "Marshall Keeble and a Grand Strategy," 39.

81 Katherine L. Dvorak, *An African-American Exodus: The Segregation of the Southern Churches* (Brooklyn, NY: Carlson Publishing, 1991), 121. Dvorak argued that the CME Church organized because of the failed effort among members of the MEC, S to achieve ecclesiastical equality.

82 Henry Holsey, *Autobiography, Sermons, Addresses, and Essays*, 2nd ed. (Atlanta, GA: Franklin Printing and Publishing, 1899), 253.

83 Ibid., 10.

84 Ibid., 23.

85 For a study of Holsey's life and a closer examination of the shift that occurred in his thought, see Glenn T. Eskew, "Black Elitism and the Failure of Paternalism in Postbellum Georgia: The Case of Bishop Lucius Henry Holsey," *Journal of Southern History* 58 (November 1992): 637–666.

86 Keeble, "Mission Work Among Negroes," 78; ibid., "The Church Among the Colored."

87 A. B. Lipscomb, "It's Not Keeble," 6.

88 Rhoads, "A Study of the Sources," 103.

89 Keeble, "A Great Opportunity," 341; ibid., "Nashville Christian Institute.," 452; ibid., "Nashville Christian Institute Commencement," 402–403; ibid., "Nashville Christian Institute Has Many Friends," 486; ibid., "Nashville Christian Institute Lectures," 503.

90 W. E. Brightwell, "The Ripest Opportunity," 1188–89.

91 A letter from Ira Rice found in Choate's biography of Keeble, for example, reflects this arrangement. See Choate, *Roll Jordan Roll*, 122.

92 Broking, "Marshall Keeble and a Grand Strategy," 50; Phillip L. Hunton, "Keeble and Boys," 398.

93 Choate, *Roll Jordan Roll*, 31.

94 Marshall Keeble, "Report of Work," *GA* 66 (3 January 1924): 22–23.

95 Choate, *Roll Jordan Roll*, 128.

96 Ibid., 53.

97 Haymes, "Introduction to the Text," n.p. [cited 14 June 2006]. Online: http://www.mun.ca/rels/ restmov /race/haymes/10.html.

98 Broking, "Marshall Keeble and a Grand Strategy," 60; Choate, *Roll Jordan Roll*, xiv; Linda T. Wynn, *Leaders of Afro-American Nashville* (Nashville: Nashville Christian Institute Reunion Committee, 2002), 17.

99 H. A. Dixon, "Marshall Keeble at the College Lectureships," *GA* 110 (1968): 455; Keeble, "Keeble's Speech," 37.

100 Keeble, "The Church Among the Colored;" ibid., "A Prepared Ministry," in *Harding College Lectures 1952* (Austin: Firm Foundation Publishing House, 1952), 261–267.

101 Keeble, "A Prepared Ministry," 261.

Chapter 3 Notes

1 Gayraud Wilmore, *Black Religion and Black Radicalism*, 163. Wilmore is not alone in his recognition of the "deradicalization of the black church" during this period. See, for example: Baer and Singer, *African American Religion in the Twentieth Century*; Frazier, *The Negro Church in America*; Mays, *The Negro's Church* (New York: Beaufort Books, 1975);

Milton C. Sernett, *"Bound For the Promised Land": African American Religion and the Great Migration* (Durham, NC: Duke University Press, 1995).

2 Dennis Dickerson, "African American Religious Intellectuals and the Theological Foundations of the Civil Rights Movement, 1930-55," *Church History* 74, no. 2 (June 2005): 217–235; Mark Chapman, "'Of One Blood': Mays and the Theology of Race Relations," in *Walking Integrity,* 233–61; Randall Jelks, "Benjamin E. Mays and the Creation of an Insurgent Negro Professional Clergy," *AME Church Review* 118, no. 387 (July-September 2002): 32–38; Thomas I. S.Mikelson, "Mays, King, and the Negro's God," in *Walking Integrity,* 154–184.

3 For detailed information on Powell's activism, see Herbert Garfinkel, *When Negroes March* (New York: Macmillan, 1969) or Charles V. Hamilton, *Adam Clayton Powell, Jr.: The Political Biography of an American Dilemma* (Lanham, MD: Cooper Square Press, 2002). For more information on Carey, see Dennis Dickerson, *A Liberated Past: Explorations in AME Church History* (Nashville: AME Sunday School Union, 2003).

4 Dickerson, "African American Religious Intellectuals," 220.

5 See Cynthia Taylor, *A. Philip Randolph: The Religious Journey of an African American Labor Leader* (New York: New York University Press, 2005).

6 Ibid., 226.

7 William Stuart Nelson, *The Christian Way in Race Relations* (New York: Harper and Brothers, 1948).

8 G. P. Bowser, "Better Outlook for Colored People," *GA* 70 (30 August 1928): 835; ibid., "Outlook Among the Colored People," *GA* 70 (1 November 1928): 1053; A. C. Campbell, "Work Among the Colored People," *GA* 53 (1 June 1911) 619; S. W. Womack, "Mission Work Among Colored People in TN," *GA* 46 (4 February 1904): 80; ibid., "Work Among Colored People," *GA* 53 (6 April 1911): 425; ibid., (20 July 1911): 798; ibid., (17 August 1911): 926; ibid., (19 October 1911): 1206; ibid., (16 November 1911): 1341; ibid., (14 December 1911): 1469.

9 For an overview of Franklin's life and work, see Dennis C. Dickerson, "Salvation and Separatism: William H. Franklin and the Presbyterian Mission to the Freedmen in East Tennessee," *AME Church Review* 120 (January-March 2004): 114–121.

10 Ibid., 117.

11 Choate, *Roll Jordan Roll,* 23; Womack, "Among the Colored Folk," *GA* 60 (3 January 1918): 18.

12 Womack, "Among the Colored Folk," 18.

13 Broking, "Marshall Keeble and a Grand Strategy"; Hooper, *A Distinct People*, 266.

14 Jackson, "Silver Point School," 684–685.

15 Boyd, *Undying Dedication*, 37; Bowser, "Work Among the Colored People," *GA* 54 (29 February 1912): 279; Ibid., 34 (4 July 1912): 793; Ibid., 55 (1 May 1913): 431.

16 Boyd, *Undying Dedication*, 59.

17 G. P. Bowser, "Work among the Colored People," *GA* 55 (1 May 1913): 431.

18 Boyd, *Undying Dedication*, 67.

19 Bowser, *Christian Echo* (1938), quoted in Boyd, *Undying Dedication*, 82-83.

20 Bowser, "The Need of Prepared Preachers," *CE* 34 (20 February 1939): 4.

21 Bowser, "The Bowser Christian Institute," *CE* 34 (20 February 1939): 4. See also ibid., "School Work," *CE* 34 (5 May 1939): 3; ibid., "What We Have Done," *CE* 34 (5 May 1939): 3; ibid., "The Bowser Institute," *CE* 34 (5 May 1939): 3; ibid., "Plain Statements Relative to the Bowser Christian Institute," *CE* 34 (5 June 1939): 2.

22 G. P. Bowser, "The Bowser Christian Institute," *CE* 34 (5 July 1939): 6.

23 Hooper, *A Distinct People*, 266.

24 Boyd, *Undying Dedication*, 44.

25 Hogan, "The Sin of Being a Respecter of Persons," 2.

26 Ibid.

27 Ibid.; Hogan, "Brother David Lipscomb"; ibid., "Is It the Law"; ibid., "Tradition Versus God's Commandments," *CE* 58 (June 1963); ibid., "Methodists Appoint Negro Pastor to All-White Church," *CE* 58 (August 1963).

28 Ibid., "The Sin of Being a Respecter of Persons," 5.

29 Ibid., "Is it the Law or Down-Right Prejudice?" 3.

30 Ibid.

31 Alvis, *Religion and Race*, 90–91.

32 Cheryl V. Cunningham, "The Desegregation of Tulane University" (master's thesis, University of New Orleans, 1982), 1.

33 Foster, "An Angry Peace."

34 Ibid.

35 Ibid.

36 Floyd, "Why I Could Not Be a Career Preacher," 167.

37 Don Haymes, "Conclusion to the Text: Why I Could Not Be A Preacher," n. p. [Cited 9 August 2006]. Online: http://www.mun.ca/rels/restmov/texts/race/haymes12.html.

38 Andrew Hairston, "Is the Race Issue Social?" *CE* 59 (June 1964): 5.

39 James Maxwell, "The Sociological Impact of the Race Issue," *CE* 59 (July-September, 1964).

40 Norman R. Adamson, "Reflections . . . Selma and Montgomery," *CE* 60 (June 1965): 2.

41 Some scholars argue that law, even more than the boycott, resulted in the desegregation of the buses. See, for example, Robert Jerome Glennon, "The Role of Law in the Civil Rights Movement: The Montgomery Bus Boycott, 1955-1957," *Law and History Review* 9 (Spring 1991): 59–112.

42 Fred D. Gray, *Bus Ride to Justice: The Life and Works of Fred Gray* (1995; repr., Montgomery: New South Books, 2002), 225.

43 "Fred D. Gray to Receive 2004 ABA Thurgood Marshall Award," n. p. [cited 26 February 2008]. Online: http://www.abanet.org/irr/tmaward/2004award/fredgray.html.

44 Martin Luther King Jr., *The Papers of Martin Luther King, Jr., Volume III: Birth of a New Age December 1955-December 1956,* edited by Clayborne Carson (Berkeley: University of California Press, 1997), 303.

45 Gray, *Bus Ride to Justice*, 41.

46 Glennon, "The Role of Law in the Civil Rights Movement," 61.

47 Pearl Gray Daniels, *The History of the Holt Street Church of Christ and Its Role in Establishing Churches of Christ Among African Americans in Central Alabama, 1928-1997* (Baltimore, MD: American Literary Press, 1997), 88–90.

48 Gray, *Bus Ride to Justice*, 10–12, 257.

49 Ibid., 257.

50 Lynn McMillon, "A Conversation with Fred Gray," *CC* 65 (February 2008): 25.

51 Keeble, "Nashville Christian Institute Lectures"; ibid., "The Church Among the Colored"; ibid., "Keeble's Speech."

52 Gray, *Bus Ride to Justice*, 260.

53 McMillon, "A Conservation with Fred Gray," 25.

54 Gayraud Wilmore, *Black and Presbyterian: The Heritage and the Hope* (Philadelphia: Geneva Press, 1983), 69.

55 Gray, *Bus Ride to Justice*, 33.

56 Carroll Pitts Jr., "A Critical Study of Civil Rights Practices, Attitudes, and Responsibilities in Churches of Christ" (master's thesis, Pepperdine University, 1969), 64.

57 Ibid.

58 Ibid.

59 Baer and Singer, *African-American Religion*, 24.

60 Gordon Allport, *The Nature of Prejudice* (New York: Doubleday, 1954), 143.

61 Evans, in interview with the author, 12 February 2008.

62 Ibid.

63 Aldon D. Morris, *The Origins of the Civil Rights Movement: Black Communities Organizing for Change* (New York: The Free Press, 1984), x, 17–25.

64 Ibid., ix.

65 *GA* 60 (18 July 1968).

66 James Fowler, "From the Midst of the Crisis," *FF* 81 (31 March 1964): 199.

67 Reuel Lemmons, "The Church and Integration," *FF* 81 (31 March 1964): 194.

68 For a sampling of these articles, see "Schools and Segregation," *Presbyterian Outlook* 135 (12 October 1953): 8; "A Moral Issue," ibid. (7 December 1953): 6–7; "Desegregation and Economic Pressure," ibid. 137 (4 April 1955): 8; "With Troops and Tanks," *Southern Presbyterian Journal* 17 (24 December 1958): 2–3; "Incident in Mississippi," *Presbyterian Journal* 24 (9 March 1966): 12–13; "This is No Way to Justice," ibid. 26 (17 April 1968): 12.

69 For a sampling of these articles, see Katherine Parker Freeman, "Christ the Answer to Racial Tension," *Royal Service* 43 (March 1949): 20–28; David M. Gardner, "Segregation's Problems," *Baptist Standard* (10 June 1954); D. Elton Trueblood, "Maker Brotherhood Real," *Light* 3 (February 1950): 1; Finley W. Tinnin, "Non Segregation," *Baptist Message* (3 June 1954).

70 PCUSA, *Minutes of the 98th General Assembly*, 1958, 37–39; Synod of Arkansas, *Minutes*, 1959, 44.

71 Mark Newman, *Getting Right with God: Southern Baptists and Desegregation, 1945-1995* (Tuscaloosa, AL: University of Alabama Press, 2001), 84.

72 Williams, "Letter to Editor," *Royal Service* 58 (December 1964): 34–35.

73 For a thorough examination of the Baptist conversation surrounding the Conventions' declarations, see Newman, *Getting Right with God*, 30–34.

74 Reuel Lemmons, "The Long Hot Summer," *FF* 85 (9 January 1968): 18.

75 Ibid.

76 Lemmons, "Letter to John Allen Chalk, dated 16 May 1968," n. p. [cited 19 August 2006]. Online: http://www.mun.ca/rels/restmov/texts/race/haymes1.html.

77 Jerry Falwell, "Ministers and Marches," sermon delivered at Thomas Road Baptist Church, Lynchburg, Virginia, 21 March 1965.

78 Lemmons, "The Church and Integration," 194.

79 Hughes, *Reviving the Ancient Faith*, 305; William C. Martin, "Shepherds Versus Flocks," *Atlantic Monthly* 220 (December 1967).

80 Hugo McCord, "A Sorry Viewpoint," *GA* 111 (20 March 1969): 190.

81 Ibid.

82 Alan Highers, "Churches and Politics," *GA* 108 (7 July 1966): 418, 428; Dale Simpson, "Let Our Preachers Lead the World on a Real Freedom March," *FF* 82 (27 April 1965): 259, 266; Rex A. Turner, "Christianity and the Races," *GA* 103 (12 May 1966): 292–293.

83 For a classic expression of this viewpoint, see Fowler, "From the Midst of the Crisis."

84 See, for example, these letters to the editor: *CC* 18 (13 January 1961): 3; (3 February 1961): 4–5; (24 February 1961): 3; (3 March 1961): 8; 21 (18 October 1963): 6–7; (25 October 1963): 2; (1 November 1963): 5; (22 November 1963): 2; (13 December 1963): 2–3. The editors also expressed their views: "Two Southern Preachers Discuss Racial Issues," *CC* (20 September 1963): 2; "Let's Discuss the Negro Issue," *CC* 21 (27 September 1963): 2.

85 Douglas Foster, "Justice, Racism & Churches of Christ," in *Unfinished Reconciliation: Justice, Racism & Churches of Christ*, ed. Gary Holloway and John York, 131–151 (Abilene, TX: ACU Press, 2003), 142.

86 Lemmons, "The Church and Integration," 194.

87 L. M. Graves, "'Without Respect of Persons': The Negro and Race Relationships," *Abilene Christian College Lectures 1950* (Austin: Firm Foundation Publishing House, 1950), 288–290; Leon Locke, "The Congregational Attitude Toward Race Relationships," ibid., 281–283; J. W. Treat, "What Does the Bible Teach About Race Relationships?" ibid., 284–287; J. Roy Willingham Jr., "What Should the Christian's Attitude Be Toward Race Relationships?" ibid., 278–280.

88 Willingham, "The Christian's Attitude," 280.

89 Banowsky, *Mirror of a Movement*, 385.

90 Spain, "Modern Challenges to Christian Morals."

91 Chronicle staff writer, "Effective Next September ACC Desegregates Graduate School," *CC* 18 (9 June 1961): 1, 6.

92 "No Hate in His Path," *CC* 17 (29 March 1960): 2–A; "Readers Tell Own Opinions of Speech on Integration," *CC* 17 (29 March 1960): 2–A; "Readers Laud Speech," *CC* 17 (5 April 1960): 2; "Reader Appreciate Policy," *CC* 17 (12 April 1906): 2; Jim Hawkins, "Dear Editor," *CC* 18 (13 January 1961): 3.

93 Pitts, "A Critical Study of Civil Rights Practices,"46–47.

94 "Background of Race Relations Workshop," *CC Supplement* (10 May 1968): 3.

95 David Jones, "Address by David Jones Jr." *CC Supp* (10 May 1968): 2.

96 Ibid., 4.

97 "Background of Race Relations Workshop," 3.

98 "Atlanta, Ga. Racial Meeting A Great Success," *CE* 63 (September 1968): 7.

99 Eugene Lawton, R. C. Wells, and Jimmy Allen, "Statement of Acknowledgement of Racial Prejudice and Proposals for Improving Race Relations in Churches of Christ," *NAC* 10 (1 July 1978): 210.

100 Walter Burch, "Neglecting the Weightier Matters," *FF* 85 (11 June 1968): 372.

101 Glenn L. Wallace, "The Atlanta Conference," *FCC* 2, no. 4 (October 1968): 1, 3.

102 The same speech was later published in the July 1970 issue of *Mission*.

103 G. P. Holt, "Tension Between the Black and White Church," *CE* 64 (June 1969): 4, 9.

104 Alvis, *Religion and Race*, 50–56.

105 Holt, "Tension Between the Black and White Church," 4.

Chapter 4 Notes

1 "The Tradition of White Presidents at Black Colleges," *Journal for Blacks in Higher Education*16 (Summer 1997): 99.

2 Alvis, *Religion and Race*, 44–45.

3 Ibid., 45.

4 Reimers, *White Protestantism and the Negro*, 40.

5 Ibid.

6 Ibid., 42–43

7 Ibid., 20.

8 Ibid.; Carter G. Woodson, *The History of the Negro Church* (Washington: Associated Publishers, 1921), 202–211; Mason Crum, *The Negro in the Methodist Church* (New York: Board of Missions and Church Extension of the Methodist Church, 1951), 64–67.

9 Brightwell, "The Ripest Opportunity," 1189.

10 A Teacher, "Interesting Facts," 1188.

11 Williamson, *The Crucible of Race*, 22.

12 Clipp, "Teacher Invests Time," 1189.

13 "Colored Singers, Speakers to Be at War Memorial Building," *GA* 89 (15 May 1947): 349.

14 Ibid.

15 Ibid.

16 Thurman Sensing, "Expert Finds Plan Sound," *GA* 90 (9 December 1948): 1188.

17 "Colored Singers, Speakers to Be at War Memorial Building," 349; "Colored Program at War Memorial, Sunday Afternoon," *GA* 89 (March 1947): 366.

18 Hunton, "Keeble and Boys," 398.

19 Gray, *Bus Ride to Justice*, 255.

20 Brightwell, "The Ripest Opportunity," 1189.

21 Keeble, "Nashville Christian Institute Has Many Friends," 486; ibid., "Nashville Christian Institute Lectures," 503.

22 Keeble, "A Great Opportunity," 341.

23 Keeble, "Nashville Christian Institute Commencement," 402–403.

24 Ibid.

25 Brightwell, "The Ripest Opportunity," 1189.

26 *Elie v. Pullias*, 615.

27 Dickerson, "Salvation and Separatism," 116.

28 Marshall Keeble, "Nashville Christian Institute to Close," *GA* 109 (16 March 1967): 166.

29 Complaint of Plaintiffs in *Obie Elie et al. v. Athens Clay Pullias et al.*, case 4794 (U. S. District Court, Middle District of Tennessee, Nashville Division, 1967).

30 *Elie v. Pullias*, 616.

31 Ibid., 617.

32 Ibid.

33 Ibid.

34 Jack Evans, in an interview with the author, 12 February 2008.

35 Hogan, "The Grab of the Century," 1–2.

36 Ibid., 1.

37 Ibid.

38 Ibid.

39 Ibid., 2.

40 Ibid.

41 Ibid.

42 Evans, "Remember N. C. I.," *CE* 63 (December 1968): 2.

43 Ibid.

44 Olivia Holt, "The Bowser Memorial Scholarship Fund," *CE* 62 (June 1967): 6.

45 Ibid.

46 Ibid.

47 Foster, "Justice, Racism & Churches of Christ," 141.

48 Pitts, "God Is No Respecter of Persons," *CE* 64 (June 1969): 5, 9.

49 Stokely Carmichael, "Black Power" (lecture, Berkeley, CA, October 1966).

50 James Cone, *Black Theology and Black Power* (New York: Harper and Row, 1969; Maryknoll, NY: Orbis, 2001), 6. Citations are to the Orbis edition.

51 Wilmore, *Black Religion and Black Radicalism*, 229.

52 Williamson, *The Crucible of Race*, 504.

53 Pitts, "God Is No Respecter of Persons," 9.

54 Holt, "Tension between the Black and White Church," 4.
55 Ibid.
56 Ibid.
57 Ibid.
58 Ibid.
59 Ibid.
60 Ibid., 4, 9.
61 Ibid., 9.

Chapter 5 Notes

1 Though no concrete numbers exist regarding the number of individuals or congregations that make up African American Churches of Christ, Edward Robinson estimates the number to be approximately 169,000 members in 1,200 congregations. Robinson, "African Americans in the Movement," *Encyclopedia of Stone-Campbell Movement*," 17. Jack Evans believes the most accurate numbers are reflected in SWCC records: 115,000 members in 1,300 congregations. Evans, "Reviewing the Garrett 'Review," *CE* 84 (September 1986): 2.

2 Jack Evans, in interview with the author, 12 February 2008.

3 Ibid.

4 Ibid.

5 Ibid.

6 Ibid.

7 Marshall Keeble, "The Great Physician," MP3 recording of sermon, n. p. [cited 3 March 2008]. Online: http://www.oldpathsmedia.org/Speakers/Keeble/Marshall.

8 An excellent record of their correspondence leading up to the forum and the events that took place at the forum itself may be found at: Ira Y. Rice Jr., "'Gold Coast Restoration Forum' Results in Blacks Withdrawing Fellowship from Ivory James," *Contending for the Faith* 17 (August 1986): 1, 3–14. This record also provides an excellent window into the separation between African American and white congregations. The phrases "black brotherhood" and "black church" routinely appear in this article indicating the common acceptance of two racially defined factions within the denomination.

9 Ibid., 3.

10 Ibid., 12.

11 Rice, "Gold Coast Forum," 13.

12 Ibid.

13 These two articles, as well as letters between Garrett and Evans, are collected in Evans' book, *"So What's the Big Issue?"* (Terrell, Texas: Jack Evans, 2005), 106–125.

14 Leroy Garrett, "The Underbelly of the Black Church of Christ," *Restoration Review* 28 (June 1986): 313.

15 Ibid., 309.

16 Jack Evans, "Reviewing the Garrett 'Review'," *CE* 84 (September 1986): 2.

17 Jack Evans, "The History of Southwestern Christian College Terrell, Texas," (master's thesis, Texas Western College, 1963), 12.

18 Ibid., 12–13.

19 Ibid., 13.

20 Ibid., 16; *Mental Diet* (November 1949): 1.

21 Vernon Boyd, "Bower, George Philip," in *Encyclopedia of Stone-Campbell Movement*, 97; Robinson, "Southwestern Christian College," in *Encyclopedia of Stone-Campbell Movement*, 695; Evans, "History of Southwestern Christian College," 3–20.

22 Other such efforts include the Southern Practical Institute and NCI.

23 "The Tradition of White Presidents at Black Colleges," *Journal for Blacks in Higher Education* 16 (Summer 1997): 93–94.

24 Jack Evans, in an interview with the author, 12 February 2008.

25 Ibid.

26 Edward Robinson, in a correspondence with the author, 4 March 2008.

27 Ibid., "Southwestern Christian College," 695.

28 Ibid., in correspondence with the author, 4 March 2008.

29 "'Christ for the Crises' at Southwestern C. C.," *CE* 62 (October 1967): 1–2.

30 A brief history and purpose of the Annual National Lectureship is presented in G. E. Steward, "History of the Lectureship," *CE* 72 (April 1974): 4.

31 Ibid.

32 See especially Evans' critique of Charles Martin and Alfred Newberry in *"So What's the Big Issue?"*

33 See, for example "Annual National Lectureship," *CE* 82 (January 1984): 1; G. P. Holt, "Purposes of Lectureships in 1977," *CE* 76 (April 1977): 4; Steward, "History of the Lectureship," 4.

34 Olivia Holt, "The Bowser Memorial Scholarship Fund," 6.

35 Ibid.

36 Steward, "History of the Lectureship," 4.

37 Ibid.

38 Roosevelt Wells, "'A Plea to My Black Brethren' (A Reply)," *CE* 68 (February 1970): 2.

39 John Waddey, "A Plea to My Black Brethren," *CE* 67 (November 1969): 3.

40 Wells, "'A Plea to My Black Brethren' (A Reply)," 2.

41 For a sampling of such articles, see Jack Evans Jr., "Jesus Christ in Black and White," *CE* 84 (August 1986): 3; Kenneth P. Garnier, "The Truth Shall Set You Free," *CE* 84 (July 1993): 2; R. N. Hogan, "The Church and Integration," *CE* 84 (May-June 1994): 2, 7; G. P. Holt, "Issues Facing the Church Today," *CE* 85 (January 1997): 4; J. Raymond Pecoraro, "Racism in the Lord's Church Is an Age-Old Problem," *CE* 10 (August 1981): 4; Carroll Pitts, "Civil Rights...In the Churches of Christ," *CE* 84 (August 1987): 2; Roosevelt Wells, "Equal Heirs, Equal Members, Equal Partners," *CE* 84 (May-June 1992): 1, 8–9; Boyd Williams, "Racial Strife Is Still With Us," *CE* 76 (July 1977): 4.

42 Wells, "'A Plea to My Black Brethren,'" 3.

43 Eugene Boring, *Disciples and the Bible: A History of Disciples Biblical Interpretation in North America* (St. Louis: Chalice Press, 1997), 2–3.

44 Holifield, *Theology in America*, 291.

45 T. Dwight Bozeman, *Protestants in an Age of Science: The Baconian Ideal and Antebellum American Religious Thought* (Chapel Hill: University of North Carolina Press, 1977), xiii.

46 Cocceius' *Summa doctrinae de foedere et testamento Dei* (1648; "Comprehensive Treatise on the Doctrines of the Covenant and Testament of God") provided the basis for covenant theology—the view that following the result of God's covenant of works through Adam, God instituted a covenant of grace in three dispensations: the Patriarchal, Mosaic, and Christian.

47 Thomas Campbell, *Declaration and Address of the Christian Association of Washington* (Washington, PA: Brown and Sample, 1809), 16. Cited 22 November 2006. Online: http://www.mun.ca/ rels/restmov/texts/tcampbell/Da/DA-1ST.HTM.

48 Alexander Campbell, "Sermon on the Law," *MH* 3, no. 9 (September 1846): 493–521.

49 Ibid., 506–507.

50 Alexander Campbell, "Schools and Colleges—No. 2," *MH* 3d ser., 7 (March 1850): 172.

51 Hughes, *Reviving the Ancient Faith*, 31.

52 See, for example, Alexander Campbell, "A Restoration of the Ancient Order of Things, No. 4," *CB* 2 (7 February 1825): 221.

53 Moses Lard, "Have We Not Become a Sect?" *LQ* 1 (March 1864): 255.

54 Lard, "Do the Holy Scriptures Authorize the Baptism of Infants?" *LQ* 1 (December 1863): 158.

55 J. D. Thomas, *We Be Brethren* (Abilene: Biblical Research Press, 1958).

56 Ibid., 6.

57 Thomas Campbell, *Declaration and Address*, prop. 4.

58 Thomas Hoyt Jr., "Interpreting Biblical Scholarship for the Black Church Tradition," in *Stony the Road We Trod: African American Biblical Interpretation*, ed. Cain Hope Felder, 17–39 (Minneapolis: Fortress, 1991), 25.

59 Maxwell, "The Sociological Impact of the Race Issue," 7.

60 Eddie S. Glaude Jr., *Exodus!: Religion, Race, and Nation in Early Nineteenth-Century Black America* (Chicago: University of Chicago, 2000), 9.

61 See Raboteau, *Slave Religion*; ibid., *Canaan Land*, esp. 41–60.

62 Martin Luther King Jr., "The Strength to Love," in *A Testament of Hope: The Essential Writings and Speeches of Martin Luther King, Jr.*, ed. James M. Washington, 491-517 (San Francisco: Harper San Francisco, 1986), 495.

63 King, *Where Do We Go from Here*, 555–633, 619.

64 Adamson, "Reflections . . . On Selma and Montgomery," 1.

65 Samuel Cassius, "Additional Acknowledgments," *CL* (17 December 1901): 13.

66 Ibid., "Among Our Colored Disciples," *CL* 17 (8 December 1903): 13.

67 Will Coleman, *Tribal Talk: Black Theology, Hermeneutics, and African/American Ways of "Telling the Story"* (University Park, PA: Pennsylvania State University Press, 2000), vii.

68 Samuel Cassius, "A Trip to the Golden Gate," *CL* 16 (12 August 1902): 13.

69 Edward Robinson, *To Save My Race from Abuse: The Life of Samuel Robert Cassius* (Tuscaloosa, AL: University of Alabama Press, 2007), 40.

70 Ibid., 52.

71 Samuel Cassius, "Unity," in F. L. Rowe, *Our Savior's Prayer for Unity: A Symposium on the Seventeenth Chapter of John* (Cincinnati, OH: F. L. Rowe, 1918), 29-30.

72 Ibid., "Among Our Colored Disciples," *CL* 5 (9 April 1901): 9.

73 By the phrase "new hermeneutic," this author does not mean to tie Churches of Christ to the "New Hermeneutic," a movement from 1950s and 1960s German biblical scholarship that attempted to relate the Christian faith to a post-Christian world. Thomas Olbricht addressed this distinction in at least two essays: "Hermeneutics: The Beginning Point (Part I)," *Image* (September 1989); ibid., "Hermeneutics in the Churches of Christ," *RQ* 37, no. 1 (1995), 14.

74 For two assessments of this phenomenon, see Ted Parks, "A Conversation with Andrew Hairston," *CC* 58, no. 4 (April 2001): 20; David Jones Jr., "Growing Their Separate Ways," *GA* 132 (January 1990): 21–23.

75 Hughes, *Reviving the Ancient Faith*, 373.

76 Everett Ferguson, "*Restoration Quarterly*," in *Encyclopedia of the Stone-Campbell Movement*, 643.

77 Russ Dudrey, "Restorationist Hermeneutics among the Churches of Christ: Why Are We at an Impasse?" *RQ* 30, no. 1 (1988): 37.

78 Ibid., 39.

79 Ibid., 40–42.

80 Michael Houston credits this essay, along with two essays by Michael Casey, as providing impetus for the renewed interest in the subject of Churches of Christ hermeneutics in "Do We Need a New Old Testament Hermeneutic?" *Christian Scholars' Conference 1990* (Abilene: Abilene Christian University, 1990), 168.

81 Ibid., 174.

82 Larry James, "Ten Principles to Consider in Developing a "New" Hermeneutic," *Christian Scholars' Conference 1990* (Abilene: Abilene Christian University, 1990), 213.

83 Don Jackson, "A New Restoration Hermeneutic—Who Really Cares?" *Christian Scholars' Conference 1990* (Abilene: Abilene Christian University, 1990); Rubel Shelly, "Apologetics and Hermeneutics: How a Properly Framed Doctrine of Inspiration Informs Sound Exegetical Method," *Christian Scholars' Conference 1990* (Abilene: Abilene Christian University, 1990).

84 J. Paul Pollard, "Recent Trends in Biblical Interpretation," *Christian Scholars' Conference 1990* (Abilene: Abilene Christian University, 1990), 317.

85 C. Leonard Allen, *The Cruciform Church* (Abilene, TX: ACU Press, 1990), 73–74.

86 Hughes, *Reviving the Ancient Faith*, 370.

87 Ibid.

88 See, for example Casey, "The Development of Necessary Inference in the Hermeneutics of the Disciples of Christ/Churches of Christ" (PhD dissertation, University of Pittsburgh, 1986); Milo Hadwin, *The Role of New Testament Examples as Related to Biblical Authority* (Austin: Firm Foundation, 1974); Robert E. Woodrow, "The Nature of Biblical Authority and the Restoration Movement," *RQ* 28, no. 1 (1986): 27–39.

89 Rubel Shelly, Mike Cope, and Phillip Morrison, "Wineskins: A Purpose Statement," *Wineskins* 1 (May 1992): 5.

90 Monte Cox, "Renewing Our Identity: Seeking and Saving the Lost," Gaylord Media Company, audiotape of lectures presented at the ACU Lectureships, 21 February 2000.

91 Mark LaValley, "A Gospel for All Generations," Gaylord Media Company, audiotape of lectures presented at the ACU Lectureships, 23 February 2000.

92 Mike Cope, "A Passion for Community," Gaylord Media Company, audiotape of lectures presented at the ACU Lectureships, 22 February 2000.

93 Harold Hazelip, "People of Proclamation and Prayer," Gaylord Media Company, audiotape of lectures at the ACU Lectureships, 22 February 2000.

94 Cox, "Renewing Our Identity."

95 Jack Reese, "May It Be According to Your Word," Gaylord Media Company, audiotape of lectures at the ACU Lectureships, 21 February 2000.

96 Ibid.

97 Royce Money, "A Vision for the Third Millennium," Gaylord Media Company, audiotape of lectures at the ACU Lectureships, 21 February 2000.

98 Cox, "Renewing Our Identity."

99 Ibid.

100 Cope, "A Passion for Community."

101 Peter Martin, "Standing at the Crossroads of Biblical Knowledge and the Knowledge of Men" (lecture, Southwestern Christian College, Terrell, TX, 19 November 2000).

102 Ibid.

103 Orpheus Heyward, "Standing at the Crossroads of Accepting a Contaminated Gospel" (lecture, SWCC, Terrell, TX, 20 November 2000).

104 Harold Redd, "The Nuts and Bolts of Spiritual and Numerical Church Growth" (lecture, SWCC, Terrell, TX, 20 November 2000).

105 Lawrence Gilmore, "Standing at the Crossroads of Denominational Influences" (lecture, SWCC, Terrell, TX, 20 November 2000).

106 Ibid.

107 See, for example, Creig Christman, "Standing at the Crossroads of Faithfulness and Backsliding" (lecture, SWCC, Terrell, TX, 19 November 2000); Jones, "Leading the Church in the 21st Century" (lecture, SWCC, Terrell, TX, 21 November 2000); Curtis

McCollum, "Standing at the Crossroads of Apostasy" (lecture, SWCC, Terrell, TX, 22 November 2000); John Tilman, "Standing at the Crossroads of Prioritizing Our Priorities" (lecture, SWCC, Terrell, TX, 21 November 2000).

108 Foster, "Justice, Racism & Churches of Christ," 148–149.

109 Michelle Morris, "'The Right Thing to Do'," *ACU Today* (Spring 2000). Cited 5 March 2008. Online: http://www.acu.edu/acu-today/spring2000/cover01.html.

110 Foster, "Justice, Racism & Churches of Christ," 149.

111 Ibid., 149–150. For Money's account of the apology, see "Reflections on Apology, Race, and Higher Education," in *Unfinished Reconciliation*, revised and expanded edition (ACU Press, 2013).

Epilogue Notes

1 Boring, *Disciples and the Bible*, 207–220.

2 Ibid., 214.

3 Ibid., 216.

4 Ibid., 216-217.

5 Lipscomb reprinted North's letter as well as his own response to North in an article: "The 'Church of Christ' and the 'Disciples of Christ'," *GA* 49 (18 July 1907): 457. Other articles of interest surrounding this event include "Meetings Extra Scriptural," *GA* 48 (30 August 1906): 552; "Divisions," *GA* 49 (28 March 1907): 201; "Divisions Must Come," *GA* 49 (3 October 1907): 633; "Divisions," *GA* 50 (23 April 1908): 265.

6 J. H. Garrison, "Things Which Make for Division," *CE* 44 (26 December 1907): 1645.

BIBLIOGRAPHY

"'Christ for the Crises' at Southwestern C. C.," CE 62 (October 1967): 1–2.

"A Moral Issue." Presbyterian Outlook 135 (7 December 1953): 6–7.

"Annual National Lectureship." CE 82 (January 1984): 1.

Annual of the Southern Baptist Convention. Nashville: Bruce Company, 1903.

"Atlanta, Ga. Racial Meeting A Great Success." CE 63 (September 1968): 7.

"Background of Race Relations Workshop." CC Supplement (10 May 1968): 3.

"'Christ for the Crises' at Southwestern C. C." CE 62 (October 1967): 1–2.

"Colored Program at War Memorial, Sunday Afternoon." GA 89 (March 1947): 366.

"Colored Singers, Speakers to Be at War Memorial Building." GA 89 (15 May 1947): 349.

"Desegregation and Economic Pressure." Presbyterian Outlook 137 (4 April 1955): 8.

"Fred D. Gray to Receive 2004 ABA Thurgood Marshall Award." No pages. Cited 26 February 2008. Online: http://www.abanet.org/irr/tmaward/2004award/fredgray.html.

"Incident in Mississippi." Presbyterian Journal 24 (9 March 1966): 12–13.

"Let's Discuss the Negro Issue." CC 21 (27 September 1963): 2.

"Nashville Christian Institute Lectureship." GA 98 (1 March 1956): 213.

"No Hate in His Path." CC 17 (29 March 1960): 2–A.

"Reader Appreciate Policy." CC 17 (12 April 1906): 2.

"Readers Laud Speech." CC 17 (5 April 1960): 2.

"Readers Tell Own Opinions of Speech on Integration." CC 17 (29 March 1960): 2–A.

"Schools and Segregation." Presbyterian Outlook 135 (12 October 1953): 8.

"The Tradition of White Presidents at Black Colleges." Journal of Black Higher Education 16 (Summer 1997): 93–99.

"This is No Way to Justice." Ibid. 26 (17 April 1968): 12.

"Two Southern Preachers Discuss Racial Issues." CC MS (20 September 1963): 2.

"With Troops and Tanks." Southern Presbyterian Journal 17 (24 December 1958): 2–3.

A Teacher. "Interesting Facts about the Negro School." GA 90 (9 December 1948): 1186–1189.

Adamson, Norman. "Reflections...On Selma and Montgomery." CE 60 (June 1965): 1.

Allen, C. Leonard. The Cruciform Church: Becoming a Cross-Shaped People in a Secular World. Abilene: ACU Press, 1990.

Allport, Gordon W. The Nature of Prejudice. New York: Doubleday, 1954.

Alvis, Joel L. Jr. Religion and Race: Southern Presbyterians, 1946-1983. Tuscaloosa, AL: University of Alabama Press, 1994.

Atchley, Rick and Bob Russell. Together Again: Restoring Unity in Christ after a Century of Separation. Abilene, TX: Leafwood Publishers; Cincinnati: Standard Publishing, 2006.

Baer, Hans A. and Merrill Singer. African-American Religion in the Twentieth Century: Varieties of Protest and Accommodation. Knoxville: University of Tennessee Press, 1992.

Bailey, Kenneth K. "Post Civil War Racial Separations in Southern Protestantism: Another Look." Church History 46 (December 1977): 453–473.

Baker, Robert A. Relations Between Northern and Southern Baptists. North Stratford, NH: Ayer Company Publishers, 1979.

Banowsky, William. The Mirror of a Movement: Churches of Christ as Seen Through the Abilene Christian College Lectureship. Dallas: Christian Publishing Company, 1965.

Barnes, William Wright. The Southern Baptist Convention, 1845-1953. 1900. Revised, Nashville: Broadman Press, 1954.

Bassett, John Spencer. "Stirring up the Fires of Race Antipathy." South Atlantic Quarterly 2 (October 1903): 297–305.

Bethel, Brian. "Local Universities Took Their Own Paths toward Desegregation." Abilene Reporter News, 16 February 2008.

Blyden, Edward W. "The African Problem and the Method of Its Solution." In African-American Social and Political Thought, edited by Howard Brotz, 126–139. 1966. Reprint, New Brunswick, NJ: Transaction Publishers, 1995.

Bodin, Jean. Method for Easy Comprehension of History. 1566. Reprint, New York: W. W. Norton and Company, 1969.

Boring, Eugene. Disciples and the Bible: A History of Disciples Biblical Interpretation in North America. St. Louis: Chalice Press, 1997.

Bowser, George Philip. "Work Among the Colored People." GA 54 (29 February 1912): 279.

———. "Work Among the Colored People." GA 34 (4 July 1912): 793.

———. "Work Among the Colored People." GA 55 (1 May 1913): 431.

———. "Better Outlook for Colored People." GA 70 (30 August 1928): 835.

———. "Outlook Among the Colored People." GA 70 (1 November 1928): 1053.

———. "The Need of Prepared Preachers." CE 34 (20 February 1939): 4.

———. "The Bowser Christian Institute." CE 34 (20 February 1939): 4.

———. "School Work." CE 34 (5 May 1939): 3.

———. "The Bowser Institute." CE 34 (5 May 1939): 3.

———. "What We Have Done." CE 34 (5 May 1939): 3.

———. "Plain Statements Relative to the Bowser Christian Institute." CE 34 (5 June 1939): 2.

———. "The Bowser Christian Institute." CE 34 (5 July 1939): 6.

Boyd, Vernon. "Bower, George Philip." In The Encyclopedia of the Stone-Campbell Movement, edited by Douglas A. Foster, Paul M. Blowers, Anthony Dunnavant, and D. Newell Williams, 97. Grand Rapids: Eerdmans, 2004.

———. Undying Dedication: The Story of G. P. Bowser. Nashville: Gospel Advocate Company, 1985.

Bozeman, Theodore Dwight. Protestants in an Age of Science: The Baconian Ideal and Antebellum American Religious Thought. Chapel Hill, NC: University of North Carolina Press, 1977.

Braxton, Brad. No Longer Slaves: Galatians and African American Experience. Collegeville, MN: Liturgical Press, 2002.
Brents, J. W. "Brother Brents' Letter." GA 83 (15 October 1931): 1289.
Brief for Defendant 5 at 10. Obie Elie et al. v. Athens Clay Pullias et al. Case 18,402. 6th Cir., 1967.
Brightwell, W. E. "The Ripest Opportunity." GA 90 (9 December 1948): 1188–89.
Broking, Darrell. "Marshall Keeble and the Implementation of a Grand Strategy: Erasing the Color Line in the Church of Christ." Master's thesis, East Tennessee State University, 2002.
Brown, William. The Crucial Race Question. Little Rock: Arkansas Churchman's Publishing Company, 1907.
Bruce, Phillip Alexander. The Plantation Negro as a Freeman. New York: Putnam, 1889.
Bucke, Emory S., ed. History of American Methodism in Three Volumes. Nashville: Abingdon, 1964.
Burch, Walter. "Neglecting the Weightier Matters." FF 85 (11 June 1968): 372.
Burton, Andrew Mizell. "The Prospects and Needs of the Putnam County Industrial School for Negroes." GA 58 (10 February 1916): 132.
Cadbury, Henry Joel. "Negro Membership in the Society of Friends." Journal of Negro History 21 (April 1936): 151–213.
Campbell, Alexander. "A Restoration of the Ancient Order of Things," CB 2-7 (1824-1830).
———. "Prospectus." MH 1, no. 1 (January 1830): 1.
———. "The Crisis." MH 3, no. 2 (February 1832): 86.
———. "Our Position to American Slavery, No. 1-VIII." MH 2, nos. 2-6 (February-June 1845): 49–53, 67–71, 108–112, 145–149, 193–196, 232–240, 257–364.
———. "Sermon on the Law." MH 3, no. 9 (September 1846): 493–521.
Campbell, Alexander Cleveland. "Work Among the Colored People." GA 53 (1 June 1911) 619.
Campbell, Thomas. Declaration and Address of the Christian Association of Washington. Washington, PA: Brown and Sample, 1809. Cited 22 November 2006. Online: http://www.mun.ca/rels/restmov/texts/tcampbell/Da/DA-1ST.HTM.
Carmichael, Stokely. "Black Power." Lecture. Berkeley, CA, October 1966.
Carroll, Charles. The Negro a Beast. St. Louis: American Book and Bible House, 1900.
Carter, Lawrence Edward. Walking Integrity: Benjamin Elijah Mays, Mentor to Martin Luther King Jr. Macon, GA: Mercer Press, 1998.
Casey, Michael W. "The Development of Necessary Inference in the Hermeneutics of the Disciples of Christ/Churches of Christ." PhD dissertation, University of Pittsburgh, 1986.
———. "From Pacifism to Patriotism: The Emergence of Civil Religion in the Churches of Christ during World War I." In The Stone-Campbell Movement: An International Religious Tradition, edited by Casey and Foster, 466–480. Knoxville, TN: University of Tennessee Press, 2002.
Casey, Michael and Douglas A. Foster., eds. The Stone-Campbell Movement: An International Religious Tradition. Knoxville, TN: University of Tennessee Press, 2002.
Cassius, Samuel Robert. "Among Our Colored Disciples." CL 5 (9 April 1901): 9.
———. "Additional Acknowledgments." CL (17 December 1901): 13.
———. "A Trip to the Golden Gate." CL 16 (12 August 1902): 13.
———. "Among Our Colored Disciples." CL 17 (8 December 1903): 13.
———. "Unity." In Our Savior's Prayer for Unity: A Symposium on the Seventeenth Chapter of John, edited by F. L. Rowe, 29–30. Cincinnati, OH: F. L. Rowe, 1918.

Chapman, Mark. "'Of One Blood': Mays and the Theology of Race Relations." In Walking Integrity: Benjamin Elijah Mays, Mentor to Martin Luther King, Jr., edited by Lawrence Edward Carter Jr., 233 –261. Macon, GA: Mercer University Press, 1998.

Choate, J. E. Roll Jordan Roll: A Biography of Marshall Keeble. Nashville: Gospel Advocate Company, 1974.

Christman, Creig. "Standing at the Crossroads of Faithfulness and Backsliding." Lecture, SWCC, Terrell, TX, 19 November 2000.

Chronicle Staff Writer. "Effective Next September ACC Desegregates Graduate School: Undergraduate School Integration Not Included in Board Decision." CC 18 (9 June 1961): 1, 6.

Clipp, Wendell V. "Teacher Invests Time." GA (9 December 1948): 1189.

Coleman, Will. Tribal Talk: Black Theology, Hermeneutics, and African/American Ways of "Telling the Story." University Park, PA: Pennsylvania State University Press, 2000.

Cone, James. Black Theology and Black Power. 1969. Reprint, Maryknoll, NY: Orbis, 2001.

———. "Black Theology and the Black Church: Where Do We Go from Here?" In African American Religious History: A Documentary Witness, edited by Milton C. Sernett, 565–579. Durham, NC: Duke University Press, 1999.

Cope, Mike. A Passion for Community. Gaylord Media Company. Audiotape of lectures presented at the ACU Lectureships, 22 February 2000.

Cox, Monte. Renewing Our Identity: Seeking and Saving the Lost. Gaylord Media Company. Audiotape of lectures presented at the ACU Lectureships, 21 February 2000.

Crum, Mason. The Negro in the Methodist Church. New York: Board of Missions and Church Extension of the Methodist Church, 1951.

Cunningham, Cheryl V. "The Desegregation of Tulane University." Master's thesis, University of New Orleans, 1982.

Daniels, Pearl Gray. The History of the Holt Street Church of Christ and Its Role in Establishing Churches of Christ Among African Americans in Central Alabama, 1928-1997. Baltimore, MD: American Literary Press, 1997.

Davis, Morris L. The Methodist Unification: Christianity and the Politics of Race in the Jim Crow Era. New York: New York University Press, 2008.

Delany, Martin R. "The Condition, Elevation, Emigration, and Destiny of the Colored People of the United States." In African-American Social and Political Thought 1850-1920, 37–101.

Dickerson, Dennis C. Militant Mediator: Whitney M. Young Jr. Lexington, KY: University of Kentucky Press, 1998.

———.A Liberated Past: Explorations in AME Church History. Nashville: AME Sunday School Union, 2003.

———. "Salvation and Separatism: William H. Franklin and the Presbyterian Mission to the Freedmen in East Tennessee." AME Church Review 120 (January-March 2004): 114–121.

———. "African American Religious Intellectuals and the Theological Foundations of the Civil Rights Movement, 1930-55." Church History 74, no. 2 (June 2005): 217–235.

Dixon, H. A. "Marshall Keeble at the College Lectureships." GA 110 (1968): 455.

DuBois, W. E. B. The Souls of Black Folk. Mineola, NY: Dover, 1994. First published 1903 by A. C. McClurg and Company.

Dudrey, Ross. "Restorationist Hermeneutics Among the Churches of Christ: Why Are We at an Impasse?" RQ 30, no. 1 (1988): 17–42.

Dvorak, Katherine L. An African-American Exodus: The Segregation of the Southern Churches. Brooklyn, NY: Carlson Publishing, 1991.

Emerson, Michael O. and Christian Smith. Divided By Faith: Evangelical Religion and the Problem of Race in America. New York: Oxford University Press, 2000.

Errett, Isaac. "Slavery—Where Does the Blame Rest?" CS 2 (17 August 1867): 258.

———. "Our Alleged Inconsistency." CS 5 (25 June 1870): 204.

Eskew, Glenn T. "Black Elitism and the Failure of Paternalism in Postbellum Georgia: The Case of Bishop Lucius Henry Holsey." Journal of Southern History 58 (November 1992): 637–666.

Evans, Dwain. "Dwain Evans: Lipscomb Is Quoted on Racial Prejudice." CC 23 (5 August 1966): 3, 6.

Evans, Jack. "The History of Southwestern Christian College Terrell, Texas." Master's thesis, Texas Western College, 1963.

———. "Remember N. C. I." CE 63 (December 1968): 1–3.

———. "Reviewing the Garrett 'Review." CE 84 (September 1986): 2.

———. "So What's the Big Issue?" Terrell, Texas: Jack Evans, 2005.

———. "Undoing Racism." No pages. Cited 5 March 2008. Online: http://www.jack evansonline.com/Undoing%20Racism.htm.

Evans, Jack Jr. "Jesus Christ in Black and White." CE 84 (August 1986): 3.

Falwell, Jerry. "Ministers and Marches." Sermon delivered at Thomas Road Baptist Church, Lynchburg, Virginia, 21 March 1965.

Ferguson, Everett. "Restoration Quarterly." In Encyclopedia of the Stone-Campbell Movement, 643.

Fleetwood, William. Unnamed Sermon. In Anglican Humanitarianism in Colonial New York. Edited by Frank Joseph Klingberg, 197–212. Salem, NH: Ayer Publishing, 1971.

Floyd, William. "Why I Could Not Be a Career Preacher." In Voices of Concern: Critical Studies in Church of Christism. Edited by Robert Meyers, 155–174. Saint Louis: Mission Messenger, 1966.

Foster, Douglas A. "The Struggle for Unity During the Period of Division in the Restoration Movement, 1875-1900." PhD diss., Vanderbilt University, 1987.

———. Will the Cycle Be Unbroken? Churches of Christ Face the 21st Century. Abilene, TX: ACU Press, 1994.

———. "Justice, Racism & Churches of Christ." In Unfinished Reconciliation: Justice, Racism & Churches of Christ, edited by Gary Holloway and John York, 131–151. Abilene, TX: ACU Press, 2003.

———. "Abilene Christian University." In Encyclopedia of the Stone-Campbell Movement, 1.

———. "An Angry Peace." No Pages. Cited 9 August 2006. Online: http://www.acu. edu/acu-today/spring2000/cover02.html.

Foster, Douglas A., Paul M. Blowers, Anthony L. Dunnavant, and D. Newell Williams., eds. The Encyclopedia of the Stone-Campbell Movement. Grand Rapids: Eerdmans, 2004.

Fowler, James. "From the Midst of the Crisis." FF 81 (31 March 1964): 199, 205.

Franklin, Benjamin. "Our Position Defined." ACR 10 (12 March 1867): 84.

Frazier, E. Franklin. The Negro Church in America. 1963. Reprint, New York: Schocken, 1974.

Freeman, Katherine Parker."Christ The Answer to Racial Tension." Royal Service 43 (March 1949): 20–28.

Gardner, David M. "Segregation's Problems." Baptist Standard (10 June 1954).

Garfinkel, Herbert. When Negroes March. New York: Macmillan, 1969.

Garnier, Kenneth P. "The Truth Shall Set You Free." CE 84 (July 1993): 2.

Garrett, Leroy. The Stone-Campbell Movement. Joplin: College Press, 1981.

———. "The Underbelly of the Black Church of Christ." Rest Rev 28 (June 1986): 309–313.

Garrison, James Harvey. "Things Which Make for Division." C Ev 44 (26 December 1907): 1645.

Garrison, Winifred Ernest and Alfred T. DeGroot. The Disciples of Christ: A History. 1948. Reprint, St. Louis: Bethany, 1958.

Genovese, Eugene. Roll, Jordan, Roll: The World The Slaves Made. New York: Vintage, 1972.

Gilmore, Lawrence. "Standing at the Crossroads of Denominational Influences." Lecture, SWCC, Terrell, TX, 20 November 2000.

Glaude, Eddie S. Jr. Exodus!: Religion, Race, and Nation in Early Nineteenth-Century Black America. Chicago: University of Chicago Press, 2000.

Glennon, Robert Jerome. "The Role of Law in the Civil Rights Movement: The Montgomery Bus Boycott, 1955-1957." Law and History Review 9 (Spring 1991): 59–112.

Goodpasture, Benton Cordell. Biography and Sermons of Marshall Keeble. Nashville: Gospel Advocate Company, 1931.

Graves, L. M. "'Without Respect of Persons': The Negro and Race Relationships." In Abilene Christian College Lectures 1950, 288–290. Austin: Firm Foundation, 1950.

Gray, Fred. Bus Ride to Justice: The Life and Works of Fred Gray. 1995. Reprint, Montgomery: New South Books, 2002.

Hadwin, Milo. The Role of New Testament Examples as Related to Biblical Authority. Austin: Firm Foundation, 1974.

Hairston, Andrew. "Is the Race Issue Social?" CE 59 (June 1964): 5.

Hale, Jess O. Jr. "Ecclesiastical Politics on a Moral Powder Keg: Alexander Campbell and Slavery in the Millennial Harbinger, 1830-1860." RQ 39, no. 2 (Second Quarter 1997): 65–81.

Hamilton, Charles V. Adam Clayton Powell, Jr.: The Political Biography of an American Dilemma. Lanham, MD: Cooper Square Press, 2002.

Handlin, Oscar and Mary. "Origins of the Southern Labor System." William and Mary Quarterly 7 (April 1950): 199–202.

Harding, Vincent. "Resistance and Religion among Ante-Bellum Negroes." In The Making of Black America, edited by August Meier and Elliot Rudwick. Springfield, IL: Atheneum Press, 1969.

Harrell, David Edwin. "The Sectional Origins of the Churches of Christ." Journal of Southern History 30 (1964): 261–277.

———. Quest for a Christian America, 1800-1865: A Social History of the Disciples of Christ, Volume I. 1966. Revised, Tuscaloosa: University of Alabama Press, 2003.

Harris, S. E., E. A. Elam, and David Lipscomb, "The Negro in Worship—A Correspondence." GA 49 (4 July 1907): 424–425; (1 August 1907): 488–489; (15 August 1907): 521.

Harrison, George B. Shakespeare under Elizabeth. New York: H. Holt and Company, 1933.

Hawkins, Jim. "Dear Editor." CC 18 (13 January 1961): 3.

Haygood, Atticus. Our Brother in Black, His Freedom and His Future. New York: Philips, 1881).

———. "The South and the School Problem." Harper's New Monthly Magazine 79 (July 1889): 225–231.

Haymes, Don. "Introduction to the Text." No Pages. Cited 14 June 2006. Online: http://www.mun.ca/rels/restmov/texts/race/negro.html.

———. "Conclusion to the Text: Why I Could Not Be A Preacher." No Pages. Cited 9 August 2006. Online: http://www.mun.ca/rels/restmov/texts/race/haymes 12.html.

Haymes, Don, Eugene Randall II, and Douglas A. Foster., "Race Relations," In Encyclopedia of the Stone Campbell Movement, 619-622

Hazelip, Harold. People of Proclamation and Prayer. Gaylord Media Company. Audiotape of lectures at the ACU Lectureships, 22 February 2000.

Heyward, Orpheus. "Standing at the Crossroads of Accepting a Contaminated Gospel." Lecture, SWCC, Terrell, TX, 20 November 2000.

Highers, Alan. "Churches and Politics." GA 108 (7 July 1966): 418, 428.

———. "The Banowsky Speech at ACU." FF 111 (1 November 1996): 1.

Hill, Samuel S. and Robert G. Torbet. Baptists North and South. Valley Forge, PA: Judson Press, 1964.

Hogan, Richard N. "The Sin of Being a Respecter of Persons." CE 54 (June 1959): 2, 5.

———. "Brother David Lipscomb Stood with God on Race Prejudice in the Church of Christ." CE 55 (June 1960): 2–3.

———. "Tradition Versus God's Commandments." CE 58 (June 1963): 1, 5.

———. "Is It the Law or Down-Right Prejudice." CE 58 (June 1963): 3.

———. "Methodists Appoint Negro Pastor to All-White Church." CE 58 (August 1963): 1, 5.

———. "The Grab of the Century." CE 63, no. 11 (November 1968): 1–2.

———. "The Church and Integration." CE 84 (May-June 1994): 2, 7.

Holifield, E. Brooks. Theology in America: Christian Thought from the Age of the Puritans to the Civil War. New Haven: CT: Yale University Press, 2003.

Holsey, Henry. Autobiography, Sermons, Addresses, and Essays. 2nd ed. Atlanta, GA: Franklin Printing and Publishing, 1899.

Holt, G. P. "Tension Between the Black and White Church," CE 64 (June 1969): 4, 9.

———. "Purposes of Lectureships in 1977." CE 76 (April 1977): 4.

———. "Issues Facing the Church Today." CE 85 (January 1997): 4.

Holt, Olivia. "The Bowser Memorial Scholarship Fund." CE 62 (June 1967): 6.

Hooper, Robert E. A Distinct People: A History of the Churches of Christ in the 20th Century. Eugene, OR: Wipf and Stock Publishers, 1993.

———. "Lipscomb University," in Encyclopedia of the Stone-Campbell Movement.

Hooper, Robert E. and G. David England. A Century of Memories: Centennial Celebration, David Lipscomb University, 1891-1991. Nashville: David Lipscomb University, 1992.

Houston, Michael. "Do We Need A New Old Testament Hermeneutic?" In Christian Scholars' Conference 1990, 167–187. Abilene: Abilene Christian University, 1990.

Hoyt, Thomas Jr. "Interpreting Biblical Scholarship for the Black Church Tradition." In Stony the Road We Trod: African American Biblical Interpretation, edited by Cain Hope Felder, 17–39. Minneapolis: Fortress, 1991.

Hughes, Richard T. Reviving the Ancient Faith: The Story of Churches of Christ in America. 1996; new edition, Abilene, TX: ACU Press, 2008.

Hunton, Phillip L. "Keeble and Boys at Albany, Ga." GA 89 (5 June 1947): 398.

Jackson, Don. "A New Restoration Hermeneutic—Who Really Cares?" In Christian Scholars' Conference 1990, 189–208. Abilene: Abilene Christian University, 1990.

Jackson, Ervin C. "Silver Point School." In Encyclopedia of the Stone-Campbell Movement, 684–685.

James, Larry. "Ten Principles to Consider in Developing a "New" Hermeneutic." In Christian Scholars' Conference 1990, 209–218. Abilene: Abilene Christian University, 1990.

Jefferson, Thomas. Notes on the State of Virginia. Edited by William Peden. Chapel Hill, NC: University of North Carolina Press, 1955.

Jelks, Randall M. "Benjamin E. Mays and the Creation of an Insurgent Negro Professional Clergy." AME Church Review 118, no. 387 (July-September 2002): 32–38.

Johnson, Thomas Cary. The Life and Letters of Robert Lewis Dabney. Richmond: Presbyterian Committee of Publication, 1903.

Jones, David Jr. "Address by David Jones Jr." CC Supp (10 May 1968): 2.

———. "Growing Their Separate Ways." GA 132 (January 1990): 21–23.

———. "Leading the Church in the 21st Century." Lecture, SWCC, Terrell, TX, 21 November 2000.
Jordan, Winthrop D. White over Black: American Attitudes Toward the Negro, 1550-1812. 1968. Reprint, New York: W. W. Norton & Company, 1977.
Keeble, Marshall. "Mission Work Among Negroes." GA 63 (20 January 1921): 78.
———. "Report of Work." GA 66 (3 January 1924): 22–23.
———. "A Great Opportunity." GA 86 (18 May 1944): 341.
———. "Nashville Christian Institute." GA 89 (26 June 1947): 452.
———. "Nashville Christian Institute Commencement." GA 91 (30 June 1949): 402–403.
———. "The Church Among the Colored." In Abilene Christian College Bible Lectures 1950. Austin: Firm Foundation Publishing House, 1950, 142–156. Cited 27 July 2006. Online: http://www.mun.ca/rels/restmov/texts/mkeeble/keeble1.html.
———. "Nashville Christian Institute Has Many Friends." GA 94 (24 July 1952): 486.
———. "A Prepared Ministry." In Harding College Lectures 1952, 261–267. Austin: Firm Foundation, 1952.
———. "Nashville Christian Institute Lectures." GA 98 (24 May 1956): 503.
———. "Keeble's Speech." In Lubbock Christian College Lectures 1958: Workers Together With God, 37-46. Jackson, TN: Nichols Brothers, 1958.
———. From Mule to Super Jet with the Gospel. Nashville: Gospel Advocate, 1962.
———. "Nashville Christian Institute to Close." GA 109 (16 March 1967): 166.
———. "The Great Physician." MP3 Recording of Sermon. No pages. Cited 3 March 2008. Online: http://www.oldpathsmedia.org/Speakers/Keeble/Marshall.
Kellam, Harry. "A Tribute to the Two Dr. K's." CE 84 (January 1987): 5.
King, Martin Luther Jr. The Strength to Love. In A Testament of Hope: The Essential Writings and Speeches of Martin Luther King, Jr., edited by James M. Washington, 491–517. San Francisco: Harper San Francisco, 1986.
———. Where Do We Go from Here? In A Testament of Hope, 555–633.
———. The Papers of Martin Luther King, Jr., Volume III: Birth of a New Age December 1955-December 1956. Edited by Clayborne Carson. Berkeley: University of California Press, 1997.
Lard, Moses. "Do the Holy Scriptures Authorize the Baptism of Infants?" LQ 1 (December 1863): 158.
———. "Have We Not Become a Sect?" LQ 1 (March 1864): 255.
———. "Can We Divide?" LQ 3 (April 1866): 336.
LaValley, Mark. A Gospel for All Generations. Gaylord Media Company. Audiotape of lectures presented at the ACU Lectureships, 23 February 2000.
Lawton, Eugene, R. C. Wells, and Jimmy Allen. "Statement of Acknowledgement of Racial Prejudice and Proposals for Improving Race Relations in Churches of Christ." NAC 10 (1 July 1978): 210.
Lemmons, Reuel. "The Church and Integration." FF 81 (31 March 1964): 194.
———. "The Long Hot Summer." FF 85 (9 January 1968): 18.
———. "Marshall Keeble." FF 85, (14 May 1968): 306.
———. "Unpublished letter to John Allen Chalk dated 16 May 1968." No pages. Cited 4 January 2007. Online: http://www.mun.ca/rels/restmov/texts/race/ haymes1.html.
Lincoln, C. Eric and Lawrence H. Mamiya. The Black Church in the African American Experience. 1990. Reprint, Durham, NC: Duke University Press, 2001.
Lipscomb, A. B. "It's Not Keeble, But the Bible Is Right." CL 45 (25 August 1931): 6.
Lipscomb, David. "The Advocate and Sectionalism." GA 8 (1 May 1866): 273.
———. "The Freedmen—Their Condition." GA 10 (13 February 1868): 147–148.
———. "Noah's Curse upon Ham, &c." GA 10 (14 May 1868): 462.

———. "The South and the Freedmen." GA 10 (9 July 1868): 649–654.
———. "A Visit to Chattanooga." GA 31 (3 April 1889): 214.
———. "Are the Negroes Neglected?" GA 68 (14 June 1906): 377–388.
———. "Meetings Extra Scriptural." GA 48 (30 August 1906): 552.
———. "Divisions." GA 49 (28 March 1907): 201.
———. "The 'Church of Christ' and the 'Disciples of Christ'." GA 49 (18 July 1907): 457.
———. "Divisions Must Come." GA 49 (3 October 1907): 633.
———. "Divisions," GA 50 (23 April 1908): 265.
Locke, Leon. "The Congregational Attitude Toward Race Relationships." In Abilene Christian College Lectures 1950, 281–283. Austin: Firm Foundation , 1950.
Loescher, Frank S. The Protestant Church and the Negro. New York: Association Press, 1948.
Lyda, Hap C. S. "African Americans in the Movement: Nineteenth Century." In Encyclopedia of Stone-Campbell Movement, 11.
Marable, Manning. Blackwater: Historical Studies in Race, Class Consciousness, and Revolution. Dayton, OH: Black Praxis, 1981.
———. How Capitalism Underdeveloped Black America. Boston: South End, 1983.
Marsh, Charles. God's Long Summer: Stories of Faith and Civil Rights. Princeton, NJ: Princeton University Press, 1997.
Martin, Peter. "Standing at the Crossroads of Biblical Knowledge and the Knowledge of Men." Lecture, Southwestern Christian College, Terrell, TX, 19 November 2000.
Martin, William C. "Shepherds Versus Flocks." Atlantic Monthly 220 (December 1967).
Mather, Cotton. The Negro Christianized: An Essay to Excite and Assist that Good Work, the Instruction of Negro-Servants in Christianity. Boston: B. Green, 1706.
Mathews, Donald. Slavery and Methodism: A Chapter in American Morality, 1780-1845. Princeton: University Press, 1965.
Maxwell, James. "The Sociological Impact of the Race Issue." CE 59 (July 1964): 1, 9; (August 1964): 7; (September 1964): 2–3.
Mays, Benjamin E. The Negro's God as Reflected in His Literature. New York: Atheneum, 1968.
———. Born to Rebel. New York: Charles Scribner's Sons, 1971.
———. The Negro's Church. New York: Beaufort Books, 1975.
———. "The Moral Aspects of Segregation." In Voices in Our Blood: America's Best on the Civil Rights Movement, edited by Jon Meacham, 123–28. New York: Random House, 2003.
McCollum, Curtis. "Standing at the Crossroads of Apostasy." Lecture, SWCC, Terrell, TX, 22 November 2000.
McCord, Hugo. "A Sorry Viewpoint." GA 111 (20 March 1969): 190.
McMillon, Lynn. "A Conversation with Fred Gray." CC 65 (February 2008): 25.
Meier, August. Negro Thought in America 1880-1915: Racial Ideologies in the Age of Booker T. Washington. Ann Arbor, MI: University of Michigan Press, 1963.
Meyers, Robert, ed. Voices of Concern: Critical Studies in Church of Christism. Saint Louis: Mission Messenger, 1966.
Mikelson, Thomas I. S. "Mays, King, and the Negro's God." In Walking Integrity: Benjamin Elijah Mays, Mentor to Martin Luther King Jr., edited by Lawrence Edward Carter Sr., 154–184. Mercer, GA: Mercer University Press, 1998.
Money, Royce. A Vision for the Third Millennium. Gaylord Media Company. Audiotape of lectures at the ACU Lectureships, 21 February 2000.
Moore, W. T. Comprehensive History of the Disciples of Christ. New York: Fleming H. Revell, 1909.

Morris, Aldon D. The Origins of the Civil Rights Movement: Black Communities Organizing for Change. New York: Free Press, 1984.

Morris, Michelle. "'The Right Thing to Do'." ACU Today (Spring 2000). Cited 5 March 2008. Online: http://www.acu.edu/acu-today/spring2000/cover01.html.

Murch, James D. Christians Only: A History of the Restoration Movement. Cincinnati: Standard Publishing, 1962.

Nelson, William Stuart. The Christian Way in Race Relations. New York: Harper and Brothers, 1948.

Newman, Mark. Getting Right with God: Southern Baptists and Desegregation, 1945-1995. Tuscaloosa, AL: University of Alabama Press, 2001.

Nichols, James Don. "A History of Harding College, 1924-1984." EdD diss., University of Arkansas, 1985.

Noll, Mark. America's God: From Jonathon Edwards to Abraham Lincoln. New York: Oxford Press, 2002.

Norell, Robert J. Reaping the Whirlwind: The Civil Rights Movement in Tuskegee. 1985; reprint, Chapel Hill, NC: University of North Carolina Press, 1998.

Olbricht, Thomas. "Hermeneutics in the Churches of Christ." RQ 37, no. 1 (1995): 1–24.

Parks, Ted. "A Conversation with Andrew Hairston." CC 58, no. 4 (April 2001): 20.

Payton, G. Michael. "Civil Rights Panel is Fair, Balanced." Toledo Blade, 7 February 2008.

PCUS. Minutes of the 98th General Assembly. (1958): 37–39.

Pearson, Chuck. "ACU Student Speaks Out." Cont F 29 (1 April 1998): 1.

Pecoraro, J. Raymond. "Racism in the Lord's Church Is an Age-Old Problem." CE 10 (August 1981): 4.

Pendleton, T. Brian. "Alexander Campbell and Slavery: Gradualism and Anti-Slavery Rhetoric in the Millennial Harbinger." RQ 42, no. 3 (Third Quarter 2000): 149–154.

Pettus, Karl. "The Memorial to Marshall Keeble." GA 60 (18 July 1968): 449.

Phillips, Paul D. "The Interracial Impact of Marshall Keeble, Black Evangelist, 1878-1968." in The Stone-Campbell Movement: An International Religious Tradition, edited by Michael W. Casey and Douglas A. Foster, 317–328. Knoxville, TN: University of Tennessee Press, 2002.

Pitts, Carroll Jr. "A Critical Study of Civil Rights Practices, Attitudes, and Responsibilities in Churches of Christ." Master's thesis, Pepperdine University, 1969.

———. "God is No Respecter of Persons." CE 64 (June 1969): 5, 9.

———. "Civil Rights...In the Churches of Christ." CE 84 (August 1987): 2.

Pollard, J. Paul. "Recent Trends in Biblical Interpretation." In Christian Scholars' Conference 1990, 305–356. Abilene: Abilene Christian University, 1990.

Poyner, Barry C. Bound to Slavery: James Shannon and the Restoration Movement. Fort Worth: Star Bible Publications, 1999.

Raboteau, Albert J. Slave Religion: The "Invisible Institution" in the Antebellum South. New York: Oxford, 1978.

———. Canaan Land: A Religious History of African Americans. New York: Oxford, 1999.

Randolph, Peter. "Plantation Churches: Visible and Invisible." In African American Religious History: A Documentary Witness. Edited by Milton C. Sernett, 63–68. Durham, NC: Duke University Press, 1999.

Redd, Harold. "The Nuts and Bolts of Spiritual and Numerical Church Growth." Lecture, SWCC, Terrell, TX, 20 November 2000.

Reese, Jack. May It Be According to Your Word. Gaylord Media Company. Audiotape of lectures at the ACU Lectureships, 21 February 2000.

Reimers, David M. White Protestantism and the Negro. New York: Oxford, 1965.

Rhoads, Forrest N. Sr. "A Study of the Sources of Marshall Keeble's Effectiveness as a Preacher." PhD diss., Southern Illinois University, 1970.

Rice, Ira Y. Jr. "'Gold Coast Restoration Forum' Results in Blacks Withdrawing Fellowship from Ivory James." Cont F 17 (August 1986): 1, 3–14.
Rivers, Richard. Elements of Moral Philosophy. Nashville: Publishing House of the Methodist Episcopal Church, South, 1887.
Robinson, Edward J. "African Americans in the Movement." Encyclopedia of the Stone-Campbell Movement," 17.
———. "Southwestern Christian College." in Encyclopedia of the Stone-Campbell Movement, 695.
———. To Save My Race from Abuse: The Life of Samuel Robert Cassius. Tuscaloosa, AL: University of Alabama Press, 2007.
———. Show Us How You Do It: Marshall Keeble and the Rise of Black Churches of Christ in the United States, 1914-1968. Tuscaloosa, AL: University of Alabama Press, 2008.
Ross, Bobby Jr. "Unity Discussion Takes Center Stage at Freed-Hardeman." CC 63 (1 November 2006): 1.
Rowe, F. L. Our Savior's Prayer for Unity: A Symposium on the Seventeenth Chapter of John. Cincinnati, OH: F. L. Rowe, 1918.
Royster, Carl H. Churches of Christ in the United States: 2006 Edition. Nashville: 21st Century Christian, 2006.
Seay, Solomon S. There by the Grace of God: The Memoir of an Early Civil Rights Activist, One of the Great African American Preachers. Montgomery: New South Books, 2005.
Sensing, Thurman. "Expert Finds Plan Sound." GA 90 (9 December 1948): 1188.
Sernett, Milton C. "Bound For the Promised Land": African American Religion and the Great Migration. Durham, NC: Duke University Press, 1995.
Sewall, Samuel. "The Selling of Joseph: A Memorial [Boston: 1700]." Massachusetts Historical Society Proceedings, 1863-1864, VII. Boston, 1864.
Shaler, Nathanial Southgate. "The Negro Problem." Atlantic Monthly 54 (November 1884): 696–709.
———. "Science and the African Problem," Atlantic Monthly 66 (July 1890): 36–45.
Shattuck, Gardiner H. Episcopalians and Race: Civil War to Civil Rights. Lexington: University of Kentucky Press, 2000.
Shelly, Rubel. I Just Want to Be A Christian. Nashville: 20th Century Christian, 1984.
———. "Apologetics and Hermeneutics: How a Properly Framed Doctrine of Inspiration Informs Sound Exegetical Method." In Christian Scholars' Conference 1990, 385–399. Abilene: Abilene Christian University, 1990.
Shelly, Rubel, Mike Cope, and Philip Morrison. "Wineskins: A Purpose Statement." Wineskins 1 (May 1992): 5.
Sherwood, Henry Noble. "The Formation of the American Colonization Society." Journal of Negro History (July 1917): 209–228.
Shields, Bruce. "The Hermeneutics of Alexander Campbell." RQ 43, no. 3 (Third Quarter 2001): 167–179.
Simpson, Dale. "Let Our Preachers Lead the World on a Real Freedom March." FF 82 (27 April 1965): 259, 266.
Sledd, Andrew. "The Negro: Another View." Atlantic Monthly 90 (July 1902): 65-73.
Smith, Arthur L. Jr. "A Rhetorical Analysis of the Speaking of Marshall Keeble." Master's thesis, Pepperdine University, 1966.
Smith, H. Shelton. In His Image, But...: Racism in Southern Religion, 1780-1910. Durham, NC: Duke University Press, 1972.
Spain, Carl. "Modern Challenges to Christian Morals." In Christian Faith in the Modern World—Abilene Christian College Bible Lectures 1960, 198–231. Abilene, TX: Abilene Christian College Students Exchange, 1960.

Spain, Rufus B. At Ease in Zion: Social History of Southern Baptists, 1865-1900. Nashville: Vanderbilt University Press, 1967.

Steward, G. E. "History of the Lectureship." CE 72 (April 1974): 4.

Taylor, Clarence. Knocking at Our Own Door: Milton A. Galimison and the Struggle to Integrate New York City Schools. New York: Columbia University Press, 1997.

Taylor, Cynthia. A. Philip Randolph: The Religious Journey of an African American Labor Leader. New York: New York University Press, 2005.

Thomas, J. D. We Be Brethren. Abilene, TX: Biblical Research Press, 1958.

Thomas, James S. Methodism's Racial Dilemma: The Story of the Central Jurisdiction. Nashville: Abingdon, 1992.

Thompson, Ernest Trice. Presbyterian Missions in the Southern United States. Richmond: Presbyterian Committee on Publication, 1934.

———. "The Struggle for Social Justice." Presbyterian Outlook 129 (12 May 1947): 13–14.

———. "Black Presbyterians, Education and Evangelism after the Civil War." Journal of Presbyterian History 51 (Summer 1973): 174–198.

Thurman, Howard. Jesus and the Disinherited. 1949; revised ed., Boston: Beacon Press, 1976.

Tilman, John. "Standing at the Crossroads of Prioritizing Our Priorities." Lecture, SWCC, Terrell, TX, 21 November 2000.

Tinnin, Finley W. "Non Segregation." Baptist Message (3 June 1954).

Torbet, Robert G. A History of the Baptists, 3rd ed. 1952; reprint, Valley Forge, PA: Judson Press, 1973.

Treat, J. W. "What Does the Bible Teach About Race Relationships?" In Abilene Christian College Lectures 1950, 284–287. Austin: Firm Foundation , 1950.

Trueblood, D. Elton. "Maker Brotherhood Real." Light 3 (February 1950).

Tucker, John Mark. "Six Black Women Who Influenced My Life: A Journey in Spiritual and Intellectual Formation." In Restoring the First-Century Church in the Twenty-first Century: Essays on the Stone-Campbell Movement in Honor of Don Haymes, edited by Warren Lewis and Hans Rollmann, 323–334. Eugene, OR: Wipf and Stock, 2005.

Tucker, Tim. "'Potsherds:' A Piece of Middle Tennessee Samizdat Literature." Working paper, Autobiography, Faculty of Columbia Christian University and Lipscomb University, 1994.

Turner, Henry McNeal. "God Is a Negro." Voice of Missions (February 1898).

Turner, Rex A. "Christianity and the Races." GA 103 (12 May 1966): 292–293.

Vaughan, C. R. "The Southern Assembly." Presbyterian Quarterly 1 (July 1887): 147.

Waddey, John. "A Plea to My Black Brethren." CE 67 (November 1969): 3.

Wallace, Foy E. "Negro Meetings for White People." BB (March 1941): 7.

———. "From M. Keeble," BB (April 1941): 5.

Wallace, Glenn L. "The Atlanta Conference." FCC 2, no. 4 (October 1968): 1, 3.

Washington, Booker T. "The Atlanta Compromise." Speech, Cotton States and International Exposition, Atlanta, Georgia, September 18, 1895. No Pages. Cited 11 July 2006. Online: http://www. historymatters.gmu.edu/d/39.

———. Up from Slavery. 1901. Reprint, Boston: Western Islands, 1965.

———. "Is the Negro Having a Fair Chance?" Century Illustrated Monthly Magazine 85 (November 1912): 46-55.

Washington, James M., ed. A Testament of Hope: The Essential Writings and Speeches of Martin Luther King, Jr. San Francisco: Harper San Francisco, 1986.

Weatherford, Willis D. American Churches and the Negro. Boston: Christopher Publishing House, 1957.

Webb, Henry. "Christian Standard." In The Encyclopedia of the Stone-Campbell Movement, 197–199.

Wells, Roosevelt. "Racism in the Churches of Christ." East Denver Herald Church Bulletin 10, no. 28 (August 1968): 3.

———. "'A Plea to My Black Brethren' (A Reply)." CE 68 (February 1970): 2.

———. "The Case for the Black Revolution." Mission 4 (July 1970): 4–14.

———. "Equal Heirs, Equal Members, Equal Partners." CE 84 (May-June 1992): 1, 8–9.

West, Earl Ervin. The Search for the Ancient Order: A History of the Restoration Movement, Volume 2, 1866-1906. Nashville: Gospel Advocate, 1950.

Whitefield, George. George Whitefield's Journals. 1960; reprint, London: Guildford and London, 1965.

Willard, Samuel. A Compleat Body of Divinity in Two Hundred and Fifty Expository Lectures on the Assembly's Shorter Catechism. 1726; reprint, New York: Johnson Reprint Company, 1969.

Williams, Boyd. "Racial Strife Is Still with Us." CE 76 (July 1977): 4.

Williams, S. A. "Letter to Editor." Royal Service 58 (December 1964): 34–35.

Williamson, Joel. The Crucible of Race: Black-White Relations in the American South Since Emancipation. New York: Oxford, 1984.

Willingham, J. Roy Jr. "What Should the Christian's Attitude Be toward Race Relationships?" In Abilene Christian College Lectures 1950, 278–280. Austin: Firm Foundation, 1950.

Wills, David W. "The Central Themes of American Religious History: Pluralism, Puritanism, and the Encounter of Black and White." In African American Religion: Interpretive Essays in History and Culture, edited by Timothy E. Fulop and Albert J. Raboteau, 7–20. New York: Routledge, 1997.

Wilmore, Gayraud. Black and Presbyterian: The Heritage and the Hope. Philadelphia: Geneva Press, 1983.

———. "Identity and Integration: Black Presbyterians and Their Allies in the Twentieth Century." In The Presbyterian Predicament: Six Perspectives, edited by Milton J. Coalter, John M. Mulder, and Louis B. Weeks, 109–133. Louisville: Westminster/John Knox, 1990.

———. Black Religion and Black Radicalism: An Interpretation of the Religious History of African Americans. 3rd ed. Mary Knoll, NY: Orbis, 1998.

Wilson, Charles Reagan. Baptized in Blood: The Religion of the Lost Cause, 1865-1920. Athens, GA: University of Georgia Press, 1980.

Wilson, John F. "Harding University." In Encyclopedia of the Stone-Campbell Movement, 382–383.

Womack, Sam W. "Mission Work Among Colored People in TN." GA 46 (4 February 1904): 80.

———. "Work Among Colored People." GA 53 (6 April 1911): 425.

———. "Work Among Colored People." GA (20 July 1911): 798.

———. "Work Among Colored People." GA (17 August 1911): 926.

———. "Work Among Colored People." GA (19 October 1911): 1206.

———. "Work Among Colored People." GA (16 November 1911): 1341.

———. "Work Among Colored People." GA (14 December 1911): 1469.

———. "Among the Colored Folk." GA 60 (3 January 1918): 18.

Woodrow, Robert E. "The Nature of Biblical Authority and the Restoration Movement." Master's Thesis, Abilene Christian University, 1983.

Woodson, Carter G. The History of the Negro Church. Washington: Associated Publishers, 1921.

Wynn, Linda T. Leaders of Afro-American Nashville. Nashville: Nashville Christian Institute Reunion Committee, 2002.

INDEX

S

T

V

W

Printed in the USA
CPSIA information can be obtained
at www.ICGtesting.com
CBHW021208020324
4853CB00003B/15

9 780891 122289